The Simplified

Book of Change

(The I Ching)

By Gu Yuan

Published by

Heart Space Publications

PO Box 1085

Daylesford

Victoria

3460

Australia

Tel +61 450260348

www.heartspacebooks.com

pat@heartspacebooks.com

Copyright © 2021 Gu Yuan

All rights reserved under international copyright conventions.
No part of this book may be reproduced, stored in a retrieval system, or transmitted in any form or by any means electronic, mechanical, photocopying, recorded or otherwise without written permission from Heartspace Publications.

Whilst every care has been taken to check the accuracy of the information in this book, the publisher cannot be held responsible for any errors, omissions or originality.

Published in January 2021 at Melbourne.

Cover image supplied by Pixaby.

ISBN 978-0-6486524-2-7

Chinese to English translation by Julio Noyola y Loya (gallochilango@gmail.com)

Original Title: 简易经

Text by: Gu Yuan

Copyright© Sichuan Tiandi Publishing House CO., LTD, 2021

This edition is published by arrangement with
Heartspace Publications.

About the author Gu yuan

Gu yuan is the pioneer of the "Chinese-style inspirational" concept, based on the inheritance of traditional classics; such as *The Four Books*; *The Great Learning; The Doctrine of the Mean; The Confucian Analects*; *The Works of Mencius*; *The Five Classics; The Book of Poetry / Songs; The Book of History; The Book of Changes; The Book of Rites;* and *The Spring and Autumn Annals;* and other classics and historical works that have a deep influence on Chinese culture. His Chinese-Style Inspirational concept is the modernisation of these, where Gu Yuan brings the deeply enduring principles for today's people.

He has published the following best-selling books; *Understand Zeng Guofan, Four Books of Life; Minimalist Zhouyi*"; and *Simple Sutra*. His Lecture and Comprehensive Guide 1: *This Is the Warring States*" and "*Gu Yuan's and Comprehensive Guide* (pertaining *to* the Qin and Han Dynasties).

In 2016, he produced China's first inspirational talk show on Chinese culture, *Gu Yuan's Thoughts on History*, which had been broadcast on iQIYI talk show channel with over 150 episodes.

Gu yuan's calligraphy is of profound merit. He has studied calligraphy for more than twenty years, and his works have been selected for many national exhibitions.

Imbued with the wisdom of the ancient sages that he studied, he is a sage in his own right, with wisdom such as; …and, in the end, you will find that we are all racing against life, and everything you get is less valuable than the life you lost running after it.

Contents

About the author Gu yuan	iii
Overview	1
A memoir of experience	3
English version – Publisher's Notes	9
Part One	11
What kind of book is the Book of Changes?	11
How The Book of Changes was written?	12
Ying and Yang	15
The Great Virtues of Heaven and Earth	16
The core idea of the Book of Changes	18
Production and reproduction is what is called the process of change	19
The Book of Changes practical applications	21
Philosophical view	25
All under heaven will be found at its time	26
The Great Virtues of Heaven and Earth	28
The Great Virtues are all of Heaven and Earth	29
Not communicating is out of the question	30
The union of the antagonist	32
Everlasting and unchanging	33
Divine retribution	34
An outlook on life; On Being Human	37
Destiny is the grasp of the overall situation of life	37
Struggle is the main theme of life	39
Noble is almost like wealthy	40
Doing good makes people happy	41
Integrity is like climbing	43
Modesty is the path of progress	44
Noble is almost wealthy	45
How to practice oriental spirituality	46
Perseverance wins	48
Perseverance is the gateway to virtue	49
Square and circle	50
The spirit of independence, the idea of freedom	52
Part Two	55
The 64 Hexagrams and Textual Explanation?	55
The 64 Hexagrams	59

Qian: The struggle of the dragon	59
classical text	59
literal translation	60
interpretation	61
Kun: The enlightenment of the Earth	65
classical text	65
literal translation	66
interpretation	67
Tun: The First step is always difficult	70
classical text	70
literal translation	71
interpretation	72
Meng: The purpose of education	74
classical text	74
literal translation	75
interpretation	76
Xu: Awaiting	79
classical text	79
literal translation	80
interpretation	81
Song: The commoner before the noble	84
classical text	84
literal translation	85
interpretation	86
Shi: When general Han Xin muster soldiers, the more the better	88
classical text	88
literal translation	89
interpretation	90
Bi: A close friend	93
classical text	93
literal translation	94
interpretation	95
Xiao Xu: The feeling of being middle class	97
classical text	97
literal translation	98
interpretation	99
Lu: the tiger's tail	102
classical text	102
literal translation	103
interpretation	104

Tai: The secret of conducting oneself calmly	106
classical text	106
literal translation	107
interpretation	108
Pi: Truman's world	111
classical text	111
literal translation	112
interpretation	113
Tong Ben: Are we all the same?	116
classical text	116
literal translation	117
interpretation	118
Da You: How to protect fortune	121
classical text	121
literal translation	122
interpretation	123
Qian: More than modesty (Qianagain;谦 in phonetic writing they have the same spelling as the first Hexagram)	126
classical text	126
literal translation	127
interpretation	128
Yu: Are you happy?	131
classical text	131
literal translation	132
interpretation	133
Sui: Follow, follow, follow	135
classical text	135
literal translation	136
interpretation	137
Gu: Chaos is an opportunity	140
classical text	140
literal translation	141
interpretation	142
Lin: Leaders' four key words	145
classical text	145
literal translation	146
interpretation	147
Guan: The way you see the world is the way you see other people	150
classical text	150
literal translation	151
interpretation	152

Shi Ke: Violence and Punishment ... 155
    classical text ... 155
    literal translation ... 156
    interpretation ... 157
Bi: Beauty is productivity ... 160
    classical text ... 160
    literal translation ... 161
    interpretation ... 162
Bo: When the foundation is not firm, it is easily shaken ... 165
    classical text ... 165
    literal translation ... 166
    interpretation ... 167
Fu: The heart of Heaven and Earth ... 170
    classical text ... 170
    literal translation ... 171
    interpretation ... 172
Wu Wang: Abide by one's station in life ... 175
    classical text ... 175
    literal translation ... 176
    interpretation ... 177
Da Xu: Pointers for officials ... 179
    classical text ... 179
    literal translation ... 180
    interpretation ... 181
Yi: How's it going? ... 184
    classical text ... 184
    literal translation ... 185
    interpretation ... 186
Da Guo: The Lone Wolf is a hidden Dragon ... 188
    classical text ... 188
    literal translation ... 189
    interpretation ... 190
Kan: Doom ... 192
    classical text ... 192
    literal translation ... 193
    interpretation ... 194
Li: Leaving the original turf ... 197
    classical text ... 197
    literal translation ... 198
    interpretation ... 199

Xian: Moving with the feeling	202
classical text	202
literal translation	203
interpretation	204
Heng: No change, no shake, no stop	206
classical text	206
literal translation	207
interpretation	208
Dun: Take a step back	211
classical text	211
literal translation	212
interpretation	213
Da Zhuang: In the prime of life people often despair	216
classical text	216
literal translation	217
interpretation	218
Jin: It's not easy coming forward	221
classical text	221
literal translation	222
interpretation	223
Ming Yi: Facing darkness	225
classical text	225
literal translation	226
interpretation	227
Jia Ren: Learning to live	230
classical text	230
literal translation	231
interpretation	232
Kui: Same same but different	235
classical text	235
literal translation	236
interpretation	237
Jian: The difficulties of the journey	239
classical text	239
literal translation	240
interpretation	241
Jie: Enmity should not endure, is better to squash enmity rather than keeping it alive	244
classical text	244
literal translation	245
interpretation	246

Sun: Life should be minimalistic	249
classical text	249
literal translation	250
interpretation	251
Yi: Life shall provide	254
classical text	254
literal translation	255
interpretation	256
Guai: About stress	259
classical text	259
literal translation	260
interpretation	261
Gou: Life is just like a First meeting	263
classical text	263
literal translation	264
interpretation	265
Cui: Avoid crowded places	268
classical text	268
literal translation	269
interpretation	270
Sheng: The two cruxes of growing up	272
classical text	272
literal translation	273
interpretation	274
Kun: The six plights of life	276
classical text	276
literal translation	277
interpretation	278
Jing: The three virtues of a leader	281
classical text	281
literal translation	282
interpretation	283
Ge: Change	285
classical text	285
literal translation	286
interpretation	287
Ding: Holding on	290
classical text	290
literal translation	291
interpretation	292

Zhen: The greatest enemy 294
 classical text 294
 literal translation 295
 interpretation 296
Gen: Self control 299
 classical text 299
 literal translation 300
 interpretation 301
Jian: Everything should be gradual 303
 classical text 303
 literal translation 304
 interpretation 305
Gui Mei: Choose life 308
 classical text 308
 literal translation 309
 interpretation 310
Feng: The wisdom of decision making 313
 classical text 313
 literal translation 314
 interpretation 315
Lu: The intention of words 317
 classical text 317
 literal translation 318
 interpretation 319
Xun: Taking advantage of the trend 321
 classical text 321
 literal translation 322
 interpretation 323
Dui: Water like friendship 325
 classical text 325
 literal translation 326
 interpretation 327
Huan: Freedom 330
 classical text 330
 literal translation 331
 interpretation 332
Jie: Temperance 335
 classical text 335
 literal translation 336
 interpretation 337

xii | The Simplified Book of Change

    Zhong Fu: Integrity wins the world ... 339
        classical text ... 339
        literal translation ... 340
        interpretation ... 341
    Xiao Guo: there are degrees for everything ... 344
        classical text ... 344
        literal translation ... 345
        interpretation ... 346
    Ji Ji: The difficulties of maintaining the achievements of our predecessors ... 348
        classical text ... 348
        literal translation ... 349
        interpretation ... 350
    Wei Ji: The path ... 353
        classical text ... 353
        literal translation ... 354
        interpretation ... 355

Part Three ... 357
  Having fun with the Book of Changes ... 357
  Divination: ... 358
  Thirty-six stratagems and sixty-four hexagrams ... 358
  How Zhou People used The Book of Changes ... 375
  I. Discourses of the States ... 375
  The part of "The Zuo Tradition" ... 382
  Divination ... 402
  Time to tell fortune, mister! ... 402

Part Four ... 411
  Leadership ... 411
  Methodology I — The way of leadership ... 411
  A general outline of Chinese leadership wisdom ... 414
  Framework of Chinese management thinking ... 416
  A framework of Chinese management consolidation ... 418
  Methodology II – The way of doing things ... 420
  One ... 420
  Two ... 421
  Acting according to one's capability. ... 423
  Striving for stability ... 425
  Simplification is the golden key to doing things ... 426
  Greatness is getting through all sorts of ordeals. ... 428
  The root of all problems is in yourself. ... 430
  Changing at the right time ... 431

Overview

A few days ago, a video of Bruce Lee was circulated on the Internet. During the interview he introduced the subject of Kung Fu, comparing it to water. "Water", Lee said, 'is one of the softest materials, yet it is able to penetrate the hardest rock, in the same way, one can adapt to defeat his opponents'.

When people hear this, they think of Laozi's concept of, "The placid and contented form of nature" and find that the king of Kung Fu, not only had a good technique, but made a real effort to raise and imbue the Kung Fu philosophical form.

This, to me can be a dilemma; once you enjoy something to its fullest, you start to enter into its philosophy. The same happens while engaging in sport, enjoying art, politics, business, etc.

The Japanese understanding in this respect seems to be particularly strong. For instance, when appreciating calligraphy, it is the Dao (the way) of calligraphy; enjoying flower arranging is the Dao of flower arrangement; all of these emphasise the Dao, which gives a mundane act a philosophical meaning.

People do not often understand modern art, so when a large white painting sells for millions of dollars, it begs the question, what is it all about? It is often because of the artists' philosophical interpretation, which once we understand it, we then join in the enthusiasm and exclaim, 'Wow, so deep. That's why is so valuable'.

Of course, these well-known artists do not dependent on the hype, so they must be deep thinkers. I like art but am no expert. I used to know very little about the great painter Wu Guanzhong. I only knew that his paintings are nice, and beautiful, and that their auction price is huge. One time, after watching a documentary about him, where he talked about his famous quote, 'pen and ink is equal to zero'. I was shocked as this is philosophy, the traditional view of the most valuable things being of zero cost and opened a new world. After that, I read more about art theory and found that almost every top painter has their own philosophical thinking.

Politics, even more so. In our education system, politics and philosophy are often not divided into separated subjects. The philosophical accomplishments of leaders, such as; Lenin and Mao Zedong need not be reminded, and political figures of all levels often relish talking about a philosophy of some kind. A great statesman, should be a great thinker, no problem with that. In recent years entrepreneurs, like the Japanese, Kazuo Inamori have built a great reputation in China. This is not because his products are used by many Chinese people, as his two Fortune 500 companies are not that well known there. His fame comes from talking about a way of living and philosophy.

What is this philosophy about? It is precisely China's own philosophy: Confucianism and Wang Yangming's philosophy, which is a sort of an export of domestic products.

Not many Chinese entrepreneurs can recall this philosophy like Inamori does, but many entrepreneurs like to talk about these ideas. For example, Jack Ma is not someone who likes to read books. He even said that except for Jin Yong's novels, he does not need to read any other books. But according to the people around him, he often turns to the *Tao Te Ching*. He learned Taiji boxing from an early age, and learnt from Taiji how the Internet can be transformed from the invisible or virtual to the real world of business. It is the secret of his success to turn virtual reality into actual reality.

A famous case of Ma Yun's combination of reality and the intangible is the investment in Haier (The invisible). Haier's Zhang Ruimin is praised by Jack Ma as a "management guru". This makes me think, Since Inamori, Matsushita Yukisuke, Akio Morita, and Honda Shoichiro are known as Japan's "Four Gurus", then who would China's Four Gurus be? I discussed this with several friends, and they all agreed upon four people: Zhang Ruimin, Liu Chuanzhi, Ren Zhengfei and Jack Ma. They have all different styles, but generally represent the highest level of corporate governance since China's reform and opening. Among the four, Zhang Ruimin is the most systematic in terms of management thinking. And which books did Ruimin's management ideas benefit most from? He said that his main non-Chinese influence is Peter Drucker. From China; *The Tao Te Ching*, *The Analects of Confucius*, *The Art of War*, and *The Book of Change*s influenced him the most. What I am about to say, was not said by Ruimin, but he suggests that there should be a relationship between "body" and "use". That is, using traditional Chinese philosophy as the body of literature, and using modern Western management ideas in practice.

A memoir of experience

So, what is philosophy? In a general sense, it is the understanding of basic principle pertaining to reality and existence; that acts as a guiding principle of behaviour. When you enjoy any kind of hobby, at first you may only rely on a feeling, passion, desire, vanity, obsessiveness, and eventually fall into helpless. The so-called beating the master by breaking the rules, even when you enjoy the task, the activity, something feels very good. It might actually be making you unstable. After all, sometimes, if you go deeper in the practice, you will find that there are some doorways, and "laws" that can be followed. By the time you get to this stage, you will be more experienced, and with greater expertise. These laws you may see as reliable? However, is there a more fundamental and more reliable law below the obvious? When you start considering this, that is when you break through to the philosophical level. Ultimately, what you comprehend and grasp at this level will in turn become a boost for enjoying this thing you practice.

So, how do enjoy philosophy? How do you comprehend and grasp the things you are trifling with from a philosophical level? There is an important saying in Confucianism 'Great Learning' – things have their root, and their branches. Affairs have their end, and their beginning. To know what is first and what is last will lead near to what is taught in the Great Learning. The meaning of this is that every good thing should have a good root, a good beginning, a good source. Like medical treatment, you have to find the root of the disease and know how the disease develops, step by step. Like when learning to compose music, you have to start from the seven notes, then progress a little bit at a time

When you reach a certain level, you can take a melody and you can figure out the notes 1, 2, 3, 4, 5, 6, and 7 of that song; or just play them differently and you can put these notes into a new melody.

In a similar way, when learning to write, you have to start from the alphabet with its twenty-six letters. Or for mathematics, why does 1 + 2 = 3? Because 1 + 1 = 2. Why is there a more complicated calculus? On a basic level, it is because 1+1 = 2. So why 1 + 1 = 2 then? For us ordinary people, this is the end, it is self-evident.

The same is true of the *Book of Changes*. For Chinese people, it is the source of all philosophy. When you study Zeng Guofan, Xue Yangming, Confucius and Laozi, if you go deeper, you will find that their source is in the *Book of Changes*. The concepts in the *Book of Changes* are equivalent to the basics of music, writing, or mathematics. It is the 1+1 = 2 of them.

It is the earliest of all Chinese classics, and it is the "prince" of all texts. Any other Chinese book is directly or indirectly affected by it, and so they are not one hundred percent original. It is the one original Chinese text, it has no other books to refer to, its only reference is nature.

In the case of Laozi's *Tao Te Ching*, his thought is almost entirely derived from the *Book of Changes*. The idea of "the movement of the Dao proceeds by contraries, weakness marks the course of Dao's mightiest deeds" is obviously derived from the *Book of Changes*.

As for Confucius; Historical Records recorded that he read *Book of Changes*. When he talks of "turning the slips three times", he is talking about the ropes of the bamboo slips that were used for the pages of early books. In *The Analects*, it is recorded he said, 'If some years were added to my life, I would devote fifty to the study of the I Ching, and then I might come to consider myself virtuous'. This means that if he could have studied *The Book of Changes* for a few more years, his accomplishments would have been even deeper.

When discussing the versions of the *Book of Changes*, scholars in the past two thousand years often think that it was written from the hands of Confucius himself, of what he learned from his experience while reading the *Book of Changes*.

After Laozi and Confucius, it is difficult to find original ideas in Chinese culture. Later generations of scholars mostly work on the basis of inheritance, incorporating new eras and new practices. This is also true of Wang Yangming and Zeng Guofan. They all invested themselves in the *Book of Changes* and benefited greatly from it. In Wang Yangming's famous, *Field of the Dragon Enlightenment*, few people know that it was inspired by the *Book of Changes*. He named the cave where he lived "The delightful lair of the I Ching". This is where he studied the *Book of Changes*. He also wrote *The Delight of the I Ching* to describe the experience of enlightenment.

In the diary of Zeng Guofan, he described in details of his study of the *Book of Changes*. On October 28, 1841, thirty-year-old Zeng Guofan and a few friends went to buy a set of Li Yidi's compilation of the *Book of Changes*, and then spent a year studying this set of books.

In the following decades, he read the *Book of Changes* almost every year, until January 1872, then he spent another twenty days reviewing it again, ten days later, he died.

In his diary, he also remembers some of the experiences of reading the *I Ching*. For example, he thinks that the six are the most meaningful (mean that those characters were Zeng Guofan's favourite hexagrams: Gua, Kun, Yi, Sun, Yi and Ding.). Moreover, he would occasionally use it for divination, and to make decisions.

There is a poem of the Confucian *Zhu Xi* that reads, "Where the channel is clear, there is a source of pure water". Why were the concepts of Laozi, Confucius, Wang Yangming and Zeng Guofan so fascinating? Because they all had the *Book of Changes* as their greatest source.

An analogy; after a chef has made a nice dish, and after you have eaten it, and sigh 'Oh, it's delicious!' This is also a wonderful experience! However, if you want to learn the skills of the chef, then you have to, at least know the ingredients in this dish. That is why the *Book of Changes* is so important.

After hearing of the merits of the book, you may ask; Will I be able to understand the *Book of Changes*? As mentioned above, if you agree that the *Book of Changes* is the 'one source of wisdom, then the "source" will indeed be complex.

But is it? How many notes are complicated? How many letters are complex? Is 1 + 1 = 2 complex? The source of the Yellow River, or the Yangtze River, is nothing but a clear spring. The source of life is nothing but a baby's innocent smile. Confucius once said, 'The path is not far from man'; Taoism says, 'the Great Path is simple'. The hallmark of this philosophy is simplicity.

The *Book of Change*s does demand an effort at the text level, or it can be understood as an egg with a hard shell on the outside, or an email that is encrypted. But this is normal. How can treasures be left in the open air? Please be assured that I have already stripped the "shell" in this book to ensure that you can understand it, learn it and use it. That is why this book is called "The Simplified" *Book of Change*s.

Another thought on this; do I REALLY understand it? Let us just say that as there are countless problems in the universe, and just because these complexities are not understood, they cannot stimulate the passion of human beings for exploration, and on the way, wisdom is constantly increasing. This may be the charm of the *Book of Change*s.

A few years ago, I began to write *Through Zeng Guofan*. Whilst writing, I got thinking about Zeng Guofan. He is just like an "Oriental Dale Carnegie", who was inspirational. However, his work was different from Dale Carnegie's Western-style inspirational books. Therefore, I coined the term of "Chinese-style inspirationalism", and wrote a preface suggesting that 'Self-improvement is the theme of "Chinese style inspirationalism".

Later, after becoming mainstream, I continued to explore the power behind Zeng Guofan's mindset and thought. Confucianism, Buddhism, Taoism, and Legalism all have their own school, but the most important is Confucianism. The *Analects of Confucius*, the *Mencius*, *The Great Learning*, and *The Doctrine of the Mean*. The *Four Books*. So I compiled a book called The *Four Books of Life*, which explore the Chinese's most basic outlook on life, namely; world view, family, wealth, self-cultivation, way of doing things, and learning. I wrote in the introduction about the Chinese-style inspirational roots in Confucianism as a preface.

Next, I did not linger in Taoism or Legalism as parallel to Confucianism. I was attracted by a force and went up the river to the source of Chinese culture. It is mysterious, and it should be a mystery. It uses only two simple symbols to create a great system that includes everything! With this basic system, it tells all the secrets of this culture with two simple statements;

- When heaven is in motion, the gentleman moves with it to improve himself.
- The strength of earth is in its receptiveness, the virtuous man helps others in such way.

While writing this, I suddenly remembered a verse "Why do my eyes often shed tears? Because I love this land deeply".

The *Book of Changes* is the source of Chinese-style inspiration. And I am proud if it.

If we could summarise the spirit of the Chinese style inspirational in one sentence, there is no better quotation than this one from the *Book of Changes*, "when heaven is in motion, the gentleman moves with it to improve himself".

First; it proposes the concept of heaven as understood by the civilised people of ancient China. As opposed to people, heaven is objective, encompassing the universe, nature, and natural law. Whereas, people are subjective, and they must maintain a harmonious interaction with heaven.

Second; suggests that the foundation of life lies in the effort and ascension of each person; the Confucian "inner saint and external emperor" or self control; Taoist "self-knowledge" and self-mastery', all emphasise this understanding.

Third; proposes that the essence of life is a state of constant resilience. The *Book of Changes* last hexagram is "Before Completion", which represents that every ending is a new beginning. In Confucianism this is the reason for the pursuit of the 'three accomplishments of; good moral, good deeds, and good speech; or, as expressed in Taoism; "He who does not resign, continues on the path, and even when he dies he does not perish, for he has attained longevity (he who has managed to live to very old age).

Fourth; suggests that the meaning of life lies in self-development and innovation. Self-improvement means maximising the value of life in a specific context.

Fifth; reflects in the minimalist language style unique to Chinese civilisation. If you can say it in a word, never use two – a single stroke right to the throat does the job. The words are many, and often pull the reader into the text to discuss with the author and together, think and contemplate.

In short, when heaven is in motion, the gentleman moves with it to improve himself contains many basic elements of Chinese culture. And it is but one sentence in the *Book of Changes*.

Throughout the ages, the interpretation of the *Book of Changes* has varied; where the benevolent see it, and call it benevolence; the wise see it, and call it wisdom.

The only reference I could find about the above statement is in Li Dingzhen of the Tang Dynasty; in Cheng Yi, Su Shi, Zhu Xi and Yang Wanli of the Song Dynasty; Wang Fuzhi (960–1279 BC) of the Qing Dynasty (1936–1911 BC), and the modern Huang Shouyi, and his contemporary Liu Dazhao as well as other scholars. Finally, in my mind, *Book of Changes* is a source of inspiration, and a book for thinking.

In this regard, in the section *The Nine Wings* I make a more detailed analysis. But first, I still hope that you will read the first part of "The Elephant", so you can go straight to the classics, and read the manuscripts, which is more flavourful and fresh.

The second last section is using the Divination, and the last is on management theory.

Of course, if you do not know anything about the *Book of Changes*, you have to first understand the symbols, and meaning of the Yin and Yang hexagrams, as these are the basis of the *Book of Changes*. The Yin and Yang constitute the Bagua, and the Bagua constitutes the sixty-four hexagrams. The sixty-four hexagrams are the verses of the *Book of Changes*. These are:

The Yin and Yang symbols are:
An unbroken line represent yang.
A broken line represents yin.

The Bagua is broken into:

Qian represent Heaven.
Kun, to represent Earth.
Zhen represent Thunder.
Xun, represents Air and Wood.
Kan, represents Water, it also represents Clouds and Rain.
Li, represents Fire and Lighting.
Dui, represents a marsh.

English version – Publisher's Notes

The I Ching or the Yi Jing, loosely translates into *The Book of Changes*. It is believed that when read with determination, life, as you know it will change, or rather, you will view life in a different way. It also describes how things change.

Gender; throughout this work most gender is masculine. As this is from the ancient, and we are not rewriting the ancient, we merely deliver its gems.

Throughout the work there are three interpretations; The Classical, Literal translation, and an Interpretation. We have retained all three as by doing so; it adds interest; offers variation from which understanding is gained to help "flesh out" the meaning. We suggest you study each. These three, The Classical, Literal translation, and an Interpretation, are reflected in the given colour.

This treatise comes from ancient China. The language that captures the treatise, not only comes from ancient China, it comes from the hearts and mouths of millions of Chinese people. The language and metaphors are the heart of the treatises, and the people.

To us Westerners, the language (even though translated to English) and metaphor will often seem incomprehensible. For instance, a description of; *he is himself subjected to the shaving of his head and the cutting off of his nose. There is no good beginning, but there will be a good end.* Yet, it is the very language that gives so much veracity and richness to the ways of imparting the information. Had we rewritten this, the language and metaphor would have remove the very foundation that emphasises the work. Additionally, our "conversion" would no doubt distance the reader from the true ethos. Besides, I am the scribe, not the sage!

The work therefore, and the presentation is a conundrum, but an interesting one. On the one hand, we have to take the time to decipher a meaning, such as; *With his relative and minister, he unites closely and readily as if he were biting through a piece of skin. When he goes forward with this help, what error can there be?* Which at second glance is not has obscure as that of the first. By doing so, it will have taken the reader closer to the core, the essence, of what those sages so long ago taught. But to help the reader, the author gives his interpretation. This therefore, is not a quick read. It is a work of determined study – one though that will be worth while for the dedicate student of the wisdom of the Tai De Ching (I Ching), and the divination methods.

The beauty that I just mentioned is in the wisdom offered and the way it is conveyed. Such as; *Bad luck is not your fault, your horse returns of its own accord. Meeting with the wicked will not make you one.* And, I would assume that you would read this book to gain wisdom.

Lastly on this. The language of description is the means to understand a collective race, called the Chinese. Within time, you will gain the ethos of "the language", and hopefully appreciate its beauty.

Part One

What kind of book is the *Book of Changes*?

Today's *Book of Changes* is roughly composed of two parts: that is classic and treatise. In this book we have three parts. Part One comprises of the classical explanation. Two discusses the 64 Hexagrams with textual explanation. Part Three is having fun with The *Book Of Changes* and Divination. Part Four, offers leadership principles.

In addition to the main text in Part One, which are an interpretation of the scriptures, including Emperor Wen's *Explanations of the entire Hexagrams*; *Great Treatise on the Symbolism of the Hexagrams*; *Lesser Treatise on the Symbolism of the Hexagrams*; *First Commentary on the Words*; *Second Commentary on the Words*; *First Commentary on the Appended Phrases*; *Second Commentary on the Appended Phrases*; *Sequence of the Hexagrams*; *Explanation of the Trigrams*; and *Miscellaneous Hexagrams*. These are called *The Nine Wings*.

The scriptures are profound and mysterious, and the treatises are profound and brilliant. The *Book of Changes* is indispensable because of its greatness. But in detail analysis, the charm of The *Book of Changes* lies in the classics. In these ten passages, there are a large number of praises and profound interpretations of both the "sage's words" and The *Book of Changes*, all of which are from the "Canon." We can learn from these to understand the ethos of The *Book of Changes*.

How The *Book of Changes* was written?

In ancient times, when Paoxi (Fu Xi) had come to rule everything under heaven, looking up, he contemplated the brilliant forms exhibited in the sky, and looking down, he surveyed the patterns shown on the earth. He contemplated the birds and beasts and the differences in the soil. Near at hand he found things that were the same to those at a distance, in all things in general. Based on this, he devised the eight trigrams, to show the attributes of the spirits and the intelligence of men, and to classify the qualities of the myriads of things.

This "Paoxi" is Fuxi, the ancestor of all Chinese people. He observed the natural phenomena of Heaven and Earth, combined them in his mind with problems encountered in his work and life, thinking about them in abstract terms, and then created the eight trigrams to analyse the various problems his people were facing.

Fuxi created The Eight Trigrams, which can be said to make for most of The *Book of Changes*. The Eight Trigrams are to The *Book of Changes*, the equivalent of axioms in mathematics. They are the basis for building the entire system. The symbols, names, and meanings of The Eight Trigrams are summarised as follows:

- Qian represents Heaven
- Kun represents Earth.
- Zhen represents Thunder.

- Xun represents Air and Wood.
- Kan represents water, it also represents Clouds and Rain.
- Li represents Fire and Lighting.
- Dui represents Lakes and Marshes.

The meaning of the Eight Trigrams goes far beyond this, but the basic meaning is roughly that. They are the same as the "Five Elements": metal, wood, water, fire, and Earth. They express a certain phenomenon and characteristics, rather than literally refer to them. I once asked an old Chinese medicine practitioner, 'Can you use the five elements in clinical practice for traditional Chinese medicine?' He replied, 'It's just like when a calligraphy practitioner begins, you have to first make a copy of the original when you first learn a script. Then when you create a calligraphy work, you do not need that copy anymore'. Theories such as "the five elements and the five internal organs" are only convenient for visualising the abstract relationship between the five internal organs.

The symbols of The Eight Trigrams are three horizontal lines. The three have profound meaning in Chinese culture. The three horizontal lines in The Eight Trigrams are considered to represent Heaven, man, and Earth, respectively. Lines that have a break in the middle indicate yin and are called yin strokes; whole lines indicate yang and are called yang strokes.

The "Yin and Yang Eight Trigrams", so familiar to Chinese people, were completed by Fuxi's hands. So, how did The Eight Trigrams become the sixty-four hexagrams? Sima Qian believes that Emperor Wen of Zhou is responsible for The *Book of Changes*. Xi Bo is another name for King of Zhou; King Wen was its ruler. At that time, he was a prince under King Shang Ye. He was put into prison by King Ye. Yet, he found time to do research in prison, so he combined his thinking about life and society. He compiled The Eight Trigrams into the Sixty-four hexagrams we see today. Emperor Wen's compilation was not complicated in form; the symbols of The Eight Trigrams were superimposed one on top of the other, so sixty-four symbols composed of six horizontal bars were obtained. Then, the meaning of the two trigrams combined with the Yin and Yang theory and how they change, has given different meanings to the sixty-four hexagrams. The sixty-four hexagrams are both a sequence and parallel, so the interpretations are constantly being expanded. From this idea, we can see that each hexagram is a life, and every word is a universe.

Two points define a straight line. Fuxi's The Eight Trigrams and Emperor Wen's sixty-four Hexagrams are such two points. They frame the path and direction of The *Book of Change*s infinite expansion.

At this time, it was completed during the Warring States period, roughly under the Shang and Zhou Dynasties, about 3000 years ago. This was the basic setting, so there were no real problems when expanded by future generations.

So, who wrote the follow-up? Again, Sima Qian has an answer; he believed that it was Confucius who elucidated the essence of The *Book of Change*s and wrote those treatises. They are known as "The Three Sages". That is to say, the creation of The *Book of Change*s was finally completed through the efforts of three generations of sages, including Fuxi, King Wen and Confucius. However, some people think that the "Three Sages" refers to King Wen of Zhou, The Duke of Zhou, and Confucius. Zhu Xi (1130–1222) believed that The Duke of Zhou was the author of *The Great Treatise*. Confucius held The Duke of Zhou as the most respected figure. He said that he often dreamt about him. I sincerely hope that Duke Zhou is the author of *The Great Treatise*. Only such a great person can say such great words as 'When Heaven is in motion. The superior man, in accordance with this, sets himself to action'. Also, 'The power of the Earth is what is denoted by Kun. The superior man, in accordance with this, uses his large virtue to support men and things'. These are really powerful sayings.

However, since the Qing Dynasty, the academic circles have been sceptical of the ancient style. They dismissed the "Three Sages". They think that the so-called "Three Sages" are just like the Yellow Emperor's (mythical character) Canon, just a big name that looks more authoritative and more convincing.

However, even if the authors of The *Book of Change*s were not the above-mentioned people, the authors of the *Book of Change*s are worthy of the name of "sage" in terms of the thoughts, and the quality of the text, and the inspiration on Chinese culture. Therefore, in this book, when referring to the authors of the *Book* *of Change*s, they are generally referred to as "sages" or "the sage" in general.

In my opinion, "sage" to Confucian culture, or Chinese culture, is like the Buddha in Buddhism. A title that should be stretched widely in our daily life. This is important for the development of modern Chinese civilisation. It will be far-reaching.

The thinking and method of The *Book of Change*s are easy to match with that of heaven and earth so that it can be the interpretation of the will of heaven and earth.

Ying and Yang

How did the ancient sages come up with the symbol of Yin and Yang? What came first? The symbol of Yin, or Yang or the concept of duality that the symbol represents? Why is the Yin and Yang symbol like this, and not something else? These issues relate to the origin of human civilisation, which can only be speculated and difficult to prove.

However, during the Shang and Zhou dynasties, the Chinese civilisation was already well developed. It is not surprising that the sages had mature yin-yang dialectical ideas from which they developed The Eight Trigrams and then the sixty-four hexagrams. So why did the sages design the symbols of yin, yang, and The Eight Trigrams? Why did they develop sixty-four hexagrams, and added a textual explanation? Why did they write a book about all this? It is actually quite simple. They did it to sum up the experience of their predecessors, so that future generations have a reference, so as to better survive and develop.

The Great Virtues of Heaven and Earth

The great grace and the great virtue of heaven, earth, and the universe lies in the production and sustains all things. Survival and development is the meaning of the universe. What is the point of a dead universe?

How can we better survive and develop? This is an eternal problem for human beings, and it is a complicated problem that can be broken down into countless sub-problems. For example; the ancient people asked: What is going on in the universe? Why are there four seasons? How do you live a good life? How can I live better? How to make things more secure? And many more. People have thought about these things since ancient times. The sages wanted to answer these questions, but there was no textbook to refer to, so what should they do? They could only observe and summarise in three aspects:

First; is the natural phenomenon.

Second; is the social phenomenon.

Third; the physical and mental phenomenon.

In my opinion, the scientific spirit of the Chinese is about observation and induction. Throughout history, there are books about face and palm reading/analysis. In them, they summarise all possible characteristics of the eyes, eyebrows, palms, etc., and certain characteristics correspond to certain personality traits and destiny. People who have these readings are often convinced by the conclusion. There is true insight to this work that cannot be denied. After five thousand years of accumulated study, no wonder there is understanding, which is the basis of ancient civilisation and modern science.

The observation and induction of the sages are fruitful and reflect three characteristics: they are simple, comprehensive, and systematic. With the attainment of such ease and such freedom after laborious effort, becoming a maser, which means acquiring of all virtues of heaven.

The sages did not have a computer or the Internet. Human beings could not analyse and process massive amounts of data in the detail required. They had no choice but to use "simplification" to simplify and manage complexity and use relatively simple forms and words to describe and analyse complex and complicated problems. However, this method of dealing with problems eventually rose into an important Chinese way of thinking and integrated into various fields of Chinese philosophy, drama, poetry, painting, and social life.

The successive movement of the inactive and active principles (Yin and Yang) constitutes what is called "The course of things".

There is a paragraph about Premier Zhou. A foreign reporter asked him the question, 'How many toilets are there in China?' Zhou responded very fast, saying, 'There are two, men's toilet and women's toilet'. This is simplification. That is the ultimate simplification, "one yin and one yang" in everything. How many kinds of people are there in the world? Man and woman. How many things are there in the universe? Good things and bad things. How many days will one live? One day or one night. And many more. All these can be collectively referred to as Yin and Yang.

So, a sage drew with a branch on the ground, one stroke, and with it, the story of the world began! This image of what later became the "one" in Chinese characters later, or the "1" of the Arabs, or the "I" of the Romans. In short, civilisation in the East and the West all started from this same image. Therefore, it is natural to use this "—" image to represent Yang. So how to express Yin? The sage stepped in the middle of the picture that he had just drawn, and that picture was broken into "— —". This is Yin, that simple it is. Of course, this is just my guess. Another famous speculation is that the sage created the "—" and "— —" from the appearance of male and female genitals. This kind of obscenity often appeared in ancient academic books, sexual depression, this is the fate of scholars. However, Yin and Yang are constantly changing, they are moving, they are full of shapes, and the two symbols for Yin and Yang alone are not enough to express the sages' insight clearly. Therefore, the sage arranged and combined the Yin and Yang symbols to form a richer symbolic system that could convey his insight and thoughts. From Yin Yang (two symbols), The Eight Trigrams (eight symbols), and then the Sixty-Four Hexagrams (sixty-four symbols), we can easily find the mathematical rules in it: the Third power of 2 equals 8, and the Sixth power of 2 is 64. So, according to this law, what the following Nth power of 2? It will probably surpass all existing experience, with infinite hexagrams, containing all problems in the universe. In fact, our entire modern science, and even economics, are based on similar mathematical rules. Mathematics is essential and closer to the understanding of the rules of nature.

The system of symbols created by our sages is not the same as mathematics. Content and form often affect each other, and the symbol system and the ideological system will inevitably influence each other. On the one hand, the sage uses this set of symbol systems to express his insight. On the other hand, this set of symbol systems must also inspire and enhance the sages thoughts, but eventually, "written words are a poor vehicle for thoughts". This is what makes the wonderful *Book of Changes* infinite in meaning, wholeness, and extensibility.

The core idea of the *Book of Changes*

The *Book of Changes* is one concept that should not be let slip from the mind. The frequent changing of its lines marks its method of teaching. They change and move without staying in one place, flowing about into any one of the six places of the hexagram. They ascend and descend, ever inconstant. The strong and the weak lines change places so that an invariable and compendious rule cannot be derived from them; it must vary as their changes indicate.

As mentioned above, the sages summarised their experiences of natural phenomena, life experiences, and human instincts in the *Book of Changes*. They gave a rough analysis of various problems faced by humanity.

At the core of all these experiences is the word "Yi" (mutation, change). Therefore, it is called "Zhou Yi" (Cycle Change), or the *Book of Changes*. Ancient scholars believe that this "Yi" word has three meanings: change, unchanging, and simple.

Simple, just as I said before, goes without saying. Unchanging refers to the basic laws that are not easy to change, that remains unchanged from ancient times. And what is apparently immutable is actually changing very slowly. Therefore, the core of The *Book of Changes* is about change and transformation, and more precisely, the law of change. What is the law of change? It is, of course, the law of the change of nature and life.

The sages emphasised the following points about the law of change: First, the basic form of change is the interaction of Yin and Yang. The successive movement of the inactive and active principles (Yin and Yang) constitutes what is called "The course of things".

How does your mood changes? Maybe it was bad yesterday, but you feel better today. Bad is Yin, good is Yang. Perhaps you feel that nothing has changed, it can only be a small degree of change, and it is not easy to detect. The change is from A to B, one being Yin and one being Yang.

So how do you get better when you are in a bad mood? According to this, when you are in a bad mood, there must also be some strength left to improve. There is Yang in Yin and Yin in Yang. Everything transforms between the two forces or elements of Yin and Yang. The second is that the result of change is development.

Production and reproduction is what is called the process of change

For humanity, there have been countless wars over the past few thousand years, and a large number of people have been killed. Various disasters have caused humanity to face numerous threats to survival; the humans have undergone many changes between survival and development, stagnation, and regression. It seems endless! For a better surviving, development is necessary. The same is true of the universe. There are many forces in the universe, full of random and chaotic variables, but in the end, the universe is expanding and developing.

The life of an individual, as small as it may be, also experiences many crises and difficulties. There are peaks and valleys. But eventually, life improves with these changes. Therefore, the ultimate result of all change is development.

There are two keys to grasping the laws of change. The operations forming the Yi (Change) are the method by which the sages searched exhaustively for what was deep, and investigated the minutest springs of things.

Learn and master the laws of change in order to improve your situation and better handle various practices. The two keys here are to be "extremely deep" and learn to "research". Extremely deep means to do in-depth study of the law of change of things. Can I do it after reading the *Book of Changes* several times? Of course, that is not all. However, many people just read it a few times, and with only a little knowledge, and emerge tell the whole story, do fortune-telling, and give advice on Feng Shui. Suddenly they become "Masters." The reading ends up being shallow. The *Book of Changes* is full of wisdom, and its value is often in the "meaning" rather than the words. To understand this "meaning", we must combine a rich social practice and apply a large number of historical examples to understand the laws of change. That is how we can have a more objective understanding.

Researching is learning how to detect things in time, catch the signs of change in time, then infer the possible results in accordance with the rules of change, and take timely counter measures to avoid disadvantage. When you see an ant nest on a river embankment, you can think that there will be many other ant nests nearby, and there may also be many rat and rabbit nests. These burrows may pose a threat to the safety of a dike, so you must quickly find them and deal with them.

A necessarily attitude to the law of change is awe.

If at the beginning there is a cautious apprehension as to the end, there will probably be no error or cause for blame. This is what is called the way of the Yi (Change).

The sixty-four hexagrams of The *Book of Changes* contain more or less worrying thoughts. While sailing with the wind, you are probably not thinking that extreme joy begets sorrow; likewise, when tragedy strikes, you probably will not believe that blessings never come in pairs or misfortunes never come singly. Do not let those things play in your head. While progressing, there is also worrying, while retreating there is also worrying. In the *Book of Songs*, it is said that, "With fear and trepidation, be cautious in handling one's business, tread carefully as if walking on thin ice". Why are the sages so careful? What is there to be afraid of? There are two aspects: one is because of the awe of nature and destiny; the other is because of a high sense of responsibility, responsibility to yourself, responsible to the cause, and responsible to the people.

The *Book of Changes* practical applications

That which precedes the material form exists as an ideal form, and that which it follows after the material form exists as a definite thing. Transformation and shaping are what we call change; carrying this out and operating with it is what we call generalising; taking the result and setting it forth for all people under heaven is, securing the success of business of life.

Tao is the supreme law of Chinese philosophy. It is "first philosophy" in terms of Western philosophy, and the Chinese usually use "metaphysics" when translating the term. The Tao transcends all tangible matter and governs all tangible matter, just as the human spirit and mind govern the physical body. The tangible matter is a vessel. The spirit guides the physical movement of the body. Such changes need to undergo numerous adjustments before it can be stabilised in a more effective form. Similarly, when the Tao acts on the vessel, the change will gradually show its pattern. This regularity will be extended, and it will further form a larger form and shape. This will ultimately push for the survival and development of human society. This is what the sages hoped for the application of *The Book of Changes*. They hope to build a system of philosophy as the core to guide the development of human society.

We look at the ornamental figures of the sky, and thereby ascertain the changes of the seasons. We look at the ornamental observances of society and understand how the processes of transformation are accomplished under the heaven; "Bi (Decoration), King Wen's Explanations of the entire Hexagrams".

Grasping change and turning the world into a beautiful new world is the application that sages seek. The benevolent see it and call it benevolence. The wise see it and call it wisdom. The common people, acting daily according to it, yet have no knowledge of it.

As mentioned earlier, once *The Book of Changes* was produced, the deduction mode it presents, allows it to transcend all existing experiences, including the experience of its authors. Just like the plot often found in Hollywood blockbusters where some scientists invent a robot. Ultimately, the robot has far more intelligence and capabilities than the human who invented it, and it becomes difficult to control, so in the end, humans are controlled by it. In short, *The Book of Changes* is similar to *The Book of Heaven* in the eyes of future generations, with various possibilities. Its text is dead. Everyone sees nothing different, but the thinking that is triggered is very different. The so-called benevolent see benevolence; the wise see wisdom.

We should set the highest value on its explanations to guide us in speaking;

- on its changes for the initiation of our movements
- on its emblematic figures for definite action as in the construction of implements
- on its prognostications for our practice of divination.

Writers see a beauty similar to the *Book of Songs*, hustlers see the secret of success in it, creators see the genius of the invention in it, and of course, many fortune tellers and Feng Shui adherents see it as their bread and butter. As the source of Chinese culture, the later sages, who wrote and spoke, could not study it properly. So Lao Tzu saw the *Tao Te Ching* inside, Confucius saw the *Analects* and the ideology of Confucianism. And so, Taoism and Confucianism were established, and Chinese thought expanded from there.

Then, what do I see in it? What I saw was "the Image", which is also part of the original title of the book.

The word for image in Chinese (Xiang) sounds very similar to the one for elephant (Xiang). There is an English saying, "The elephant in the room". It refers to the things that are obvious and easy to see but are ignored by people. There is quite a big elephant in "The Image" in *The Book of Changes*, the first sentence of which is "Heaven, in its motion, it gives the strength. The superior man, in accordance with this, sets himself to ceaseless activity". And the second sentence is, "The capacity and sustaining power of the earth is what is denoted by Kun. The superior man, in accordance with this, with his large virtue, supports men and things". These great words are popular and deeply integrated into the psyche of the Chinese nation. However, in today's reading and understanding of *The Book of Changes*, they have been ignored to a certain extent. Even in the ancient *Book of Changes* research, *The Great Treatise* was not given enough attention.

In my opinion, *The Great Treatise* is the highest of the *Nine Wings*, and it is truly a high-rise building. It should be used as an entry point to interpret the sixty-four hexagrams. Moreover, the living truth and self-cultivation thoughts clearly expressed in *The Great Treatise* are the "The images of The *Book of Changes*, which is the main spirit of The *Book of Changes*. With this in mind, understanding the sixty-four hexagrams is imperative.

Therefore, in my eyes, *The Book of Changes* is the most important inspirational book in the world! When I say that, I am not trying to win publicity. In fact, as a classic of Confucianism, the mainstream Confucian scholars for more than 2,000 years mainly focused on its "righteousness", which is the principle of repairing oneself and governing others. I once said that the foundation of Chinese-style inspiration lies in Confucianism, and I meant this is only to inherit their relics.

However, it is undeniable that the value of *The Book of Changes* lies in rationality, and the charm of *The Book of Changes* lies in its openness, inclusiveness, and its mystery of divination.

[...] when living quietly, contemplates the emblems and studies the explanations of them; when initiating any movement, he contemplates the changes that are made in divining, and studies the prognostications from them.

In the earliest historical books, *Discourses of the States* and *The Zuo Tradition*, there are a lot of cases for using *The Book of Changes* for divination. So evidence of the original use as an oracle is undeniable. Confucianism avoids ghost talks and superstitions, but does not exclude the use of divination in *The Book of Changes*. SiMa's *Historical Records*, tells that Confucius was obsessed with the study of *The Book of Changes* in his later years and he studied it diligently. *The Analects of Confucius* also records Confucius himself saying, 'If some years were added to my life, I would give fifty to the study of the Yi, and then I might become to be without so many faults". Therefore, later generations believed that The Great Commentary of *The Book of Changes* came from the hands of Confucius.

Moreover, there are new unearthed historical materials that prove that Confucius himself also used it as a divinatory tool, and that is how he became a half-immortal, haha. The great Confucianist, Zhu Xi (1130–1200), of the Song Dynasty also commented on *The Book of Changes* referring to it as a book of divination. From a folk perspective, for more than 2,000 years, divination based on *The Book of Changes* has been a profession and has supported many people. But can people really predict the future with a single book? If they could, would not those people be able to escape from a huge disaster like an earthquake? Or even if some people do it, with 7 billion people, would not the streets be always full of panic? Confucius said, 'Hear much and put aside the points of which you stand in doubt, while you speak cautiously at the same time of the others – then you will afford few occasions for blame'. As for the divination of *The Book of Changes*, we might as well hold a spirit of tolerance and a playful attitude. Occasionally, my friends and I gather for divination, and they feel it is accurate and suggestive. In my opinion, this is a psychological issue.

Moreover, interpreting hexagrams requires many insights. In short, it is fun to play with it. So I also spent a lot of effort to sort out the cases of divination in the early history books for your reference. In Part Three, I introduced a simple method of divination. You can play with it and conduct divination yourself. Maybe you can also become a "Master", haha.

In all these operations forming the Yi (the change or mutation), there is no thought and no action. It is still and without movement; but, when acted on, it penetrates forthwith to all phenomena and events under the sky.

*The Book of Change*s is like a game of Go, with only black and white pieces, with nineteen straight and vertical lines forming a chessboard. I believe that the person who invented Go is definitely also a master, but it should not be the highest, because there is no such thing as being the best. There is only being better. And, certainly, the person who invented Go could not exhaust the possibilities of Go.

In ancient times, the sages compiled *The Book of Change*s. Then countless researchers, many from different perspectives, also wrote books about it. In my opinion, these studies are equivalent to a certain game of Go. The charm of Go is not in the white and black pieces and the board but the mental struggle between the players. Similarly, the charm of *The Book of Change*s lies not in these hexagrams and words. Still, in that, it gives us a simple and infinitely extensible framework. Once the mind enters this framework, it will be affected by it and will follow involuntarily. This framework runs as an infinite exploration channel. Just like Chinese poetry, books, and paintings, you can study it all your life, yet you cannot exhaust it; you will always have a sense of freshness, interest, and playfulness until death. You will never feel bored or tired.

*The Book of Change*s lies not in what it tells us, but in what it makes us think.

Philosophical view

*The Book of Change*s carries an important idea found all over Chinese culture: harmony between men and nature. This "harmony" refers to the notion that the faith of heaven and man is interlinked and consistent. Therefore, there is a constant threat, of "bolts out of the blue"; a person's fate is as uncertain as the weather; life is full of vicissitudes. All of these refer to the interaction between heaven and men. The problems encountered by human beings are accompanied by certain omens, including astrology, natural phenomena and disasters, and other unexplainable phenomena. Or plain calamity. A disaster was often an opportunity for self-examination for ancient rulers.

This understanding is not necessarily scientific, but it makes sense. All reasonable people must be scientific, but there may be doubt too of things that have not yet been thoroughly studied. Based on the idea of "harmony between man and nature", the Chinese have regarded the earth and the universe as one since ancient times.

Humanity is a single living body, which should be the consensus reached by human beings today when facing environmental issues. Heaven and humanity are both the Tao (The Way). By observing and summarising the ways of heaven and earth, we can have a deeper understanding of how people do things.

So, what is this important Way for Heaven and Earth that the sages emphasise in *The Book of Changes*? As mentioned above, "Yi" (change) is the core of the entire ethos, and it is also the core of the Way of Heaven and Earth. Around this core, the Tao of Heaven and Earth also includes some important principles, namely: time, creation, exchange, correctness, recovery, balance, agreement, and many more.

All under heaven will be found at its time

All under heaven will be found at its time. King Wen's *Explanations of the Hexagrams* Profits and losses take place in harmony with the conditions of the time.

Sun, King Wen's Explanations of the entire Hexagrams' When the sun has reached the meridian height, it begins to decline. When the moon has become full, it begins to wane. The interaction of heaven and earth is now vigorous and abundant, now dull and scanty, growing and diminishing according to the seasons. How much more must it be so with the operations of men!

Feng, King Wen's Explanations of the entire Hexagrams; When a sage observes the change between heaven and earth, the first thing he notices is the day and night and the four seasons, and then an abstract concept dawns on him – time. Einstein said that time is an illusion of human cognition. We feel time in change, and then we have the perception that time leads and drives change. This is what the sages call "the world at any given time". All change and movement unfolds on the axis of time. What if time is zero? Like a superhero screaming in a science fiction movie, "Time has stopped!" Then everything stands still; can the whole universe stands still?

A seed germinates, grows, sometimes bears fruit, and then withers over time.

A worm crawling on the ground becomes a butterfly flying in the sky over time and then becomes still. A baby girl, over time, becomes a girl, then a beauty, then a pregnant woman, a mother, an older woman, and then a pile of bones after death. Over time, a ship sailing from one dock to another may change several captains, or even be refitted, and eventually, be sold as scrap iron. An enterprise gradually develops, grows, or transforms over time, and finally becomes a completely different company than the one it was at the beginning. Heraclitus said that one person could not step into the same river twice because time makes everything no longer the same thing over time.

One time, someone crossed a river by boat, then they accidentally dropped the sword into the river. Then he made a mark on the ship's side where the sword had dropped and later waited for the boat to come back to try and salvage the sword using that mark.

The well-known parable in *Master Lü's Spring and Autumn Annals* was included in the textbooks of elementary school. I thought it was ridiculous during school, but who of us did not make such a mistake?

Today's friends only represent today's friendship. Tomorrow may be different. The successful experience of the ancients may not be applicable to modern times. Copying may be unfortunate. Someone today is a gentleman, and tomorrow maybe a villain. The fastest changing thing in the world is the human heart. Lots of corrupt officials were once zealous youths; a lot of grief turned into sorrows that passes through their hearts when they laugh now. Times change; it is a brave new world.

What is evil at one time, becomes good at another time. What to do? Keep up with the times! The theory of the ruling party must keep pace with the times. It is necessary to update it constantly, optimise it, and achieve harmony with the social development of the times.

Traditional culture and Confucianism must also advance with the times. It seems that the revival of Confucianism, the study of scriptures, the promotion of ancient Chinese clothing in society, etc. All measures that have been taken without regard to changes in circumstances. Now is the era of globalisation. We cannot go back. Confucius would be wearing a suit and tie today. The new Confucian must be able to stand in a new way to adapt to modern society. Companies must keep pace with the times, constantly adjusting, and always following the beat of the age. Haier's Zhang Ruimin has a famous saying, 'there is no successful company, only the company of the times'. Otherwise, just like Kodak and Nokia, they were the industry leaders last decade and then be dumped this decade.

So is marriage. A married woman is often troubled and thinks: when he was not married, he was so good to me and made me so happy, but now he is unbearable? In fact, love has the faint joy of love, marriage has the ephemeral happiness of marriage, but the way to get along must be adjusted over time.

If the time is good, luck is good, and life is good. Among the elements of success or failure that Chinese people agree upon, timing is the first. It is invisible and intangible, but always affecting everything.

The Great Virtues of Heaven and Earth

Heaven and earth nourish all things. The sages feed men of talents and virtue for them to reach to the myriads of the people.

Yi, King Wen's Explanations of the entire Hexagrams; We also have in it heaven dispensing and earth producing, leading to an increase without the restriction of place.

Yi, King Wen's Explanations of the entire Hexagrams Production and reproduction is what is called the process of change.

[...] in the system of the Yi (the change) there is the Supreme Ultimate, which produced the Yin Yang. Those two forms produced the Four emblematic Symbols, which again produced the eight Trigrams. The eight trigrams served to determine good and evil in issues, and from this determination produced the prosecution of life.

The Great Virtues are all of Heaven and Earth

When we discuss all issues, the central premise is survival. King Louis the XV of France, once said, 'After I die, the flood will come'. It sounds awkward, but it was true. If human beings cannot survive and become extinct, then it matters little what science or wisdom is. There would not be any meaning, and the universe has in itself no meaning. The meaning lies in survival.

Many people are confused. Why do people live? What is the meaning of life? The meaning of life in life itself. What better reason to live on every day than this?

The sages said that the universe originated from an origin, and this origin is called "Tai Chi" (Supreme Ultimate). Out of the Yin and Yang, "the two symbols", there came "four images". The four images are the four seasons, the four directions, etc. It is the quadratic power of Yin and Yang. Then the cubic power becomes the "The Eight Trigrams", which continuously develop and generate the universe and everything.

The Taoist thought of the universe that it was continuously improving: "All things under heaven sprang from nothingness; everything sprang from It". The Tao produced One; One produced Two; Two produced Three; Three produced All things.

Later, Confucianism, during the Song Dynasty, further improved this: Nothingness engendered Tai Chi, Tai Chi engendered Yin and Yang, and Yin and Yang engendered the five elements, which in turn produced everything. No matter how it is expressed, the basic point is the same: the universe is constantly developing. In fact, modern science also proves that the universe is constantly expanding.

We produce in order to survive and develop. This is a primitive standard for measuring good and evil. All thoughts and practices that are conducive to survival and development will be carried forward. All those that violate this principle and are not conducive to survival and development will eventually die. In line with this trend, the value of each individual's life lies in creation and innovation, and in helping as many people as possible to improve their survival and development. The most ordinary person, trying to train children, providing for the elderly, and helping others is the way to realise the value of life.

Maybe you have to ask, since survival and development are the keys to heaven, why are so many species extinct, or so many people die in various disasters? It can only be said that, on a higher level, all death is for a better life, just like suffering can make people stronger.

Food and sex too. Eating and sex, and all human instincts are to ensure survival, and the source of human strength is precisely for survival.

Not communicating is out of the question

Heaven and earth in communication with each other, and all things, in consequence, having free course, and also the high and the low, superiors and inferiors, in communication with one another, and possessed by the same aim.

Tai, King Wen's Explanations of the entire Hexagrams; Heaven and earth meeting together, all the variety of natural things become fully displayed. His *Explanations of the Hexagrams*; If heaven and earth were to have no intercommunication, things would not grow and flourish as they do.

Gui Mei, King Wen's Explanations of the entire Hexagrams; The first part talked about the question of "engendering", but did not mention how it happens. How to engender? Can a woman have children by herself? Of course not. If a woman wants to have a child, she must have intercourse with a man, and the sperm and egg interact to form a fertilised egg before she can turn it into a foetus.

Can we hatch chickens from the eggs bought from the market? Generally, it is not possible, because the hens laying these eggs have never seen a rooster in their lifetime, and of course, they have not mated.

The same is true of plants. The flowers that bloom also involve male and female; all things have to have a similar process of mating and conception. Of course, there are also problems with hermaphrodites and cloning. But we are not studying biology. There may be exceptions in everything; there is always something unknown. The vision of the ancients was great. They paid attention to the interaction of heaven and earth in the production of all beings.

Plants are rooted in the ground. Animals eat and rest on the ground, but they cannot do without sunlight and rain. Plants need photosynthesis. Even the fish in the water cannot survive without the sun. Heaven and earth, no one can do without them.

Nothing is possible without interaction. On the other hand, if you set your mind to get something by "interacting', and you devote all your energy, you will be able to produce and prosper. We discussed this below in the hexagram of "Tai".

All chemistry is based on this theory. When several chemical elements are matched together, a new thing emerges. As in the kind of branches that can be grafted on an apple tree, which becomes a new variety, and the fruit produced is large and sweet.

Education in China is for the body, what education in the West is for practical application. Stones from other mountains can be used to make jade millstones. By bringing in advanced Western ideas and combining them with Chinese traditions, the country developed well.

Often the more isolated things are blended, the more interesting the result is. There is a fashionable saying among the Internet community, "cross-border", that's what it is all about. Besides, "crossing" is not limited to mating. It is not necessary to produce new things. "Interaction" can also be communication and exchange, which can improve the relationship between things. Make friends, keep close relationships with your boss or subordinates, and have a more heart-to-heart relationship with your family. The relationship will be improved, efficiency will be improved, and you will find new opportunities and feel better. For the average person, intercourse may be more attractive, but connecting is more useful.

The union of the antagonist

Heaven and earth are separate and apart, but the work that they do is the same. Male and female are separate and apart, but with a common will, they seek the same object. There is diversity between the myriad classes of beings, but there is an analogy between their several operations.

Kui, King Wen's *Explanations of the Hexagrams*; "The way of heaven, calling the lines Yin and Yang; the way of earth, calling them the weak or soft and the strong or hard, and the way of men, under the names of benevolence and righteousness".

Explanation of the Trigrams; "Heaven and earth are different, but they work together to produce and nurture all things". Men and women are also different, but they are attracted to each other, and they have a heart and soul. All creatures are different, and some even use each other as food, but coexist, maintaining an ecological balance.

Heaven is divided into Yin and Yang, things are divided into rigid and soft, and humanity is divided into righteousness and evil. Benevolence is yin and tender; righteousness is yang and rigid. In fact, it is better to say that humanity is divided between good and evil. Man is a complex kind of devil and angel, and both strive to maintain a balance between self-interest and altruism. Regardless of heaven, earth, man, nature, or human society, everything is made up of elements that are both contradictory and complementary.

Contradiction, the unity of opposites, dialectics, splitting into two, and combining two into one, all these are all-important philosophical concepts. All the problems we face can be analysed using this framework. It is a powerful tool that makes our thinking more comprehensive and more inclusive. All negative things have a positive meaning. The so-called misfortune and fortune are mutually dependent. You might ask an extreme question: Is death something positive? This issue has been discussed in the analysis of "the great virtues of heaven and earth". At a higher level, the significance of death lies in better survival. Maybe that is its meaning.

All things have meaning. At the beginning of liberation, the four pests (flies, mosquitoes, mice, and sparrows) were eliminated. This endeavour was carried out, and it may not hurt, but if these species were to be extinct, humans might also be finished. It is said that a scientific research group in the United States worked in a sterile environment for a long time, and they all died young.

The ancient Chinese used this idea as a tool to flourish in many fields such as military, architecture, medicine, and art.

Everlasting and unchanging

The way of heaven and earth is to be long continued in their operation without stopping.

Heng, King Wen's *Explanations of the Hexagrams*; Even modern science cannot tell when the universe started, and even more difficult to tell when it will end. The universe seems endless.

Many things in nature embody eternal characteristics. The sun, the moon, stars, mountains, and lakes. They do have their beginning and end, and they have maintained long-term stability. Long-term stability is persistence, which is a necessary condition for everything to survive and develop. For example, a foetus must have stable amniotic fluid. If not, it will be aborted.

Why did our republic not develop before 1978, but have been able to maintain rapid development for more than thirty years? It was because of the change it underwent before, the "Great Leap Forward" and the "Cultural Revolution" that social instability was like a catalyst, and after decades of reform, it remained stable for decades.

Stability is not being static, but to maintain a certain state, such as the state of struggle, the state of research, and the state of learning. Doing things at a fixed time, every day, every month, every year. This is stability.

Of course, another key is the long-term. When we buy a house, we will encounter the issue of the time we can use the land. There are forty years, fifty years, and seventy years state leases, and most people do not think it matters, because there is no knowing what society will become at that time. The Japanese seem to have long-term literacy. They invest in a project and plan to recover costs in fifty years. At that time, the person that develops it may have died. The Japanese tycoon Sun Zhengyi, who invested in Yahoo and Alibaba, made his fifty-year life plan at the age of nineteen, and then made it all happen. Regarding investment, Sun Zhengyi said that to plant an apple tree, plant it this year, but will you have an apple this year? Definitely not. It must grow for three or four years before it can produce apples. After a day of work, when the money can be earned on the same day, it usually for the lowest level of business.

Divine retribution

Do we not see in Fu the mind of heaven and earth?

Fu, King Wen's *Explanations of the Hexagrams*; as mentioned earlier, eternity is a major feature of heaven and earth. Many things between the universe and the nature of heaven and earth have a very long existence, which is almost eternal. However, logically, anything on the axis of time must have a beginning and an end.

So is there an infinite distance between the start and the end? Or logically, the starting point of the universe must be infinitely small, otherwise what would be smaller than the one thing before the starting point? And if the universe is infinite, then its end must be infinitely big, otherwise what would be outside the boundary? In fact, the universe is an infinitely small point, its inner edge is the starting point, and its outer edge is the endpoint. In Zhuangzi's words, it means, 'That which is so great that there is nothing outside. It may be called the Great One; that which is so small that there is nothing inside it may be called the Small One'. The big one and the small one are all one.

When we were in elementary school, when we learned the allusion that "the South is the North", we heard of that the person who was going to the south but ended up going north. He had no problem with the theory. He would go around the earth and finally get to the other side. You can always go back to where you started. The way of the earth and all the stars is almost the same – starting from a starting point continuously and going back to the starting point in a cycle.

We can imagine that in a large, stable, and organised systems, to maintain unlimited long-term movement, the most likely way is to go round and round or to go back and forth. In the words of *The Book of Changes*, it means that "everything goes on". All beginning from the starting point will return to the same point. So, will light travel in circles? Will time bend back to the beginning? It seems that modern theoretical physics holds this argument.

Mo Yan was inspired by Buddhism's *The Six Great Divisions in the Wheel of Karma* to conceive a novel. Reincarnation is Buddhism's understanding of eternity. A man starts naked and ends naked. Where was it before? Where will it go? The starting and ending points are both zero. In physics, the effect of all forces is mutual, how much force you exert, and how much force you will receive simultaneously. Similarly, your thoughts, actions, and energy will definitely return to you.

Mencius said, 'What proceeds from you will again return to you'. Therefore, kind deeds pay rich dividends; evil is repaid with evil; this is divine retribution.

Every time Zen master Lkkyu encountered a difficult problem, he would sit down quietly and draw circles on his head with both hands. Tai Chi is also a circle. Many questions may be answered by drawing a circle. Do not try it during the exam though.

In all the processes taking place under heaven, what is there of thinking?

All roads lead to Rome. This "Rome" can be truth, success, or some other goal. Just like a geometric problem, there are several ways to solve it. From a higher level, these different paths, or methods, are consistent. Just like the more than seven billion people in this world; some live by the sea, some live on a plateau, some are poor, some are rich, some are blind, and some are sloppy; there are all kinds of skin colours, and all sorts of faces, each have a life and a different way to live it. Still, in general, we are all the same; we go from foetus to babies, to teenagers, to youth, and old age. We have all emotions, joys, and sorrows, we all have to die.

There are many religions with a long tradition in the world, such as Buddhism, Taoism, Christianity, Islam, Confucianism, etc. The basic teachings are similar. Think positive.

All philosophy hope to solve such problems as to where do I come from, and where do I go. All reach the same goal by different paths. From this, Zhu Xi (1130–1200) put forward an important philosophical point, "There Is But One Universal Principle, Which Exists in Diverse Forms". He also made an analogy, there is only one moon in the sky, and countless lakes and ponds on the ground have the reflection of the moon. There is only one heavenly way, but it exists in various shapes in different forms. There is also an image in "Zhuangzi". Someone asked him where Tao was. He replied that Tao was everywhere, in ants, rubble, and faeces.

Everything has "Tao" (A path): playing chess has a technique to play chess, writing has a method to write, fitness has a way to keep fit, driving has a way to drive. The Japanese like to use the word "Tao". They put it in chess, martial arts, and tea ceremony, they are all connected and with the way of life it entitles, because they are all the original way, they are all the ways of heaven and earth.

Looking to the interpretation of the sixty-four hexagrams in *The Book of Change*s, there are various schools of thought, with heavy images and heavy meanings. Still, the final interpretation of the top masters should be consistent. Just like for a patient, Chinese medicine has its treatment and methods, and Western medicine has its treatment methods. Still, ultimately the disease has a cure because the Tao is union.

In the Northern Song Dynasty, Shao Yong (1011–1077) and Cheng Yichuan (Cheng Yi, 1033–1107) were the two great masters representing the schools of interpretation of *The Book of Change*s. In Qian Mu's book he tells this story about them: When Shao Yong was dying, Yi Chuan gestured to Yi Chuan with both hands, saying, 'The path in front must be wide, if it were narrow, it wouldn't be enough for everyone on the road'. Shao Yong's meaning is that no matter what the approach is, it should not be sectarian. Everyone will get on the road (to death). My experience is the same. I take a hexagram and interpret it, then look at the written meaning. The conclusion is the same.

An outlook on life; On Being Human

As a broad conclusion, all philosophies are human life studies. They are all about how people live, how they should live, how they look at problems, and how they go about them.

If the saying, 'Tao is not far from the people', and something has been spoken for a long time, but does not touch people's hearts, then it must not be "Tao", and it must not have spread.

The Book of Changes is a classic of Chinese philosophy. It is a summary of the experience of ancient sages. It includes both heaven and earth, and its roots are both humane and divine.

There are so many comments on being a human. Modern times are full of text such as *Chicken soup for the soul*, and all these things that are uploaded on Weibo and WeChat, there is too much. So what is different about *The Book of Changes*? In my opinion, *The Book of Changes* is more flavoursome, deeper and more comprehensive.

The significance of revisiting these doctrines lies in the fact that these doctrines are of eternal value and cannot be surpassed, and we better be absolutely determined to practice them. There are ten themes of development: fate, endeavour, good deeds, integrity, modesty, caution, patience, perseverance, harmony, and independence.

Destiny is the grasp of the overall situation of life

Be happy with your fate, it is inevitable.

Recently I read SiMa's *Comprehensive Mirror in Aid of Governance*, and the biggest feeling was that the history of the Chinese people is really a history of war, fighting every year. In this life, ordinary people can survive without war. A large number of people died in war, and even the words "cannibalism" often appear in history books. The official ranks are also uncomfortable with the idea. Being in the king's company is like living with a tiger. Many people in history have been killed, or their relatives have been killed. Many of Su Dongpo's (1037–1101) handed down letters in which they told the recipients to burn them or not show them to others. In this background of suffering and tragedy, people lived – on the one hand, relying on survival instincts, and on the other hand, spiritual conviction coming from comfort and self-motivation. Therefore, the more troubled the times are, the bigger markets religion has. Both Buddhism and Taoism developed in a troubled times like the Three kingdoms and the Two Jin Kingdom.

Even in the heyday of peace, everyone faces the plight of old age, illness, death, and life vicissitudes. It is a consensus that people live to suffer. Therefore, the market for religion is always vast. And the hope that all religions give these lies: Be happy with your fate. Fate is to believe that God will help you, or that God will redeem you, or that Buddha will bless you, or that Allah is with you.

To know one's life is to know the basic principles in life, such as birth, illness, death, inevitable sorrows, joys and tragedies, luck, good fortune, and happiness. I call this "positive fatalism". I believe that many things are decreed by fate, so do not be arrogant. Failure is also mentioned in *The Book of Changes*. It may be that you are or are not incompetent. Or it may be your destiny that will lead you to a more suitable path, or let you lay the foundation for you to improve. Just follow those basic principles.

The Great Virtues of Heaven and Earth. The destiny of everyone is survival and development. It is positive, not destruction. Is there any reason to be pessimistic?

Lao Tzu said that the Tao makes up for all harm it does. Fate will compensate you for your shortcomings in various ways. Those who carry heavy shovels and live off their hard work are dirty and tired, but they all have strong muscles and are fitter; they do not eat fancy food, but they do enjoy sweets; some women might not be beautiful, but their sex life could not be better.

The so-called "Heaven dispenses wealth and rank are matters of destiny", you can be happy one day and sad the next, so why not laugh? We have no reason not to be an optimist.

More than ten years ago, I ended my student days. I was selling books in a small town, renting a room with only a small bed. I asked my friends to write a banner (幅贴 a four characters scrolls meant for decoration) on the wall, it read: Reality is cruel, there no room for vanity or romance, but you must smile regardless. Looking at it today, it still feels relevant, and maybe it will last a lifetime.

Struggle is the main theme of life

When heaven is in motion, the gentleman moves with it to improve himself! This first sentence in *The Book of Changes* and *Treatise on the Symbolism of the Hexagrams* sets the tone of the book. It also sets the tone of traditional Chinese culture, and sets the tone of Chinese philosophy of human life – which is struggle.

I chose the following sentences to help understand this topic: The superior man, advancing in virtue and cultivating the sphere of his duty, yet wishes to advance only at the proper time.

Zeng Guofan educated his children and used this maxim often. He said that fame, profit, power, and affection are all things arranged by destiny that we cannot control. That he can grasp only two things: progress in morality and self-cultivation. Moral virtue is working within oneself, that is, internalising what you study. Self-cultivation comes from doing your current job well. With a little more effort on these two things, there will be more gains that support each other.

So, "at the proper time", we have to catch up. Time does not wait for people, years do not forgive. The fairness of the world can be seen on those with grey hair, and they do not have time to spare. The time God gives to people is almost the same. In fact, struggling is mainly a matter of time management. Using time for meaningful things is struggling; using it for meaningless things is a waste of life. As mentioned earlier, "time" is a big concept in *The Book of Changes*.

Their wisdom was deep, and their rules of conduct were solid. That loftiness was after the pattern of heaven; that solidity, after the pattern of earth. The meaning of this sentence in today's words is: high-profile work, low-key life. People's causes should be meaningful, govern the country, bring peace to the world, and benefit as many people as possible. To imitate heaven, there is only sublime ideals and a strong spirit.

Human cultivation should be modest. The *Tao Te Ching* says that, "The highest excellence is like that of water". Isn't Mother Earth like this? It is always at the feet of people, but people can never live without it.

Complete is its abundant virtue and the greatness of its stores! Its rich possessions are what are intended by the greatness of its stores; the daily renovation, which it produces, is what is meant by the abundance of its virtue.

Noble is almost like wealthy

[...] Among the honoured and exalted there are none greater than he who is rich and noble.

The sages in *The Book of Changes* are different from the sages of Confucianism.

So you can be happy to lead a simple virtuous life, you can pay attention to your own moral uplifting without thought for others and be independent. The sages in *The Book of Changes* are similar to the so-called "King Philosophers" of the West. They have the thoughts and virtues of the sages, as well as power and wealth. Only in this way, can we gather manpower, transform society and benefit the world.

Fighting for power and wealth is natural. In reality, the vast majority of people struggle this way throughout their lives, and this process is of course noble! The value of life is not reflected in the result. Throughout his life, the accumulated wealth reaches a certain point and then becomes legacy. This has no meaning to that person anymore, and all meaning left is in history.

The same is true of virtue. Reputation left behind is valuable, but the process of accumulating virtues and doing moral studies is more meaningful. Confucius said, "To be fond of learning is to be near to knowledge". Wisdom is reflected in a dynamic process, not a fixed indicator, as it is moral virtue. Do not waste your life, have the strength to live it, and fight!

Doing good makes people happy

From the classical text; "The family that accumulates goodness is sure to have superabundant happiness, and the family that accumulates evil is sure to have superabundant misery".

"People who are good and have good will definitely have good things coming their way. People who lack morality and do evil will suffer badly in the future".

In The Zuo Tradition it is said, "Unjust behaviour leads to self-destruction. Doing too many bad things will surely lead to a dead end".

As mentioned in a previous section, "Divine Retribution", Mencius said, "What proceeds from you, will return to you again". Whatever seed you sow, you will harvest. Make good, and this good will surely return to you; make evil, and this evil will surely return to you. This principle, which cannot be demonstrated by science, it is a summary of the experience of ancient sages. This is the Confucian way. Buddhism puts forward the theory of "retributive justice" (Karma). There are many amazing stories, such as the famous *Liao-Fan's Four Lessons*, which is deeply rooted in people's hearts, and has a profound and positive impact on our culture.

Is it true that "good deeds pay good dividend?" Many people doubt it, including Sima Qian. Of course, he must doubt it. He had to be loyal to his lover, but if he had to express affection for his friend, he was tortured. He wrote with great emotion in the Biography of Boyi and Shuqi, in the Historical Records: do good people walk the heavenly path? If so, aren't Boyi and Shuqi good? They both starved to death. Isn't Confucius' most respected Yan Hui a good person? He had the shortest life. The robber Zhi was a real killer, but he lived long. Since modern times, countless treacherous people have been rich and long-lived, and those gentlemen who met tragedy are innumerable. I am so confused! Is this the way to heaven?

Today's ordinary people are thinking – good people do not live long, they inherit bad luck, they face corrupt officials, con artist, and wicked people. In this regard, Buddhism has cleverly answered that there are three types of retribution: First, there is instant karma where bad things that are done in the morning pay the price in the afternoon. Good things that are done yesterday, get good results today. The second is retribution in one's lifetime, where the bad things in this life are punished before death. The third is the karma from previous lives. The evil from a past life has to be repaid in this one. Good and evil come to balance in the end, deeds are not left unpunished, it is that the time has not yet come.

This statement may not convince Sima Qian, but it works for most ordinary people. People who do good deeds, even if they do not do well all their lives, will eventually bless their children or grandchildren. And the strong ones, such as some kings, will become famous. Behind the imperial power are countless souls, and their children and grandchildren will either inherit the throne or be crown ministers and enjoy good wealth. How can there be evil like this? As a matter of fact, most of the descendants of the royal family had some sort of physical disability, and will eventually be killed by the newly-emerged king several years later.

Let us just believe that it is overall good to have both good and evil, but when doing good things, do not think too much about the future. However, something that we can firmly believe (and I have personal experience with is) when doing good things, you will feel relaxed and happy; when you do evil things, you will feel uneasy.

This is due to human nature. Based on this, how can we be reluctant to do good? One of CCTV public service slogans is: Help others and be happy!

Integrity is like climbing

Who is it but the superior man that, though straitened, still does not fail in making progress to his proper end?

"Kun" King Wen's *Explanations of the Hexagrams*; "The superior man, in his intercourse with the high, uses no flattery, and, in his intercourse with the low, no coarse freedom.

From the classical text; who knows to advance and to retire, to maintain or to let perish; and that without ever acting incorrectly. Yes, he, the sage!

In fact, many people, including the ancients and the sages, doubted, can an upright person win in social struggle? Now that the media is well developed, a corrupt official is exposed within a few days. No matter how positive his image is in the people's view, once he falls, he will reveal his true nature. Does anyone believe they are the exception?

Lin Zexu (1785–1850) is a national hero. However, historians have discovered that his gifts to his subordinates of "three festivals and two birthdays" (Spring Festival, Dragon Boat Festival, Mid-Autumn Festival, and birthdays of officials and their wives) are not mistakenly received, and they represented tens of thousands of silver coins.

Zeng Guofan (1807–1872) was willing to "be not a sage, but a beast". He was a clean official himself, but his brother Zeng Guoquan was called, "a glutton" because he was greedy. Was he not responsible? He often taught his children to be able to stand up for themselves. That "Achievement" means to be well connected, to work well, and to give gifts.

Understand the intrigue to gain one's ends. It is said that the sage taught his disciples that the true knowledge is not written in the book. The implication here is to have a suspicion of "righteous". In this regard, I wrote an article ten years ago, thinking that in the officialdom, bad coins are used to eliminate good coins. Often, trivial officials win, even corrupt officials win.

In life, people generally think that the gentlemen cannot fight villains. In the end, few people stand firm. People sigh. There are straight trees in the mountains, but there are no straight people in the world. So why are so few people uphold integrity? In fact, it is like knowing that climbing is dangerous, but still some people do it.

What is the point? The well-known entrepreneur Wang Shi has climbed to the highest peak of real state business. His answer to this question is ridiculous. The general meaning is: in order to endure hardship, he needs to know the happiness of an ordinary life. There is pride in his words. The more things others cannot do, the more I feel I have to do them; the more sins others cannot bear, the more I have to suffer. This is not masochism, this is a heroic heart.

It is so boring when you are comfortable; you have to find yourself some hardship. You may not have the money to suffer the hardship of climbing, but you can always suffer the hardship of integrity. Many people in history have died for their integrity. There is a sense of excitement and a sense of superiority, which is not strange to the mountaineering experience.

Of course, just as mountaineering tempers people's will, it will promote careers and uphold integrity, so it will even motivate people's ability to be flexible and balanced without losing their integrity.

Modesty is the path of progress

He toils with success, but does not boast of it.

Noble is almost wealthy.

The sage said that the one who has merit does not need to boast, and does not want others to thank him.

This is not only modesty, but "thoughtfulness". Kindness is a big concept for the Chinese people. *The Book of Changes* talks about "virtues", like being kind, loyal, and sincere. Kindness is the most recognised quality for Chinese.

A small bottle was filled with half a ladle of water, and a large water tank, even with a few ladles of water would not get its bottom wet. Bridges erected with ordinary wooden boards can hold only pedestrians; while bridges erected with reinforced concrete can hold cars and trains. The cylinder is large relative to the bottle; the reinforced concrete bridge is large relative to the wooden bridge (the Chinese character Hou, means large, deep and kind). Deep is like the earth. It has a large body and a large heart. It can tolerate and bear. Only in this way can people be humble. Modesty is not a pretence, the modest person always is referred to as having a larger self and regards himself as simple.

It is the way of heaven to send down its beneficial influences, where they are brilliantly displayed – Qian, King Wen's *Explanations of the Hexagrams*.

Because the sun shines on the earth, people know its light. When climbing, a person standing tall, if he would bend down and lean down a little, he would be more at ease. People in the mountains have felt this way.

And a person at the lowest point, no matter where he goes, can only go higher and higher.

[...] those are also modest and respectable.

Noble is almost wealthy

The law of nature is the survival of the fittest, and so prevails in human nature. Everyone makes his life story, and what they get after is a feeling of exultation. The flexibility to make words of the Chinese language is extremely high. This feeling can be expressed plainly as being proud, but generally speaking we mean honour, face, and so on. However, if you are good and others are good...

[...] those are also modest and respectable.

If you are happy, others will not be happy, and if he is not happy, he will find a way to trouble you. Humility is to leave more opportunities for others, so he can be as happy as you, and everyone will be happy. If you can be proud, but you keep a low profile. You have to learn to pretend to be a smaller person in order to keep your position and the fruits of your work, then you can be great person.

How to practice oriental spirituality

'Be undefeated', said Xu, Lesser *Treatise on the Symbolism of the Hexagrams.*

There is a master in a Jin Yong's novel, known as "the unbeaten of the East". How did he become so? Jin Yong said that he obtained a rare martial arts book, and the title was *The magic guide of the prodigious sword master*, and so he was inspired. Some netizens criticised him, saying that he needed to be a master himself, 'If you can write about it, you can practice it', so the discussion went viral.

There are many similar situations in martial arts novels. For example, many eunuchs had very high martial arts skills, and some kung fu fanatics strive to be ruthless in order to maintain their standards or to improve. But for writers, they write this because it makes sense. Only by restraining lust can one concentrate on improving one's ability and surpass ordinary people.

Of course, life is not martial arts, we do not have to be so extreme, but self-denial and hard work and also applying respect and carefulness to overcome our various shortcomings; and overcome the weaknesses of human nature so that we can be undefeated.

Truly, it is what really matters. The object of your practice can be a variety of people such as parents, elders, leaders, customers, colleagues, friends, etc.. It can also be a variety of major events in work and life; it can also be laws, morals, and beliefs values and dreams. All these objects are to be taken seriously, anytime, anywhere.

Go all out and deal with it. Being cautious means being circumspect. Zhuge Liang was revered by the common people as a "sage of great wisdom", while historians rather see him as "cautious character". Human intellect is often manifested when being cautious.

The superior man, thus represented, by his self-reverence maintains the inward correctness, and in righteousness adjusts his external acts.

The gentleman has a strong faith and worships the Tao, the sage's instructions, and those ancient moral principles in his heart. A gentleman works with conscience and works according to belief. Such a person may seem treacherous and shifty at first, but will eventually make many friends.

Actions proceed from what is near, and their effects are seen at a distance. Words and actions are the hinge and spring of the superior man. The movement of that hinge and spring determines glory or disgrace. His words and actions move heaven and earth; may he be careless in regards to them?

When disorder arises, it will be found that ill-advised speech was the steppingstone to it. If a ruler does not keep secret his deliberations with his minister, he will lose that minister. If a minister does not keep secret his deliberations with his ruler, he will lose his life. If important matters are not kept secret, that will be injurious to their accomplishment. Therefore, the superior man is careful to maintain secrecy, and does not allow himself to speak.

Regarding sincerity and prudence, the ancients spoke tirelessly and talked about many things, but the better the truth, the harder it is to deal with it. How to do it better? It is said that Jack Ma once pointed out an expert and insisted on not speaking for three days. He felt that experience was wonderful. We might as well learn from it. Hold your mouth shut and do not open it.

Of course, another important thing: keep it secret. The story of the famous three little golden statues has been heard by many people. These three little golden statues look exactly the same. Which one is more valuable? A wise man pricked the straw through the ears of each of the three little golden statues, and so coming out from the other ear, but one of them came out of its mouth, and the last one came out of his stomach. We want to be like the last little gold statue, otherwise no one will trust you. The superior man, when resting in safety, does not forget that danger may come; when in a state of security, he does not forget the possibility of ruin; and when all is in a state of order, he does not forget that disorder may come.

In short, no matter how perfect your situation is now, never be too proud, your fate is fickle, and life will be different if you do not pay attention. The "Invincible East" was undefeated and finally lost to the unknown Ling Wu Chung?

Perseverance wins

When the worm coils itself up, it thereby straightens itself again; when worms and snakes go into a state of hibernation, they thereby keep themselves alive.

The superior man keeps his weapon concealed about his person, and waits for the proper time to move.

The crawling of the Geometer moth is flexible, while the Dragon Snake has a period of hibernation and dormancy. The meaning of this sentence is simple: a man of fortitude and courage must be able to flex and stretch. When you are in your early stages, you just watch from the side. The summary of all human wisdom is to hope and wait. Waiting is uncomfortable. In the process of waiting, people are despised and bullied, it can be uncomfortable. This is normal, why should you all of a sudden be better than others? Can you count on God to recognise you for doing something? You can only hope you are not committing more sins, more offences, and more evil deeds than others.

There is a folk story that says: the gods will choose a person among commoners to be the Jade Emperor, inspected from many of people, and finally selected a person from an honest family. This person is nicknamed Zhang Bai Ren, and he could bear anything. He was getting married that day, and the Lord of Heaven was dressed up as a monk and went to him, saying that he was seriously ill and only lying with a young bride could help him. What did Zhang Bai Ren do? Accept it. And so he ascended to heaven. The comic sketch, "If you want to work well, you must endure some unpleasant things", is roughly the same as the story of the Jade Emperor.

I have not seen geometer moths, but only similar caterpillars, like soybean worms. I saw many in my childhood, and they all crawled forward like this. The ancient cultural classics that were created more than 2,000 years ago were written in a background of an agricultural society. There are many examples about crops and fields in the texts. I am fortunate that I grew up in the countryside. Only by being aware of these things, can I be more familiar with these classics. However, thanks to the Internet, we can quickly supplement information and fill in the blind spots. I checked the geometer moth and found that its flexion and extension did not have any strange ways, but its camouflage was excellent, and its body straightened at rest, just like a dead branch. The sage did not mention this characteristic, but it certainly gave him a deep impression. Is that not this the ultimate "blending"?

In fact, the characteristics of motions in sports are the same as those of the geometer moth: in order to jump high, you must first squat; if you want to jump long, you must step back and get momentum.

Countless heroes in history have had experiences of bearing humiliation, compromising, concealing, and keeping a low profile. After their success, these experiences have been passed down as stories. In short, bend, wait, bear, back, listen to instructions, all of these are the keys to perseverance!

Perseverance is the gateway to virtue

The successive movement of the inactive and active operations constitutes "the course of things". That which ensues, as the result of their movement is goodness

The nature of man having been completed, and being continually preserved, it is the gate of all good courses and righteousness.

Under the control of heaven, everything has a goal and motivation to be good. And then, this development process is to give raise to their different instincts, so in the end, they can blend in perfection.

All of our studies and experiences are actually not adding things that are not already part of us, but refining and sublimating our original nature. This is our "second nature". This is not for once and for all, but for "storage", to be saved and to be kept, and to be repeated and replicated, such is the way where constant effort brings success. Only by relentlessly accumulating in order to make perfection. It is the only way to seek the truth from the heart and work from the outside.

I have been practicing calligraphy for more than 7000 days. Every day I set time aside to practice it. It is not unreasonable, but I still have high aims but low skill, and I am far away from becoming a master calligrapher. There are millions of people practicing calligraphy in China, and many people have written for a lifetime. I believe that no one thinks they have reached their maximum level. How to go about it? Only "preserve the practice". Even the ancients were the same. In the early Qing Dynasty, Wang Duo was considered to be one of the top ten scholars in the Chinese millennium, but in his later years, he still practiced every day.

This is the Chinese way, in short, constant perseverance. Based on this, Chinese believe in tales like the one of old Yi Gong moving a mountain, and the turtle and the hare race. The Chinese may not be strong in creativity, and there may be many shortcomings. But based on perseverance, the Chinese will eventually stand among the nations of the world in a proud manner.

"If acts of goodness be not accumulated, they are not sufficient to give its finish to one's name".

In 2011, I wrote the first book, *Understanding Zeng Guofan* and proposed the idea of "Chinese inspirationalism". Although the book is still selling well, almost no one knows me, and there are no more than 30,000 or 40,000 followers on Weibo. How to do it? Being good is not enough to become famous, so I went on to write the second *Chinese-style inspirational,* book *Four Books of Life*, then this was the third, and then the fourth and fifth books were written into a series. I firmly believe that transforming traditional classics into "Chinese-style inspirational" books is suitable for modern people and will eventually win wide public praise.

If you win once, do not call it a victory, people will only remember those that win many times. All that is valuable is because of its scarcity. Nothing is impossible.

Square and circle

[...] the inner is the symbol of strength, and the outer of docility; the inner represents the superior man, and the outer the small man. Thus, the way of the superior man appears increasing, and that of the small man decreasing – Tai, Emperor Wen's *Explanations of the Hexagrams*.

A man can be masculine and strong inside, but he can show softness and obedience on the outside; there can be a gentleman's cultivation and sentiment on the inside, such as a beautiful jade stone that is covered in dirt. People from all walks of like can achieve a high spiritual level.

The sage admires this kind of personality. Why? Because of two aspects: First; the outer and the inner circle of the human life are consistent with the heavenly path of the "Round Heaven and Earth Square", meaning that things are different outside and inside. The second, the sage is well aware of the characteristics of disagreement in human nature.

"Affairs are arranged together according to their tendencies, and things are divided according to their classes".

Regardless of the ideology or any specific things, people are gathered or separated because of their identity or differences, and contradictions arise in the process of differentiation. "In all relations, if two are near and do not blend harmoniously, there may be all these results, evil, or something injurious".

Regardless of space or social relations, people who are closer to each other will inevitably hide a crisis if they do not have mutual affection and tolerance. If both sides are rigid, like two pieces of steel, it will be difficult to fit together. At least one side needs to be fitted with soft things, such as rubber pads. Man must have a soft side, an ambiguous side, and a flexible side. This is not to say that appearance can be different, because if his inherent nature is good and positive, there will not be anything to hide. This is sad. Why should people be so afraid? Or, is it so dark that we now regard most people as villains? Everyone's situation is different; these principles are "like people drinking water, they do not need to be told how to do it".

[...] "the inner is the symbol of weakness, and the outer of strength; the inner represents the small man, and the outer the superior man. Thus, the way of the small man appears increasing, and that of the superior man decreasing" – Fou, *Emperor Wen's Explanations of the Hexagrams.*

Of course, some people are just the opposite. They are either strong and sturdy on the outside, but cowardly inside. Like wolves in sheep's clothing, or sheep in wolf's clothing. The inner might not be true, just pretending to look like it is, and people who are unable to persist will become increasingly humble and small.

The spirit of independence, the idea of freedom

His will is set on following others, "what he holds in his grasp is low" – Xian, Emperor Wen's *Explanations of the Hexagrams*.

The seventeenth hexagram in *The Book of Changes* is the hexagram of Sui (Following), which discusses the issues of following, imitating, continuing and such, which all have its positive meaning. However, if a person's ambitions stop here, if he becomes a copycat at the end of his life, he will "have done what the other have done".

Oriental culture emphasises learning, including Japan, South Korea and other countries that are deeply affected by ancient Chinese culture. They attach great importance to learning, so the pressure on primary and secondary school students is the largest in the world. And the foundation of learning must be based on inheriting and imitating the knowledge of our predecessors.

Chinese calligraphy is a remarkable example. Many learners of calligraphy copy the books of their predecessors, and they are willing to be their followers for life. Everyone like Qi Baishi (1854–1957), it is said that he was willing to be a "slave" for the art of his predecessors. His book *The slave book* refers to this. Throughout the ages, such "book slaves" can still become famous, but they are certainly not first-rate.

First-class scholars, such as Wang Xizhi, Yan Zhenqing, Huai Su, Su Dongpo, Huang Shangu, etc., have all worked hard in following Lintong. In their appearance and in their own family.

As mentioned above, Qi Baishi blindly followed during the learning stage, but he warned the younger generation, 'Those who learn from me will die as if they were vulgar'. The implication is; if you want to surpass me, you have to be different.

At present, the most fashionable theory in the corporate world is "positioning". Successful positioning can occupy a place in the minds of consumers. How to do it better? It is impossible to be a follower or an imitator. But the best way is to create a new product category. Just as Sina did when it launched Weibo first; later, Tencent could not surpass it no matter how it followed up; then Tencent launched WeChat first, and Alibaba had no chance.

Back to life. The Confucian *Book of Rites* says that a Confucian believer must have the spirit of "independence in mind and action" and dare to be transcendent to the world, not just follow the current, but to be do something different.

"Zhuangzi" is even more proud of the fact that "Independence is in contact with the spirit of heaven and earth". Many young people have a problem: they like to go chasing stars. Not only are singers and movie stars chased, but also various celebrities, including the wealthy and high officials.

Everyone gets together and talks about these people with joy. Some people even take pride in knowing more about a celebrity than others. Such a person does not have good prospects. Try not to care too much about how others are good, but care about how you become as good as others. We talked about the sages such as Confucius, Mencius, etc. If we just talked about it, it would be equally unproductive.

Mencius mentions Kngs Yao and Shun, but he said that Yao and Shun are also real people. And I am also a person, so, why cannot I do like them? As a result, he really became a sage after like the legendary monarchs Yao and Shun. Zeng Guofan said that, 'A man must not lose his stubbornness, and only if he has persistent energy all his life can be a success'.

Once I talked to a friend about Mao Zedong's calligraphy. My friend said that we cannot compare with others. They are "kings" and most are bold and imperious "monarch spirits" in calligraphy, which mortals cannot learn. I say, we are all our own kings. In the past three thousand years, China has had a lot of people who could not come on board and receive the call of the king. Chen Yin, a famous historian, has a famous saying, 'An independent spirit is free in his own mind'. Everywhere there are countless outstanding figures, but you should look at the present. Do you dare?

If the stroke is too high, do it again. Anyone who is good at reading is liable to fall into a trap, which is to let other people's thoughts be in their own brains. Giving free reign to other people's thoughts makes it easy for others' thoughts to lead your own away. In fact, even if the author is Confucius, Laozi, or another historical figures, learning with an open mind is good, but you must never forget yourself! Life is boundless, and knowledge is boundless. The truth is inexhaustible, and knowledge is inexhaustible. Keep yourself alive and let your awakening bloom. This life is enough.

Reality is always more cruel than theory. Today, we are not only facing the problem of "following people", we are also "following things". This kind of "control" is really a prelude to this world being ruled by machines.

Part Two

The 64 Hexagrams and Textual Explanation?

So, let's get started! Here are the 64 Hexagrams (To see all sixty-four hexagrams, go to page 404), and below that is the contextual explanation of each.

Qian:	The struggle of the dragon
Kun:	The enlightenment of the Earth
Tun:	The first step is always difficult
Meng:	The purpose of education
Xu:	Awaiting
Song:	The commoner before noble
Shi:	When general Han Xin musters soldiers, the more the better
Bi:	A close friend
Xiao Xu:	The feeling of being middle class

Lu:	the tiger's tail
Tai:	The secret of conducting oneself calmly
Pi:	Truman's world
Tong Men:	Are we all the same?
Da You:	How to protect fortune
Qian:	More than modesty
Yu:	Are you happy?
Sui:	Follow, follow, follow
Gu:	Chaos is an opportunity
Lin:	Leaders' four key words
Guan:	The way you see the world is the way you see other people
Shi Ke:	Violence and Punishment
Bi:	Beauty is productivity
Bo:	When the foundation is not firm, it is easily shaken
Fu:	The heart of Heaven and Earth
Wu Wang:	Abide by one's station in life
Da Chu:	Pointers for officials
Yi:	How's it going?
Da Guo:	The lone wolf is a hidden dragon
Kan:	Doom
Li:	Leaving the original turf
Xian:	Moving with the feeling
Dun:	take a step back
Da Zhuang:	In the prime of life people often despair
Jin:	It is not easy coming forward
Ming Yi:	Facing darkness
Jia Ren:	Learning to live
Kui:	Same same but different
Jian:	The difficulties of the journey
Jie:	Enemies should not end. It is better to squash enmity rather than keeping it alive

Sun:	Life should be minimalistic
Yi:	Life should provide
Guai:	About stress
Gou:	Life is just like a first meeting
Cui:	Avoid crowded places
Sheng:	The two cruxes of growing up
Kun:	The six plights of life
Jing:	The three virtues of a leader
Ge:	Change
Ding:	Holding on
Zhen:	The greatest enemy
Gen:	Self control
Jian:	Everything should be gradual
Gui Mei:	Choose life
Feng:	The wisdom of decision making
Lu:	The intention of words
Xun:	Taking advantage of the trend
Dui:	Water like friendship
Huan:	Freedom
Jie:	Temperance
Zhong Fu:	Integrity wins the world
Xiao Guo:	There are degrees for everything
Ji Ji:	The difficulties of maintaining the achievements of our predecessors
Wei Ji:	The path

Note; All hexagrams are composed by two trigrams.

The 64 Hexagrams

Qian: The struggle of the dragon

CLASSICAL TEXT

(This is the direct text from the ancient {classical} text (reflected in blue). Being with less filter, it may seem convoluted)

Qian the great, the smooth, the advantageous and the firm.

Nine in the First line; A capable person biding his time.

Nine in the Second line; The dragon in the field, time to meet with an important person.

Nine in the Third line; the great man remains active and vigilant during the day, then careful and apprehensive in the evening. A dangerous situation, there should be no mistake.

Nine in the Fourth line; The dragon seems to be about to soar, but is still in the low. If it continues, there should be no problem.

Nine in the Fifth line; The dragon is in the sky. The great man rouses himself to work.

Nine in the upper line; The dragon is exceeding the proper limits. There will be regret.

Nine in all lines; One is his own master. There will be good fortune.

The image; When heaven is in motion, the gentleman moves with it to improve himself.

(The image is the phenomenon the hexagrams represents)

LITERAL TRANSLATION

(To make the ancient {classical} easier to understand we have put these through an edit filter.)

Qian represents what is great, the smooth, the advantageous, and the firm.
Nine at the First line; The dragon dives down in order not to be seen.
Nine in the Second line; The dragon in the field, time to meet with an important person.
Nine in the Third line; The great man works hard all day and remains cautions at night, he is free from evil in the face of danger.
Nine at the Fourth line; Whether you remain still or advance, you will not be harmed.
Nine at the Fifth line; The dragon is in the sky. The great man rouses himself to work.
Nine at the top Line; The dragon flies too high, there shall be remorse.
All lines are nines; A group of dragons flying freely without a leader, a good auspice.
The big picture; Qian is the movement of heaven with full strength, a time for the greater man to strive for improvement.

INTERPRETATION

(The interpretation is the authors understanding of the ancient {classical} text.)

Qian has the two heaven trigrams stacked together. Meaning that knowledge capabilities are limitless. The sage appears aloft, high above all thing, the vast universe, moon and stars, numerous galaxies flows eternally, never stagnant, never slacking. If we imagine the universe as a person, then that person will be masculine and strong. Traditionally the sage assumes that this kind of masculinity and vitality is essence of the cosmic spirit and the will of the universe. It possess the four great qualities: 'the great', 'the smooth', 'the advantageous' and 'the firm'.

The great; is at the origin of all progress.

The smooth; display of excellence.

The advantageous; is the harmony of all that is right.

The correct and firm; the faculty of action.

Only by upholding these spiritual values, one can understand the value of life. Therefore, the sage recites, 'When heaven is in motion, the gentleman moves with it to improve himself'.

Sages referred to this self-improving way of life as the struggle of the dragon and divided it into six stages from weak to strong:

First stage; A capable person bids his time. At the beginning, even if you are a dragon, you are still weak. Although you have the potential of a dragon, you are still weak, and any ability you might have is still poor. You may even be vulnerable. At this time, the most sensible choice is to sink deep into the water. Other dragons may be in the air, they may be worshipped by people, but you are still far from that. Loneliness is inevitable, and there may be some sense of inferiority. You might be eager and wanting to get ahead and show your skills, but you should not be hasty. It is time to sit down and work on yourself. You can only clench your fist and be patient. It is time to work hard in the dark, study hard, practice, accumulate energy, and wait for the right opportunity.

Second stage; The dragon in the field. This state of mind is like pregnancy. In due time it will naturally be noticed by people without a hint of a doubt. At this time, the dragon's golden scales are exposed at water level, so they shine brightly under the sun, and under the water a strong body can be seen. You now stand conspicuously in the spotlight, and your worth can be seen – a value people will want to exploit. The weak and the strong will come to you to gain benefit. They will take the initiative to support you, make you stronger, and bring more rewards because of it.

Third stage; Remaining diligent all day. A wise man once said, 'neither in the sky nor in the field', not being up or being down, this uncertainty is something difficult to withstand. In terms of career, when something is improved it becomes a thing of the past. If you do not keep up, you may have to give up.

In terms of family, when parents become old, it is often only when one of them becomes ill that they suddenly realise that they are old. At this time, no matter how old you are, in your heart you are already middle age. Youth is a most beautiful things, but like goodness, always scarce and short-lived. If you do not pay attention, you will not know this until you are middle age. It is my deepest realisation of this year. What to do? As the pillar of the whole family, no matter how busy, how tired, we have to hold on.

Fourth stage; Despair perhaps? After being through hell, the dragon is now experienced and strong. You have almost achieved the goal of your youth. Sometimes you cannot believe what you have achieved. But you cannot stop. The next goal is the "dream". It is the tip of the pyramid. You have to raise to the challenge. For facing this challenge, the wise man reminds you to prepare for the opportunity. You may only have one chance, if you achieve it, so be it, but if you do not, you will get to it some other way.

Fifth stage; The soaring dragon. The dragon is soaring in the sky, and everyone is watching. You stand on top of the pyramid. You are helped by many people, and you also serve many people. This kind of success is something that very few people achieve, it is like the lottery jackpot. As long as you go after it, no one can say that it is impossible. Just like what Jack Ma said, 'What if your dream comes true?'

Sixth stage; The regret of the arrogant dragon. A dragon is indeed beautiful in the sky, but it is a lonely feeling to be so high, and it cannot fly forever, it must rest or die of exhaustion or exposure. To stand on top of the pyramid and shout victory, and then engrave a, "I was here", is fine, but what is the point? However, the reason why people can win in competitions is because there is a strong desire to win. Such people are achievers. But the person who never thinks about stepping down, this is what is called arrogance. Caught in this excitement, you keep pushing forward, advancing and pushing until you pay a heavy price. When looking at the history books, we find that heroes rarely have a happy ending, they either are killed, or they live long enough to become the villain. Zhuge Liang was so wise, and yet his children and grandchildren were all killed. Today's heroes do not have to worry about being beheaded, but many do not understand the right moment for advancement and retreat in life, they live to become lonely old people.

And, in the end, you will find that we are all racing against life, and everything you get is less valuable than the life you lost running after. Birth, old age, sickness and death – in life you can only neglect one of them, for the last three you need to prepare yourself.

In the end, the sage summarises it as: A group of dragons flying without a leader it is a good omen. You are not alone. There are countless dragons in the world who have the spirit of self-improvement. They are moving in their own way towards an ideal future. The sea is wide, the sky is high, and the birds fly freely. No one can be in the lead or walk in front forever. This is a world with infinite possibilities, a colourful life drama.

In any case, the struggle for life is something great!

Kun: The enlightenment of the Earth

CLASSICAL TEXT

Kun represents what is great and engendering, penetrating, advantageous, correct and having the firmness of a mare. When a great man intends to make a move, at first it will seem like he is going astray; if he continues, he will find his fortune. He will gain friends in the south-west, and lose friends in the north east. If he remains firm on the right path, there will be good fortune.

Six at the First line; Shoes are treading on hoarfrost. There will be strong ice to overcome.

Six at the Second line; A sign of rectitude, squareness, and greatness. A well-rounded operation will be advantageous in every respect.

Six at the third line; By keeping his greatness under restraint, but firmly maintaining it, the king's subject should engage in service, he will not claim the success for himself, but he will bring affairs to a good outcome.

Six at the fourth line; The symbol of a sack tied up. There will be no ground for blame or for praise.

Six at the fifth line; The yellow lower garment (the emperor's colour) can be seen. There will be great fortune.

Six on top; Shows dragons fighting in the wild. Their blood is purple and yellow (the king's colour).

Six in all lines; If those involved remain firm and righteous, there will be good fortune.

The image; The capacity to sustain the power of the earth is what is denoted by Kun. The superior man acts alike and uses his power to support people and things.

LITERAL TRANSLATION

Kun Earth over earth, all yin lines: a calm mood, not doing anything but being everything.

Six at the first line; Step on frost now, it will be ice later.

Six at the second line; At the right place, at the right time. Actions should be straightforward and uncontrived. Respond effortlessly to circumstances and your actions will be correct.

Six at the third line; Work in the background, now is not a time to claim the credit.

Six at the fourth line; Beware of taking on new responsibilities, keep silent. Keep what is in the sack.

Six at the fifth line; The embroidered yellow dress is a good omen.

Six at the top line; Dragons fighting in the wild, restoring balance will spill blood.

Six at all lines; For those who remain always firm and right there shall be profit.

The image; Earth is receptive, generous and unselfish. The great man handles things based on these qualities.

INTERPRETATION

Kun represents the Earth, what is coming out of the earth. The underlying layer of the earth. For the ancients, Earth is as infinite as the universe with different levels below and above. Because the earth is infinite, it can engender and nurse everything, including countless mountains, rivers, animals, plants, food, drink, etc., and of course humans. Its purpose is to engender, and its bearing will be solid. This is the main quality of Earth. The sage believes that great men should take responsibility for all life, "the righteous shall bear his burden with gravity", and understand the six key revelations:

First revelation: step firmly through soft snow until you feel the ice as your little feet first stepped on the earth, and your life was just beginning. Actually, did you know when you took the first step toward the future, the end point seemed to be out of reach, mysterious and vague, but it was already destined? Just like when you step on the frost of the first night of the late autumn, the harsh winter is already in sight. Sima Guang wrote in his *Comprehensive Mirror in Aid of Governance* about the development of human history; Regardless of historic events or trivial matters, everything develops in a certain direction on the axis of time. The starting point, the path, and the end point are a whole. Seeds that are planted yield their specific fruit and that is inevitable. This is an underlying argument of the *Book of Change*s. The first step is important, the first step must be a good one. There is a general intuition or gut feeling about how things develop, which is the root of basic wisdom.

Second revelation: Straight, square and great. "Straight", the earth is thick and straightforward. It reveals itself openly. There is nothing to hide. Under the light of day all is fully visible and the horizon is always straight. The heaven is a circle and square is the place of earth. The ancients taught that the earth was a square. Solid and reliable, different from the round things that roll and turn and cannot rely on their stability; "great" is the vast, the vast that can receive everything. And this is how a person should be! Bold and bright, honest and solid, vast and inclusive, these people will not be disadvantaged.

Third; revelation: Keeping its tinder flint firmly held. Where is the energy of the earth stored? At its core. It is a survival wisdom to hide your own beauty. Constantly improving one's inner beauty is also a survival wisdom. Practicing such wisdom will win the long-run.

Fourth revelation: A sack tied up. Take the sack and fill it with grain. When it is full, use a string to tie the opening of the bag.

Tie it tight. This is a sack tied up. The earth is like this sack. It can only produce so much food. The rest is simple. When there is no more, it is finished and nothing can be said to change this.

There is only doing, not saying. For all the glory and sin that has occurred on Earth, can you put the blame on Earth? The answer is no. When, through his efforts he achieves, and thereby gains a reputation, he pays little attention to his own merits. This is truly amazing; where someone did something of value, but no one knows that he did them all. No one has attributed his merits to him. This is even more remarkable.

A sack tied up, has also another meaning, retreat. Life is like gambling; a constant flow of money, of losing and winning, yet, you never know how much you will end up with. "A sack tied up" is to put a cap and no longer bet, holding back, no matter what you might win. Regardless of how much you win, you should be content and enjoy the end results.

Fifth revelation: The sighting of the yellow garment (the king's colour). The leaves in autumn are golden, the sky is high, the clouds are soft, and the wind is light. It is the season of ripeness and the season of harvest. It seems as if the earth wears yellow clothes. People mature, how can it be otherwise? After experiencing many things in life, the heart has turned a thousand times, and in the final harvest season, one should welcome his own maturity and return to the natural state of calm.

Sixth revelation: the dragon battles in the wild, its blood yellow. There has always been bloodshed throughout history, for every inch of territory there is an ounce of blood. The old drama of Earth has always been the survival of the fittest, and the week becoming their meal. How to be humble? How to make concessions? And how to focus on yourself? Can it be done without locking oneself in an ivory tower? Will you really quit all pleasures and dramas of life? Those people on the TV who wash their hands in a golden basin, are they forced to pick up the gun again? The true warrior can face a bleak life, and turn his back to the warmth of an emotional life, but he can never forget this cruel truth.

These six revelations, that unfold during the years, summarise human life.

"Qian" and "Kun" are the general principles of the *Book of Changes*. Being heavy in yang nature, and proactively doing things in an external upwards process is a Confucian key principle. Kun is Yin, the introverted and low-key man. Focusing in an internal perfecting process and is a key principle of Taoism. One yin and one yang is what makes The Path – the two complement each other and give birth to each other. This is what the *Book of Changes* is all about, and the core of Chinese culture, a summary of life as a whole.

After reading for ten minutes about Qian and Kun, can you see it now?

Tun: The First step is always difficult

CLASSICAL TEXT

[Zhun] Great progress, success, and advantages for those who are correct and firm. Any forward movement should not be lightly undertaken. The appointing of a princess is auspicious.

Nine at the First line; Difficulties are advancing. It will be advantageous for the noble to be made a ruler.

Six at the Second line; A maiden in distress is forced to return; even the horses of her chariot seem to be retreating. But not by her spoiler, but by someone who seeks her to be his wife. The young lady maintains her virtue, and declines a union. After ten years she will be united, and have children.

Six at the third line; Someone following the deer without the guidance of the forester, and only to find himself lost. The superior man, acquainted with the lurking risks, thinks it better to give up the chase. To go forward, could be to regret it.

Six on the Fourth line; The maiden's horse appears to be in retreat. She seeks the help of him who wants to marry her. Make advances will be fortunate; all will turn out advantageously.

Nine in the Fifth line; Difficulty is experienced by one bestowing rich favours. With firmness and correctness there will be good fortune in small things, and in great things there will be evil.

Six at the top line; The horses of the chariot are in retreat, and the raider weeps tears of blood in streams.

The image; Clouds and thunder form Zhun. The superior man, in accordance with this, adjusts his measures of government.

LITERAL TRANSLATION

The hexagram Water over thunder. Thunder is a dynamic force and next to water is dangerous.

Nine at the First line; A strong person in an uncertain position. It is better to ask for help.

Six at the Second line; A raiding party approaches, but they come not to plunder, but to seek a wife. Resist being pressured into a partnership, in time the maiden will find a good suitor.

Six at the third line; Hunting a deer without a guide will get you lost. Insist on it and you will regret it.

Six at the fourth line; Riding a horse is good enough, no need to plunder, waiting for the right time is not negative.

INTERPRETATION

This hexagram contains: in the upper part is Kan (the abysmal), meaning water or cloud; the lower is Zhen (the arousing), indicating thunder. Under the clouds, the lightning glimmers, no doubt a heavy rain is coming. At this time, the sage thinks of the new sprouts from the rain. The hexagram is "Tun", a Chinese character formed by Che (number of characters), which means grass, above a horizontal line that represents the ground: a sprout coming out from the earth.

This new grass is just like the beginning of our life, or the beginning of a career. No one seems to appreciate, no one seems to help, it is weak, but eager to grow, there is a lot of resistance. What to do? A wise man taught:

First; do not be anxious or aggressive. Young people eager to succeed can understand the mood, but the conditions are not ready yet, there is no need to be anxious, just get through it and lay a good foundation. The foundation is nothing more than two aspects: one is the purpose, get good at whatever you are to do.

Second; is the connection with the people around you, the networking. The best moment for building this foundation is in the twenties. Then stagnation is not such a bad thing. In the words of a farmer, this is called "growth restraint", where the roots can develop better, which is conducive to future growth. When the cadres in an organisation are promoted, the leaders often use this line to comfort young cadres who are not yet mature enough. For those who have been grounded for a long time, the moment they fly they will soar. Do not worry.

Second, everything is difficult at the beginning. Primitive accumulation is a long process, earning the first 100,000 is often more difficult than earning the first one million. In the early days, when opportunities come, because of their lack of experience, young people often hesitate and worry that it is a trap. Sometimes, traps are seen as opportunities. The problems at this time is to hurry and fail to check impulses.

Third; generals do not chase rabbits. Before finalising a business it is easy to make it look like a high mountain and get dizzy. You might want to seize any money you can, any opportunity you see, and try everything. But if you go about life with a club in one hand and a hammer in the other, you will not be able to nail anything. Since strength and resources are limited, it is more important to focus on one area. Put all eggs in the same basket and then you will have a chance.

Fourth; when you are self-reliant, hard-working, and start to develop character, then the so-called professionals, such as investors, partners, big customers, etc., may start to come.

Fifth; when the grass has grown, do not rush to enjoy it. Leisure and rest after work are good, but do not lose yourself in self-indulgence.

Sixth; entrepreneurship is a path with no return, and often a story of blood and tears. The same is true of life, either stay still and die, or to move forward with no turning back.

What is hard is hard. This little seedling is just beginning, there is hope, there is a future, as the old saying goes, "worry about old age, not about small things" just persist and you will see how time flew once it is fully grown. After a few years, when you look back at the hardships of this beginning, you will find that it was not the most profound experience in your life.

Finally, the sage concludes by saying, "the great man is economically motivated". Early in life and career, he must weave dreams, plan well, acquire knowledge, and redouble efforts. Just like weaving, we must strive for the perfect fabric.

Meng: The purpose of education

CLASSICAL TEXT

[Meng] indicates that there will be progress and success. I do not go and seek the youthful and inexperienced, but he comes and seeks me. When he shows sincerity, I instruct him. If he gets rejected a second and third time, that is troublesome; and I do not instruct the troublesome. There will be advantage in being firm and correct.

Six at the first line; The dispelling of ignorance. It will be advantageous to use punishment for that purpose, and to remove the shackles from the mind. But going on punishing in that way will give occasion for regret.

Nine at the second line; This shows its subject exercising forbearance with the ignorant, there will be good fortune. Admitting the goodness of women will also be fortunate. He may be described as a son able to sustain the burden of his family.

Six at the third line; Seems to say that one should not marry a woman who seeks a man of wealth, she will not keep her loyalty, and no advantage will come from her.

Six at the fourth line; shows its subject as if bound in chains of ignorance. There will be occasion for regret.

Six at the fifth line; This shows its subject as a simple lad without experience. There will be good fortune.

Nine at the top line; Here we see one smiting the ignorant

LITERAL TRANSLATION

[Meng] Go smoothly. The teacher does not ask the student to learn, the student asks the teacher for teaching. The wise man knows that the first teaching should not be ignored, if it is, then more advice will be of no benefit.

Six at the first line; Understanding frees the mind from mental shackles. Rushing through without clearing ignorance will bring regret.

Nine at the second line; Be kind to the ignorant. You are ready to take over responsibilities such as marrying and starting a family.

Six at the third line; It is not appropriate to marry the kind of woman that when she sees a handsome man, loses herself. It is unprofitable.

Six at the fourth line; You have lost touch with reality and have taken on too much.

Six at the fifth line; The ignorant is starting to learn, now he should be able to accept advice.

Nine at the top line; A good teacher does not use violence, this only instills violence and passes on regret.

The image; Water under the mountain. Water is like youth and the mountain is the wisdom to attain.

INTERPRETATION

This hexagram contains: in the upper part is Gen (keeping still), indicating the mountain; in the lower part is Kan (the abysmal), indicating water. At the foot of the mountain, a clear spring is like a child's innocence, ignorant and pure of mind. At this stage, people are, Meng, which literally means ignorant. When they go to school, they are called "Fa Meng." (deliver from ignorance). The teacher is seen as the inspiration for the ignorant. So the sage here tells the emperor about education. He puts forward several points:

First; learning begins by imitating. Give children a role model or paradigm. Teaching is important, and reading the classics is interesting. Learning to paint and calligraphy all start by copying the great scripts. Let the children know what they cannot do, such as not touching a bottle with hot water, and then emphasise in the legal system and moral education to ensure that they have self-control and awareness in the future. In addition, beginners should not be eager to rush to progress, and should first lay a solid foundation.

Second; family education is important and there must be an atmosphere of love. Also, establish filial piety and other family ethics is an important part of education.

Third; is to cultivate the child's skills and work ethics. It is necessary to understand that good families and marriages can be achieved through having a good career. They should be encouraged to make money and not to rush to marriage.

Fourth; learning should be combined with practice and targeted at specific problems and difficulties. On the other hand, life is constantly facing difficulties, which are opportunities to learn from. Confucianism emphasises that 'learning is knowing how to solve problems'.

Fifth; the adult should not lose the heart of a child. One should always maintain a childlike curiosity and seek one's deepest dreams.

Sixth; strategy education. All higher knowledge is learned from a text. Those that we do not follow, we should at least know them. Bohemian life does not harm anyone, but we must learn how not to get harmed by it. In addition, if a child does comply, he should be forced. The "sudden strike" (name of a Zen practice) of Zen is often used for instant awakening.

The sage believes that teaching and learning are present in all situations of life. From the perspective of teaching, we must pay attention to two points.

First; do not be a teacher all the time, always looking to give pointers to others, unless people come for advice, do not sell yourself too cheap.

Second; the teaching points are so far, to be inspired, to let the other engage in thinking, do not cram everything in, so the person being taught develops interest for the subject. If you do not think it, you cannot learn it.

Finally; the sage concluded that the purpose of education is to 'grow' some virtues, like to be productive, help people and guide others to virtue. However, Confucius once said, 'In a hamlet of ten families, there may be found one honourable and sincere as I am, but not so fond of learning'. For most young people, morality is not a problem, the problem is acting upon it. In other words, the significance of cultivating morality is to follow with moral actions.

The text looks weak, small, nothing flashy, but the source of any big river in the world is just like this. The same is true of life. The great historical characters grew up from being babies and toddlers, growing up a bit at a time. The gap between success and failure in life is often determined from the beginning, what is the decisive factor? The capacity of action.

A young man has to compete with middle-aged and elderly people. There is no comparison between the knowledge, experience, connections, wealth and resources of the first and the later. But we can see that most great people in history have succeeded at a very young age. Xiang Yu was a great warlord, he was only thirty-one years old when he died. He was defeated by Han Xin, a soldier. He was only thirty years old! The great scholars of the late Qing Dynasty and the early Republic of China, such as Liang Qichao and Hu Shi, were already leading figures in their early twenties. Einstein developed his theory of relativity is in his twenties. So, what are the advantages of those young winners? The capacity of action. The newborn calf is not afraid of the tiger, the ignorant is fearless, rules and regulations are for the old. Dare to imagine and dare to just do it – that is how you overtake and win.

Careers develop by doing things, and the truth is something that can be practiced. In the classic book *Records of the Grand Historian* we can read; Break free and do it, avoid the evil spirits. As long as you dare to do it, evil spirits will not dare to block your way.

Why do Japanese people observe Wang Yangming's *Integration of knowledge and action*? It is because Wang Yangming emphasises that knowledge is also a matter of doing things, acting, being proactive! Do it.

Being earnest is the result of a successful education. If you start to act now, you do not have to stay at your desk.

Act now while you still can. If there are several failures in life, then let these failures come early. Do it while there is plenty of time and energy to defeat it.

Xu:

Xu: Awaiting

CLASSICAL TEXT

[Xu] dictates that with the sincerity that is declared in it, there will be brilliant success. With firmness there will be good fortune, and it will be advantageous to cross the great stream.

Nine at the first line The subject is waiting in the distant border. It will be well for him to maintain its purpose, in which case there will be no error.

Nine at the second line The subject is waiting on the sand by the stream. He will suffer a small injury, someone will speak against him, but in the end there will be good fortune.

Nine at the third line The subject is in the mud by the stream. He thereby invites injury.

Six at the fourth line The subject is waiting in a bloody spot. But he will get out.

Nine at the fifth line The subject is waiting amidst the appliances of a feast. Through his firmness and correctness there will be good fortune.

Six at the top line The subject entered the cave. Three people will come, and if they are well received, there will be good fortune in the end.

The image Xu denotes waiting. The image shows danger ahead, but notwithstanding the firmness and the strength indicated by the inner trigram. The subject shall not get involved in dangerous defiling.

LITERAL TRANSLATION

[Xu] Waiting. Timing is the most important. When the time is right, it will be advantageous to cross a great river.

Nine at the first line It is not the right time to move. Stay in safety and wait for danger to pass.

Nine at the second line Close to danger, but not in danger. Just like being criticised but letting it slide off. Keep firm and let it pass.

Nine at the third line You moved too quickly to cross the river and got stuck in the mud. You are vulnerable to attack.

Six at the fourth line After finding refuge for healing from your wounds, you have to find the moment to come out, eventually. You have to make a decision.

Nine at the fifth line You managed to cross the river, but the danger is not over. You can enjoy yourself, you have done well.

Six at the top line Some people might have influence over your life, you need to treat them with respect and accept what comes with it.

The image Water over the sky. The trigram for water is over the one for sky. Heavy rain makes a river hard to cross and it is wise to wait.

INTERPRETATION

This hexagrams contains: in the upper part is Kan, the cloud (water); in the lower part is Gan, indicating the sky. The sky is high, and the weather is clear and with few rain clouds. Things might take some time. In agricultural societies that rely on the sky to eat, all agricultural farming activities require rain. The less rain, the more you have to wait. Therefore, the sage named this phenomena as Xu (needing), meaning waiting.

Life is generally a process of decomposing, a process of waiting for death, of something waiting for something else. People often think the meaning of their lives is waiting for something, longing is the one big footnotes of every life.

Regarding waiting, the sage advises, being optimistic, believing in the future, I believe that what you are waiting for will come one day. Waiting is a journey in itself, and people who are good at waiting will get further in life. The sage pointed out that the process of waiting is not comfortable, it is full of challenges and makes people feel anxious. He reflects on this the following:

First; at the beginning of the wait, be prepared for waiting for a long time. This is very important. Just as Mao Zedong pointed out on his essay *On the Protracted War*, that the War of Resistance against Japan will be long-term and arduous, and it is necessary to make long-term strategic arrangements.

Second; during your wait, there will be a lot of criticism. People will tell you that the things you wait for will never come, so you have to believe in yourself.

Third; your waiting will become a signal that calls people's attention to the things you wait for, so many people will join in and compete with you. There will also be some people who will copy your path and take advantage while you are concentrating on your goal.

Fourth; when your waiting is finally over, there will often be another evil waiting for you. You must use your last strength to take them on, or you will lose your strength and give up. Zeng Guofan's friend Dou Lanquan had a saying, 'When a great accomplishment is to be fulfilled, the devils will wait, make them think it is not ready and they will lose'.

Fifth; summary of all human wisdom is hope and patience. Wait calmly and hope will meet you, you must believe in your fate.

Sixth; expect incidents, there will be surprises, and there will also be unexpected worries. It is necessary to respond with a calm mind and respect.

Finally; the sage believe that the essence of the Xu is "enjoy the pleasure of a simple life". Life needs to be relaxed. When we start a long wait, relax and enjoy life along the way, eat, drink, and play. This in itself is also a path to a good life.

The first is physiological. "Eat, drink, man and woman, it is all part of people's life. The pleasures of food are not as stimulating as the pleasure of sex, but they are more persistent and essential. You can live without love, but cannot live without eating. Hinduism believes that vital energy comes from the universe. This energy is obtained through food and sleep, and is consumed by working, thinking, and labour. Balance between acquisition and consumption is essential. Li Dazhao (Chinese Marxist) says, 'Learn to be practical and play happily'. Being happy increases productivity. Therefore, it is necessary to let yourself be connected to earth, to receive energy, to get the most out of your positive energy, and to recharge your positive energy.

The following is regarding personnel matters. Whether these are between family, friends, colleagues or customers, eating and drinking are good opportunities for everyone to share and improve their mood. Every day at work, you may have been alone for a long time, you may have felt alienated. Like water without a stream or a tree without roots! One of the most important things for Chinese people is, make no distinction between public and private interests. Emotions are mainly cultivated in a leisurely state of mind. Find emotional balance, and everything will be OK. On the other hand, if a leader invites you to join his leisure activities, or a customer becomes friends with you, then everything is easier.

Once again, this is wisdom. If you do not live fully, you lack wisdom. If you do not know how to live, you will not understand human nature. If you do not understand human nature, you will not be invited by important figures, and you will not be able to accomplish anything big. At least half of the meaning of life is in living it with plenitude, five years of good life is equivalent to living for decades.

Song: The commoner before the noble

CLASSICAL TEXT

Though there is sincerity in one's contention, one will yet meet with opposition and obstruction; but if he cherishes an apprehensive caution, there will be good fortune. While, if he must prosecute the contention to the bitter end, there will be evil.

It will be advantageous to consult a great man; it will not be advantageous to cross a great stream.

Six at the First line; suggests the subject not perpetuating the matter about which there is contention. He will suffer of being spoken against, but the end will be fortunate.

Six at the Second line; shows its subject unequal to the contention. If he retires and keeps himself concealed where, and the inhabitants of his city are less than three hundred families, he will fall into no mistake.

Six at the third line; offers its subject firmly keeping in the old place of support. Perilous as the position is, there will be good fortune in the end. Should he perchance engage in the king's business, he will not claim merit for the achievements.

Nine at the Fourth line; shows its subject unequal to the contention. He returns to the study of Heaven's ordinances, changes his wish to contend, and rests in being firm and correct. There will be good fortune.

Nine at the Fifth line; suggests its subject contending and with good fortune.

Nine at the top line; shows how its subject may have the leather belt conferred on him by the sovereign, and thrice it shall be taken from him in a morning.

The image; The trigram representing heaven and that one representing water, moving away from each other, form Song. The superior man, in accordance with this, in the transaction of affairs takes good counsel about his First steps.

LITERAL TRANSLATION

The Song hexagram; Someone is going to the mandarin's court to present a complaint. You are not in a powerful enough position to necessarily direct things the way you would like. Be willing to compromise and mediate.

Six at the First line; Avoid misunderstandings by knowing when to retreat. You do not have the upper hand. You might suffer criticism because of this, but it will all be well in the end.

Nine at the Second line; conflict is beyond your control. The opposition you are facing is stronger than you. Retreat while you can to a safe and familiar place.

Six at the third line; Your position is weak, you are afraid. Rely on your own means only and follow strategies that have worked well before.

Nine at the Fourth line; Your attempt to carry out a complaint has been unsuccessful. Do not linger on the grievance and keep moving. You should accept the course of things.

Nine at the Fifth line; Litigation can be auspicious.

Nine at the top line; You have been awarded a leather sash (a symbol of force and punishment), it shall be recalled thrice in a day.

The image; Sky (The authority) is over water confronting it, this represent disagreement.

INTERPRETATION

This hexagram contains: in the upper part is Gan, indicating the sky; in the lower part is Kan, meaning water (river). I go out for a walk every night to places where there are no street lights. The stars in the night sky are bright. I do not know about astronomy or astrology, but every night, I can see at least a feature: the starry sky preceding West. So, of course, the actual motion of the earth is towards the east. However, the ancients also relied on this intuitive feeling that the sky is going west, and the river is flowing eastward. One going westward and another one eastward, so the sage saw in this a scene of conflict and litigation, so he defined this as a "dispute."

Then the sage said about a lawsuit that:

First; "a lawsuit should not be too long", a lawsuit cannot be dragged on for too long, there should be compromise, early termination, even if it is criticised, it is better; if it takes long, certainly both parties will see loses. Even if you win, you may sow hatred.

Second; the people should not need to sue officials, people should not fight with the officials, yet they are somehow defeated. When you look at the situation, you have to move quickly, get out of the way, and avoid the spotlight.

Third; it is better to cut a loss, try not to go to court, and know that it will pass. It is important to remember that when you threat superiors and leaders, you will be at a disadvantage.

Fourth; if the lawsuit is lost, then accept the facts calmly, steady your mood, continue to work hard, and make your life better.

Fifth; a lawsuit must be conducted in appropriate conditions where the judges are fair, and the evidence is sufficient.

Sixth; relying on bribes to make a profit is risky and easy to be caught. In short, if it is time to go to court, you have first to think well. So, it is best not to come to this.

What to do? The sage pointed out that; 'things should be done diligently from the beginning', you should think clearly about the things that may be in dispute and make a contract.

As the saying goes, "A villain at first glance, but a gentleman in the end". Harsh words should be said early. From these two sayings, we can see that the Chinese do not like contracts and believe that these are ugly, though it restricts a villain. The contract depreciates the confidence of both parties.

In life, when friends come to borrow money from you, tell me, 'Let me write you a receipt'. Keep it in mind, though I am afraid it is difficult to say it. What to do? I will teach you a trick: You may borrow money from all your friends, and take the initiative to give them a receipt, then you will set the example! The joke might seem ridiculous, but in reality, it is hard to set a standard. Who has had a dispute over a lawsuit where there were only good intentions? Either friends or business partners. It is unlikely to go to court with a person to whom you have no relationship at all. The paradox is nothing more than a way to focus on the point. Therefore, if everyone was of excellent moral quality, there should be a consensus among brothers, clear accounts, and everybody should have a sense of a contract. Do not overestimate each other's ability to do wrong, and do not overestimate their personality.

"A thousand miles journey begins with one step," A good start is half the battle. At the beginning of affairs, a tone should be set. This tone will only be strengthened in the future and should not change. Be careful to remain right at the end.

Zeng Guofan has a valuable insight: to seek a prior defeat. Do not think about how you will succeed, but consider what you could eventually lose. Among many other factors, disputes are the main factor in a defeat. Therefore, it is especially important to establish a contractual awareness from the beginning. To make a broad generalisation, that is the reason why the West surpasses China in modern times, because of the rule of law developed under the contractual consciousness.

Shi: When general Han Xin muster soldiers, the more the better

CLASSICAL TEXT

Shi; With firmness and correctness, and a leader of age and experience, there will be good fortune and no error.

Six at the First line; The army acting according to the rules. If these are not good, there will be evil.

Nine at the Second line; The leader among the army. There will be good fortune and no error. The king has thrice conveyed to him the orders of his favour.

Six at the third line; shows how the army may possibly, have many inefficient leaders. There will be evil.

Six at the fourth line; The army in retreat. There is no error.

Six at the fifth line; suggests birds in the fields, which it will be advantageous to seize and destroy. In that case there will be no error. If the oldest son leads the army, and younger men idly occupy offices assigned to them, however firm and correct he may be, there will be evil.

Six at the top line; The great ruler delivering his charges, appointing some to be rulers of states, and others to undertake the headship of clans; but small men should not be employed in such positions.

The image; The trigram representing the earth and in the midst of it that represents water, form Shi. The superior man, in accordance with this, nourishes and educates the people, and collects from them the multitudes of the army.

LITERAL TRANSLATION

Shi; When keeping the right, the wise and the elders in the army, there is no harm.

Six at the First line; The military must be disciplined but military discipline can be bad.

Nine at the Second line; A fair leader is rewarded for his dedication and service. It is time to equal to the demands of an important mission.

Six at the third line; Disorder due to incompetent leadership, there are casualties now.

Six at the fourth line; The army retreated and there was no harm in that.

Six at the fifth line; There are birds in the field, which can be caught without harm. The seniors led the division to advance, and the enemy left their dead.

Six at the top line; The emperor issued an order to summon the hero to establish a clan, and the enemy cannot benefit from this.

The image; Earth over water. A great man keeps people united.

INTERPRETATION

This hexagram is formed by Kun, the Earth on top; and the lower is Kan, indicating water. Under a vast land, there is abundant groundwater resources for requirements. What the sage thinks of this image is that there is a rich source of troops to draft from the people. As long as there are enough people, the military can be strong, and the country can be strong. This principle was generally good in the cold war era. The sage named this "teacher" Shi, which also means the army, and then elaborated on some of his military ideas:

First; military discipline must be strict.

Second; the general is to be unselfish.

Third; to avoid low morale that can be frustrated by failure.

Fourth; to be flexible to retreat.

Fifth; if the strategy is clear, it will be easier to be put into practice.

Sixth; after victory, the military merit is not equal to the rule of law, and the military cannot decide on appointing official positions. However, the sage finally emphasises an essential problem, that is that to "accommodate the livestock", the general mind must be like that of the Earth; just like the story of general Han Xin points out: the more soldiers, the more significant the accomplishment.

Following this idea, Mao Zedong formed the strategic manoeuvring of the "People's War," and he firmly believed that the more people that come together, the more powerful they are. This concept does have problems under the constraints of non-renewable resources of the land; however, in most situations, there is no problem. In Keynesian economics, it is believed that if population is large enough, then the economy has ample room for development.

Things need to be done, and quantitative growth is a must. In terms of business, if sales volume increase, product types will increase, the investment will increase, equipment will grow, customers will increase, and the market will expand. When these quantities increase to a certain degree, they will form a "scale advantage": the cost will decrease, the collaboration will be more comfortable, the influence will be stronger, and so on. Making the volume bigger is the key of commercial success. Why are Internet companies loved so much by investors? It is because these companies have a user base of hundreds of millions of people, and billions of dollars, which is unmatched by traditional enterprises. The Internet industry has a famous "long-tail theory", which is looking for business opportunities in quantity.

However, among all the variables, the most fundamental is the person, which is the primary variable that drives other variables. It is necessary to recruit enough people to develop, profit, and create value in this platform. Zeng Guofan lived long and experienced countless things. He concluded that the only thing to do is to win the people over. And "getting people" is like eating. If you want to eat enough, you must eat more and more. A leader, when watching over people and employing people, must be independent. You cannot get used to it. Seeing who is not pleasing or not, that is all right. But if you look at yourself, you are still not pleasant to others. Then you will find you are alone.

Why is Li Ka-shing's company named "Cheung Kong Holdings"? Because the Yangtze River "does not merge into smaller rivers," the smaller rivers flow to it. Everyone wants to!

For the sake of being a good human being, the "teacher" inspires us to make friends, to build good relationship, to stick to basic principles, to do things the right way, and to have a balanced view. The resources of life can be abundant enough.

Of course, the original meaning of "Shi" is still military. The essence of the *Book of Change*s is to serve the ruling party. The ruling is based on two points: the internal rule of the country and the external use of the army, together they make the country both rich and strong. Therefore, not only this hexagram among the book's sixty-four hexagrams contains the army, directly relating to the ancestors and other military figures. Each of the famous *Thirty-six stratagems* (see below) corresponds to a glimpse only. It can be seen that the ancients had a deep understanding of the sixty-four hexagrams and their use. It is very interesting. I have sorted out this aspect and attached it later in the book.

Bi: A close friend

CLASSICAL TEXT

Bi; Under the right conditions this is good fortune. But let the main person involved re-examine himself, as if by divination, whether his virtue be great, constant and firm. If it be so, there will be no error. Those who are restless will come to him; and those who come late will be ill.

Six at the First line; Shows its subject sincerely seeking to win the attachment of his object. There will be no error. Let it be full of sincerity as an earthenware vessel is of its content, and in the end it will bring other advantages.

Six at the second line; Showing the movement towards union and attachment proceeding from the mind. With applied wisdom (virtuous, virtue, pure, acting with virtue) there will be good fortune.

Six at the third line; We see its subject seeking for union with such as ought not to be associated with.

Six at the fourth line; We see its subject seeking for union with the one beyond himself. With applied wisdom there will be good fortune.

Nine at the Fifth line; Afford the most illustrious instance of seeking union and attachment. The king seems to be urging his pursuit of the game only in three directions, and allowing all the animals before him to escape, while the people of his towns do not warn one another to prevent it. There will be good fortune.

Six at the top line; We see one seeking union and attachment without having taken the first step to such an end. There will be evil.

The image; The trigram representing the earth, and over that representing water, form Bi. The ancient king, in accordance with this, established the various states and maintained an affectionate relation to their princes.

LITERAL TRANSLATION

Bi; Agreement. In accordance with the tradition, families will live together and live cooperatively. Those who hesitate, and the latecomers, are not fully welcomed and trusted.

Six at the First line; A plain cup overflowing with sincerity. Sincerely believe that if you are fully stocked with wine, you will end up with the attachment of others and this will be auspicious.

Six at the Second line; Remain on the inside, keep auspicious.

Six at the third line; Close to the wrong person.

Six at the fourth line; Close to the outside, keep auspicious.

Nine at the Fifth line; The King allows some of the game to escape. Villagers do not prevent it, which is auspicious.

Six at the top line; People who are close to each other have no leader, if an unqualified person is in charge, there will be problems.

The image; Water over the earth. The King remains close to the princess in times of trouble.

INTERPRETATION

In this hexagram, the upper part is Kan, indicating water; the lower is Kun, meaning the ground. The water is on the ground. Naturally, it is close to the ground, so the sage named this "Bi." There is a poem that says: "to have friends afar, be with each other even though far apart", this is close to the meaning of Bi. Bi is about the matter of being close to people. The sage believes that:

First; to be close to people should be about honesty, should be "close" not for a particular purpose, but you should at least give yourself a reason to be close to each other.

Second; being close is the only way to win the hearts of the people. The highest form of closeness is to be intimate.

Third; being honourable and keeping your distance from mean people. Sometimes, I will focus on the moon and its features.

Fourth; the farther away you are, the more you should pay attention to the small issues.

Fifth; whether close to the leadership or other people, we must strive to achieve two points:

First; it is understandable that others need to be fully recognised.

Second; each is in full trust of the other because of their closeness.

Sixth; for those who deserve to be close, as Zeng Guofan said, 'Keep them strong and attached!' Close people should pay attention to the hierarchy of each other; otherwise, they will easily hurt each other.

The sage finally raised this issue to a different height and proposed that, 'The king should first build the kingdom and then keep the princes close'.

We all know of the "feudal society". But what is it? For example, Wu Wang overturned the Shang Dynasty, established the Zhou Dynasty, and then divided his relatives and heroes into the government. For instance, Zhou Gong and Jiang TaiGong were appointed to Shandong, each of whom established a vassal state, the Lu state, and a Qi state. This is "feudalism". What is the purpose of doing this? In today's words, it helps to establish grassroot organisations to be close to the government and to manage the people. In Mandarin Chinese, it is to adhere to the masses, closely be connected with the people, unite with the people, and serve the people wholeheartedly. In short, the ruler must be close to the people. Only when you are close can you fully understand, trust, and entrust. Then you can connect like life and death. When the body is close, the mind will be close.

A country is the same, and a company is the same, it is necessary to invest resources, establish a robust first line service system, fully get closer to the customer and serve them, to win over your customer support.

How close? Close in terms of service, especially free services. 360 is very powerful nowadays, today at war with QQ, and tomorrow with Baidu PK (Chinese brands). What is it that is so powerful? It is free. Other anti-virus software costs money, they are expensive, but 360 is free, and the quality is excellent. All the people have been won over, and this is amazing. Yu Minhong's secret to starting a New Oriental is that it is also free. The students are attracted to the class with free lectures. Then the course is excellent, and it starts from there.

Nowadays, the so-called "Internet thinking" is very hot. If you refer to the hexagrams "Shi" and "Bi", you will be inspired.

Xiao Xu: The feeling of being middle class

CLASSICAL TEXT

Xiao Xu indicates progress and success. We see dense clouds, but no rain coming from our borders in the west.

Nine at the First line; The subject returns and pursuing his own course. What mistake should he fall into? There will be good fortune.

Nine at the Second line; shows its subject returning to the proper course. There will be good fortune.

Nine at the third line; suggests a husband and wife looking upon each other with averted eyes.

Six at the fourth line; shows its subject possessing righteousness. The danger of bloodshed is thereby averted, and his grounds for apprehension dismissed. There will be no mistake.

Nine at the Fifth line; Suggests its subject possessing righteousness, and drawing others to unite with him. Rich in resources, he employs his neighbours to join them under the same cause with himself.

Nine at the top line; shows how the rain has fallen, and the onward progress continues. So we value the full accumulation of virtue. But a wife exercising restraint, however firm and correct she may be, is in a position of peril, and like the moon approaching fullness. If the superior man prosecute his measures in such circumstances, there will be evil.

The image; The sky, and that represents wind moving above it, form Xiao Xu The superior man, in accordance with this, adorns the outward manifestation of his virtue.

LITERAL TRANSLATION

Xiao Xu Clouds are gathering in the west, there will be rain, but not yet.

Nine at the First line; Return to the right path, is there anything that might harm you? This is auspicious.

Nine at the Second line; Getting traction on the right path, this is auspicious.

Nine at the third line; The spokes of the wheels fell off and the couple lost sight of each other.

Six a the Fourth line; A sincere approach avoids bloodshed.

Nine at the Fifth line; Integrity and love, and get rich with neighbours.

Nine at the top line; It finally rained, you weathered the storm; remain cautious, the moon is not quite full yet. If you risk it now, you will suffer.

The image; Wind in the sky. The gentleman needs to be exemplary in receiving the influence of learning and the arts.

INTERPRETATION

This hexagram is formed by Xun (The Gentle) in the upper part, indicating the wind; the lower is "dry", meaning the day. The wind blew gently in the sky, and the clouds gathered with the wind, and gradually gained strength of the next light rain. What the sage sees here is that people have a certain amount of savings (the "livestock" and "stores" for the small animals), the material living standard has reached a certain level, and a well-off society has the feeling of being middle class. There may be problems with the poor while getting rich. It is easy to get lost and go wrong. It is like arriving at a crossroads. How to know where do you go from here? The sage believes that:

First; do not forget your heart, remember your original intentions and dreams, and calm your restless heart.

Second; hold hands with your loved one, just like the first few times; in fact, everything is still beautiful.

Third; it is not easy to go back at this time. Just like a car that has been maintained for a long time, it should be tuned. The emotions between husband and wife must be managed too. It is also necessary to check the oil. The seven-year itch is a high-risk period of quarrelling and divorce. Work hard to get through. Other interpersonal relationships and emotions also need to be worked on and maintained.

Fourth; to reciprocate with sincerity is the secret to maintaining healthy interpersonal relationships.

Fifth; home and everything, relying on friends and working together, will create a better future.

Sixth; the husband and wife should have a correct relationship, and if the family has a good and happy wife, then the husband is safe.

The sage summarised by saying; that when issues are small, people should pay attention to "receiving a positive influence of learning and art", whether they solve problems or seek development. After civilisation has developed in the material front, and spiritual side must keep up. After enriching the pockets, it is necessary to enhance the head and improve cultural life.

This matter does not require the sage's input to know how it should be. In terms of Maslow's pyramid theory, material wealth only solves the physiological and security needs. At this point, people still have social, self-esteem, self-fulfilling, and other necessities, which cannot be realised by money alone. Therefore, many people who were sloppy at school have become like a nouveau rich, and they like calligraphy and painting and Zen tea. They do not think that this is pretentious and artsy. They have an inner demand for these cultural things.

The meaning of culture is not limited to the satisfaction of demand; it has a rich practical significance. For an entrepreneur, "Xiao Xu" is like a small business that has experienced a relatively cruel rushed and painful success. Now might not be as embarrassing as it was when it started. However, to further develop, the situation is equally grim. The second venture generally comes at this stage. Whether a second venture is successful or not, it is crucial to see if the same kind of mindset can be applied.

On the one hand, you have to study and learn, to understand those more advanced things, to improve management, technology, and other aspects, you can no longer use an old mindset; on the other hand, to develop a corporate culture, use a fresh culture to manage people, one that can adapt. There is always a loophole in relationships. There is still a loophole in the system. On the other hand, it is necessary to use friendship. Culture is the communication tool of the elites. Without culture, there is no way to communicate with those higher-level people, and they cannot enter the circle of others. No better resources are available.

The seven-year itch also needs "the exemplary refining influence of learning and art," read more books, see things through a little more, and put your mind on to serious things to successfully pass this hurdle.

Lu: the tiger's tail

CLASSICAL TEXT

Lu; Someone treading on the tail of a tiger, which does not bite him. There will be progress and success.

Nine at the First line; shows its subject treading his accustomed path. If he goes forward, there will be no error.
Nine at the Second line; The subject treading a path that is level and easy – a quiet and solitary man, to whom, if he be firm and correct, there will be good fortune.
Six at the third line; suggests a one-eyed man who thinks he can see clearly; a lame man who thinks he can walk well; one who treads on the tail of a tiger and is bitten. All this indicates ill fortune. We have a bravado acting the part of a great ruler.
Nine at the Fourth line; shows its subject treading on the tail of a tiger. He becomes full of apprehensive caution, and in the end there will be good fortune.
Nine at the Fifth line; we see resolute footsteps. Though he be firm and correct, there will be peril.
Nine at the top line; this tells us to look at the whole course that is trodden, and examine the presage which that gives. If it be complete and without failure, there will be good fortune.
The image; The sky above, and below, the waters of a marsh, form Lu. The superior man, in accordance with this, discriminates between high and low, and gives settlement to the aims of the people.

LITERAL TRANSLATION

Lu Treading on the tiger's tail but the tiger does not bite.

Nine at the First line; walking with honestly, go forward there will be no harm.

Nine at the Second line; walking on a flat road, remain honest and it will be auspicious.

Six at the third line; The one-eyed man thinks he can see clearly, the lame man wants to run like an athlete. That is how you get eaten by a tiger.

Nine at the Fourth line; Tread on the tiger's tail, remain in fear and caution, and it will be auspicious.

Nine at the Fifth line; Go on easy and steady, be careful of possible dangers.

Nine at the top line; Examine your steps, examine the gains and losses, continue and find prosperity.

The image; Sky over the lake, this forms Lu. The gentleman distinguishes between the lower and the higher, this is how it helps to deal with public matters.

INTERPRETATION

This hexagram is formed by Xun (The Gentle) in the upper part, indicating the wind; and the lower is "dry", meaning the day. Above is the vast sky; below is the boundless lake, the lake his high, you can step on it, there are also low-lying puddles, and unfathomable mud. Going this way is like following the tiger's tail. Only when you take extra care, you will not be bitten by it, and you remain safe. Therefore, the sage named this hexagram "Xu" (needing), meaning "waiting". In one of the oldest Chinese dictionaries, the entry for "Elegant, refined and cultured", is also annotated as Xu. China has a long history of etiquette, of ritual and music, with many ancient books, such as the *Book of Rites*. So what are rites? Basically a ritual is a set of rules and order. How to walk properly? You need to behave in accordance with rules and laws. In this regard, the sages put forward a few points;

First; in general, if there is honesty while obeying the rules and order, obeying the law, and not violating morality, there will be no problem.

Second; even if you take the Middle Path, you should be cautious and be low-key to avoid tripping to the ground.

Third; if you do something, but do not understand the rules, do not act rashly. Every time Confucius arrived at a new place, he first ask about the local customs and taboos. Unless you are powerful, you cannot ignore rules.

Fourth; make sure you understand the official rules, and the unspoken rules; be sure all are clear, and strictly abide by them. This is like a tightrope, although dangerous, as long as you know what you are doing, you can walk safely.

Fifth; is to create rules and obtain pricing power. Risks and opportunities are directly proportional.

Sixth; for the road you have travelled, you should always look back and reflect on how you made it to where you are.

The sages further promoted this idea, arguing that "the gentleman distinguish between the lower and the higher, and helps the common people to make the difference". This is how you can help society reach its goals.

Confucius said, 'The monarch rules, the minister carries out governmental duties, the father takes care of his family, and the son studies and obeys. The monarch is in the position of the ruler, doing what the ruler should do; the minister is in the position of the minister, doing what the minister should do; the father is in the position of the father, doing what the father should do; the son is in the position of the son, doing what the son should do'.

This is the rite, and this order allows things to work in harmony. Otherwise, the king does not rule; the minister does not do his duty, the father is not a good father, the son is not a good son, none can distinguish between the upper and lower, and then all is chaos. Modern people criticise Confucian's "The three cardinal guides and five constant virtues", but most of them are blind. The "five guides" are certainly no problem to follow: Benevolence, Justice, Politeness, Wisdom, and Faith. These are all good things. What can be wrong with these? The "three guides" seem to be awkward: The monarch is obeyed by the minister, the father is followed by the child, and the wife obeys the husband, but it is not so absolute in practice. The order emphasised behind it should be flexible.

In any business or organisation, this order is required. Who is the boss, who is the employee; who is the leader, who is subordinate? If this is unclear, how can an office function? Moreover, there must be detailed behavioural guidelines, rules, and regulations, or there will be no rule! There is no exception to the family. There is a saying: A mountain cannot accommodate two tigers, except for one male and one female. But this male and the female must also have an agreement, such as men and women and so on. When something happens, it is good to discuss it among equals. When the consultation is inconsistent, you must have a clear leader-subordinate order. Who will listen to whom? This is how to ensure a long-lasting family.

This "rite" is set and must be carefully maintained.

Tai: The secret of conducting oneself calmly

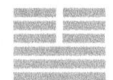

CLASSICAL TEXT

Tai The small one is gone and the great comes. This indicates that there will be good fortune, with progress and success.

Nine at the First line; suggests the idea of grass pulled up, and bringing with it other stalks, which to whose roots are connected. Advance will be fortunate.

Nine at the Second line; One who can bear with the uncultivated, will cross the river without a boat, does not forget the distant, and has no selfish friendships. Thus does he prove himself acting in accordance with the course of the due mean.

Nine at the third line; shows that, while there is no state of peace that is not liable to be disturbed, and no departure of evil men so that they shall not return, yet when one is firm and correct, as he realises the distresses that may arise, he will commit no error. There is no occasion for sadness at the certainty of such changes; and in this mood, the happiness of the present may be enjoyed.

Six at the Fourth line; shows its subject fluttering down – not relying on his own rich resources, but calling in his neighbours. They all come not as having received warning, but out of the sincerity of their hearts.

Six at the fifth line; reminds us of Emperor Di-yi's rule about the marriage of his younger sister. By such a course there is happiness and there will be great good fortune.

Six at the top line; shows us the city wall returned into the moat. It is not the time to use the army. The subject of the line may, indeed, announce his orders to the people of his own city; but however correct and firm he may be, he will have cause for regret.

The image; The trigrams for heaven and earth in communication together form Tai. The wise sovereign, in harmony with this, fashions and completes his regulations after the courses of heaven and earth, and assists the application of the adaptations furnished by them in order to benefit the people.

LITERAL TRANSLATION

Tai; Small offering and big returns, prosperity.

Nine at the First line; The roots are connected and this attracts others. Good fortune.

Nine at the Second line; Inclusive, you can walk across the river and not get lost. Follow the Middle Path and you will receive help.

Nine at the third line; There is no plain without a mountain. There is no harm in being in a difficult situation, no need to worry if you have the basics.

Six at the fourth line; Not boasting of wealth in a life that is not rich, neighbours can help if you communicate in good faith.

Six at the fifth line; The king married a daughter with his blessing, great auspicious.

Six at the top line; The city wall falls on the dry moat. It is not necessary to send troops, reduce orders and guard against regrets.

The image; Heaven and Earth intermingled; the monarch manages affairs to achieve the balance between heaven and the earth and to guide the people.

INTERPRETATION

This is the most wonderful one of the sixty-four hexagrams: above is Kun, indicating the land; the following is Qian, meaning the sky. At first glance, the ground is up, and the sky is down, isn't this upside down? In the eyes of the sage, on the contrary, what he saw was heaven on earth, and he saw it as peaceful and stable! Why? Because it is impossible to turn upside down, this is beyond the scope of human experience. What the sage saw from this image is that the sun and the rain in the sky are given to the earth, and the atmosphere of the earth evaporates to the sky. Everything grows towards the sky, so the heavens and the earth meet. You have me, I have you, and we are in harmony. Producing for each other, one is full of vitality, and thus covering the way between heaven and earth, "nothing is always flat, nothing goes on forever", Yin and Yang follow each other. When you see this, you should be able to think of the Taiji figure (the yinyang) composed of black and white Yin and Yang (see image in this book).

The Taiji diagram is rich in meaning, and Tai is the same. The sage emphasises a few points.

First; anything that grows up will take root. The upper branches seem to be independent, but in fact, the roots are connected and tangled.

Second; there are several keywords for Tai: tolerance, skill, thoroughness, independence, and the right path.

Third; is to understand the truth that things must be reversed, and prosperity will weaken. Everything starts to fail once it has reached the zenith.

Fourth; is not to be happy with stuff, neither be sad about them, remain respectful and serene, modest and courteous, be close to others, and eliminate barriers.

Fifth; is to make the best of the marriage and alliances to consolidate the foundation of their relationship.

Sixth; when glory and the decline are inevitable, you should take advantage of the situation and be supportive. However, these are fundamental: communication, conversation, making friends, trading, exchanging, being intimate, interacting, coordinating, fighting, communicating, and dealing with each other.

Wei period literary genius, Cao Pi said, 'The relationship between Ying and Yang is like all things; the king and the ministers; the country and the government; the scholar and the virtue, they all show the moral example. These are not only to be practiced by these, but by anyone with a strong will'.

There is no human being without sexual intercourse. There is no political power without the exchange of monarchs and ministers. What is life without friends? I cannot live without market transactions. So, we have to give up our blind reason.

The second is easy, that is, change and transformation. The sky will fall to the ground, and the underground will rise to the sky — thirty years on the east bank of the river, thirty years on the west side. The extremes must be reversed; the monthly surplus must become deficit, and everything in the universe does not change instantly, but it will do it in the opposite! Many things we pursue, such as success, wealth, status, fame, and security, are not once and for all. If you do not get it, you will not know where to go. It is not changing for changing sake; it is just like you riding a bicycle; it seems that the bike is steady and moving forward. But in fact, your hands and body are the centre of gravity, constantly fine-tuning at every moment to ensure the balance of the bike. Therefore, Zeng Guofan emphasised to his children a thousand times to maintain one's good position by restraining. So, how to protect this state of peace? "Tai" gives us an answer: Being arduous has no blame.

This word has been mentioned several times in the *Book of Changes*, meaning: bitter, tired, and suffer some unsatisfactory things, such people will not have big problems and suffer great disasters. Zeng Guofan often said that gentlemen do not seek perfection. This is the way to conserve the peace of Tai.

Deeply understand the truth of the above and your knowledge of the people will be spotless, everything can be achieved, can be overcome, can bend and stretch, can be big and small, can be soft, can go up, can enter and retreat, can be Grandpa can also be a grandson, such a talent can really work!

"After all the richness of the world", when I read this sentence, I was attracted by this "financial" word, and immediately came down to earth: there is money to keep afloat and money to be able to settle down. Moreover, using money to allocate natural and earth resources also coincides with today's market economy. Of course, the ancient scholars believed that this "financial" word [Cai] should be connected with the word "reduce" [Cai], and it is reasonable to use it. My opinion is only to complain.

Pi: Truman's world

CLASSICAL TEXT

Pi; In Pi there is the want for good understanding between the different classes of men, and its indication is unfavourable to the firm and correct course of the superior man. We see in it the great one leaving and the small one coming.

Six at the First line; suggests the idea of grass pulled up, and bringing with it other stalks with whose roots it is connected. With applied wisdom on the part of its subject, there will be good fortune and progress.

Six at the Second line; its subject patient and obedient. To the small man behaving the way is appropriate; there will be good fortune. If the great man acts as the distress and obstruction of a situation requires, he will have success

Six at the third line; The subject ashamed of the purpose folded in his breast.

Nine at the Fourth line; shows its subject acting in accordance with the ordination of Heaven, and committing no error. His companions will come and share in his happiness.

Nine at the Fifth line; we see him who brings the distress and obstruction to a close, the great man and fortunate. But let him say, 'We may perish! We may perish!' so shall the state of things become firm, as if bound to a clump of bushy mulberry trees.

Nine at the top line; shows the overthrow and removal of the condition of distress and obstruction. Before this, there was that condition. Hereafter there will be joy.

The image; Heaven and earth, not in intercommunication, form Pi. The superior man, in accordance with this, restrains his virtue, and avoids the calamities that threaten him. There is no opportunity of conferring on him the glory of emolument.

LITERAL TRANSLATION

Pi; the person who is closed is not the right person. It is not conducive to be a gentleman, the big one is leaving, the small one is coming.

Nine at the First line; The roots are connected and this attracts others. Good fortune.

Six at the Second line; Tolerance. Lowly people must make humble offerings.

Six at the third line; Be oneself without shame.

Nine at the Fourth line; There is life, so no harm, and everyone is blessed by each other's support.

Nine at the Fifth line; be at one with your fate, remain firm, secure your position and be firm like a mulberry tree.

Nine at the top line; No obstacles, happiness ahead.

The image; Sky over the earth, they appear to be in the right place, but they do not interact.

INTERPRETATION

This phenomenon is the opposite of "Tai": the upper is Qian, indicating the sky; the lower is Kun, meaning the ground. The above part is the sky; the bottom is the earth; this is normal; their place is right, the feeling of the monarch and the minister doing their duty. But these are particularly salient persons. If 1 + 1 = 2, what can be wrong? It is complicated to know that it is not that simple, so... funnily this is kind of cute if you think about it. The depth of the sage's thoughts is not to be wondering about this. However, we should see that his ideas are worrying about the future. From such a normal phenomenon, he considers the separation between the top and bottom, the centrifugal separation. "ErYa ancient dictionary" we can read, "Pi, separation" is the definition of a barrier. For example, for an official person, if there is no one to protect the platform, no one to maintain it, no one is covered, even if its prominent position, it is already dangerous. At this time, we must pay close attention to observing ourselves. We must "look to have good morality and not be proud of it". We must be notably low-key, support the blessings, and not be illusory, not to be greedy for power, and it is best to keep safe.

The saint describes "Pi" as a situation of life:

First; In the beginning, you can be rooted with a group of brothers and a group of friends.

Second; Then, you tried to climb up and tried your best to please the boss and tolerate your colleagues. All the work was spared.

Third; In the meantime, you also bear the burden of humiliation, and personality and dignity make way for success.

Forth; One day, you finally climbed up. Many people surrounded you because of their interests. Those who used to be friends and those who really loved you were squeezed out of the circle.

Fifth; at this time, a few people discovered the problem in time and made changes, and finally had a good ending. When Zhang Ruimin talked about using Internet thinking to transform traditional management, he said, 'Go for the inferior first, then for happiness'. Only by actively subverting oneself and suffering from pain can you achieve a new life.

Sixth; most people will be lost, and eventually fall into a desperate situation of rebellion, loneliness, and embattled songs. All the struggles are in vain. However, never despair!

The meaning of Pi when it comes to human life is twofold:

> **First;** is to learn the way of thinking of the sages and to calmly examine your situation through a balanced view, including the relationship with others and the nature of heaven and earth. This is very difficult. Famous Hollywood comedian, Jim Carrey starred in the movie *The World of Truman*. He lived a normal life like all ordinary people, and one day he found an incredible secret. It turned out that Truman was born as a protagonist of a reality show. Everything he saw, the blue sky, the sea, the supermarket, etc. all was a prop, even his lover, colleagues, friends, strangers, and so on. He was the only non-actor of the show; only he did not know the truth. This film reflects a spiritual dilemma of human survival: it is difficult to understand how it relates to ourselves. It is said that the daughter of the richest man, Zong Qinghou, is still single in her early thirties because it is difficult to determine which man is chasing after her only for the money. Behind every

marriage story, there is a husband who makes money for his wife.

Second; when we realise that our relationship with the outside world changes, we must adjust in time. At this time, you do not love "earning face", you love vanity, do not be greedy for what you have now, and dare to give it up and trace back. For those relationships that can be recovered, you have to put down your mask to recover them — fall from where you climbed. The method of recovery is nothing more than working hard on the "crossing" and reopening relationships. No matter how good it seems, as long as it is appropriately handled, everything will be fine.

Tong Ben:

Are we all the same?

CLASSICAL TEXT

Tong Ren; The "Union of men" appears here as we find it in the remote districts of the country, indicating progress and success. It will be advantageous to cross the great stream. It will be advantageous to maintain the applied wisdom of the superior man.

Nine at the First line; shows the representative of the union of men just issuing from his gate. There will be no error.

Six at the Second line; suggests the representative of the union of men in relation with his kindred. There will be occasion for regret.

Nine at the third line; shows its subject with his arms hidden in the thick grass, and at the top of a high mound. But for three years he makes no demonstration.

Nine at the Fourth line; its subject mounted on the city wall; but he does not attack, he contemplates. There will be good fortune.

Nine at the Fifth line; The representative of the union of men first wails and cries out, and then laughs. His great host conquers, and he and the subject of the second line meet.

Nine at the top line; representative of the union of men in the suburbs. There will be no occasion for regret.

The image; The trigrams for heaven and fire form Tong Ren. The superior man, in accordance with this distinguishes things according to their kinds and classes.

LITERAL TRANSLATION

Tong Ren; People united, out in the open but together. People gather and the great man leads them rightfully.

Nine at the First line; Meeting friendly people outside the gates. No harm will come.

Six at the Second line; Trouble with friends and family at the hall. Beware of danger.

Nine at the third line; Behind friendly faces there can be an ambush. Do not wait for too long.

Nine at the Fourth line; Climbing the ramparts, but not calling an attack. Good fortune.

Nine at the Fifth line; After great tragedy, there was laughing. Victory will come.

Nine at the top line; The leader out in the open with friendly people around him. There will be no occasion for repentance.

The image; Fire under the sky, the leader meets his people around a fire to sort things out.

INTERPRETATION

In this hexagram: the upper is Qian, indicating the sky; the lower is Li, meaning the fire, and also the sun. Flames rushed up to the sky, just like the mutual attraction between like-minded people; the sun hangs in the sky, just like a person relying on his group to be more radiant. Therefore, the sages named this hexagram as "the same person" [Tong Ren]; that is, people who are the same in some respects, such as classmates, colleagues, peers, comrades, associates, fellows, companions, and so on. In most cases, "the same person" means a cooperative relationship. The sage has some thoughts on this relationship:

First; as early as possible, students, small children, and friends should form a sense of cooperation to complete a specific job at an early stage. Many entrepreneurs are like brothers with their associates and have built a solid trust, a complementarity one, or a leader-subordinated relationship. Bill Gates and Paul Allen started learning and working together at the age of fifteen.

Second; getting along can be a source of trouble. Family cooperation has advantages and disadvantages, and it is easy to hurt feelings because of work.

Third; an alliance will enhance its strength and cooperation when they create a common cause.

Fourth; partnerships do things in order, friendship first, success second. If the friendship is not stable, progress is difficult; if the friendship is gone, then success is also leaving.

Fifth; a friendship must be tested on the field, and an alliance that does not test on the field is certainly not stable.

The same is true for husband and wife. After a few sorrows, we will see the true feelings, and the future in the long-term.

Sixth; people without interests can relax together. Although "the same person" may not be sweet, but people with the same attributes "act in unison, birds of the same feather flock together." They will always come together unconsciously.

People alike attract people like them. The sage finally emphasised that "the gentleman distinguishes between classes," which reminds us that we must have a deep understanding of the "same group" human nature.

Everything in the universe, including things, including people, are not alone or isolated. It is through similar attributes that a variety of groups distinguishes itself.

This feature has helped us greatly simplify the universe in our eyes and reduce things for our understanding.

The difficulty of making a difference. For example, as of now, there are only 119 elements of all the substances we know. Through this simplification, chemistry can be carried out.

There are 7 billion people on the earth. We have to study human problems. Can we look at them one by one? No, it has to be simplified. First, there are two kinds among these 7 billion people – men and women, or people who are not divided between men and women; then, seven billion people can also be divided into four kinds – white, black, yellow and brown; and then, it can divided into five continents, divided into more than two-hundred countries, divided into several regions, and so on. Only through similar divisions can we think and study large problems in order to carry out the corresponding work.

In order to promote a local portal that I operate (Huang Wei Network), I checked a QQ group of Huang Wei every day. I was surprised to find that these QQ groups particularly clearly reflect the characteristics of interpersonal communication in real society. The names of these QQ groups can be seen:

Huang Qi Photography Group, Huang Qi Hai Fishing Group, Huang Qi Calligraphy Group, Huang Yi doctors, Huang Yi job group, Huang Wei pet group, and so on. The inspiration for us is that we all know that interpersonal relationships are important to the development of life. How do we develop our interpersonal relationships? It is simple: sort out the qualities of yourself and find people with the same attributes. There is a natural attraction between people alike. When you are together and have the same qualities, you will be continuously strengthened and enhanced.

Da You: How to protect fortune

CLASSICAL TEXT

Da You; Under the circumstances which it implies, there will be great progress and success.

Nine at the First line; There is no approach to what is injurious, and there is no error. Let there be a realisation of the difficulty and danger of the position, and there will be no error in the end.

Nine at the Second line; we have a large wagon with its load. In whatever direction advance is made, there will be no error.

Nine at the third line; shows us a feudal prince presenting his offerings to the Son of Heaven (the king). A small man would be unequal to such a duty.

Nine at the Fourth line; shows its subject keeping his great resources under restraint. There will be no error.

Six at the fifth line; the sincerity of its subject reciprocated by that of all the others represented in the hexagram. Let him display a proper majesty, and there will be good fortune.

Nine at the top line; The subject with help accorded to him from Heaven. There will be good fortune, advantage in every respect.

The image; The trigram for heaven and that of fire above it forms Da You. The superior man, in accordance with this, represses what is evil and gives distinction to what is good, in sympathy with the excellent Heaven-conferred nature.

LITERAL TRANSLATION

Da You; Having everything.

Nine at the First line; No compromise made, no harm, no difficulty.

Nine at the Second line; You are carrying a heavy load, but you can go forth slowly.

Nine at the third line; The princes are offering tribute to the king, and the enemy cannot take advantage of this.

Nine at the Fourth line; No boasting will avert harm.

Six at the fifth line; Acting in mutual good faith, a good reputation pays.

Nine at the top line; With heaven's help anything can be accomplished.

The image; Fire in the sky. The superior man pedals the bad and cite the good in people.

INTERPRETATION

In this hexagram: the upper part is Li, indicating the fire; the lower part is Qian, meaning the Sky. Fire brings a feeling of prosperity. Whoever has useful life is called "having the fire set everyday" In Chinese, those who are famous, it is called "on fire," Who is in good business, that is called "Red fire." The fire here also means the sun, and the sun is high in the Sky, which means "every day". Therefore, the sage named this as "great," meaning significant wealth.

Everyone wants to be rich and wealthy, but there are not many people who can be rich and wealthy, even if they save for the rest of their lives. In this regard, the sage believes that the following points should be noted:

First; do not provoke things, do not cause trouble, suck it up, bury your head, and work hard. Confucius said, "behave in accordance with your position".

Second; it is necessary to have a high morality to be able to afford to be rich and wealthy. Confucius said, "The gentlemen should have a broad and strong mind; that is how you can carry the burden of wisdom". A famous saying goes, 'The poor cannot bear the burden of the rich'. It is like gambling; it depends on how much money you can bet. Be careful to be bold; if you inherit two million dollars, you spend them, and then, how can you make more money? For making money, you need a mix of certain qualities, IQ, EQ, physical health, psychological resilience, skills, connections, and opportunities, no exception. If the weight is light, you can make it bigger if you have more energy.

Third; is to connect up and down. Confucius said that, "only the gentleman shall be appointed high office, the lower position should be for the lower people", but you have to make a lot of money, you have to get up and down, both to the upper level, but also to the lower level.

Fourth; is that you should not boast and suffer from pride. Lao Zi said, 'It's hard to be rich and not arrogant'.

Fifth; is to treat others with sincerity and respect. Confucius also said, 'get rich and healthy'.

Sixth; beware of fate, be thankful. A Chinese saying goes, 'Life and death are predetermined'. The reason why you are rich is not how great you are. In the end, it is because of luck, because of destiny.

Matsushita Yukisuke said that his success is 5% hard work and 95% on fate. With this thought in mind, words and deeds will not cause big problems, and you can be rich.

The sage further emphasises that the rich want to protect the rich, especially to "suppress evil and promote good", to curb ugliness and promote charity, to conform to the heavens, and praise the value of life. As the saying goes, "money cannot make you a better person, but it can make you worse". Feng Xiaogang said, 'The poor are rich in virtues', my first thought was: I can be rich! I have been poor for so many years, endured a lot of anger, suffered countless tragedies, almost succumbed to death, and finally got rich. Do I still have to vent all that? Those virtues that persist after reaching success could get weak, so I let the desires that are at the bottom of my heart come out and breathe. The sage understands this kind of human weakness; thus, he emphasises that the first thing to protect the rich is to "suppress evil". You must hold yourself, control your desires, do not do anything evil.

Else, how can this evil energy of impulsiveness be contained? The best way is to do good. The satisfaction of doing good is far and wide, far beyond the short-lived pleasure of doing evil.

The good of the rich is to conform to the heavens. What is heaven? Lao Tzu said, 'It is the Way of Heaven to diminish superabundance and to supplement deficiency. It is not so with the way of man'. You are rich. You have the money and spare power to make up for the inadequacy of others. This is heaven. In the *Book of Change*s, "the great virtue of heaven and earth". The right path of Heaven and Earth is to develop for subsistence – not the survival and development of one person, but the survival and development of all humankind. You contribute to your own strength and help others to survive and develop together. Those who submit to heaven's decree will prosper, defy the laws of heaven and you shall suffer. Act in accordance with the heavens, there will be good fortune. The wealthiest people in the West know this truth. Bill Gates and Buffett are both charitable. The more you donate, the more you earn! As the saying goes, "Go out and clear yourself from sin, and you'll be coming back inside your true self" (more on this later in the book). In the *Book of Change*s, the sages also said, 'A family given to charity and kindness will have good fortune". Follow this precept.

Furthermore, the rich and the poor are, relatively speaking, good in deeds and are closer to heaven even if they do not have wealth. If there is a brick on the road, it is dangerous for bicycles. You can take it out of the way. This is a good deed. This is to give roses and receive the fragrance. It is to follow heaven, to add up to life, and to help others.

Qian: More than modesty

(Qianagain; 谦 in phonetic writing they have the same spelling as the first Hexagram)

CLASSICAL TEXT

Qian; This indicates progress and success. The superior man, being humble as it implies, will have a good issue to his undertaking.

Six at the First line; that the superior man who adds humility to humility. Even the great stream may be crossed like this, and there will be good fortune.

Six at the Second line; shows us humility that has made itself recognised. With applied wisdom there will be good fortune.

Nine at the third line; the superior man of acknowledged merit. He will maintain his success to the end, and have good fortune.

Six at the fourth line; one, whose action would be in every way advantageous, stirring up even more his humility.

Six at the fifth line; one who, without being rich, is able to employ his neighbours. He may advantageously use the force of arms. All his movements will be advantageous.

Six at the top line; shows us humility that has made itself recognised. He who follows this principle will have advantage in putting his people in motion; but he will only punish his own towns and state.

The image; The trigram for the earth and that of a mountain in the midst of it form Qian. The superior man, in accordance with this, diminishes what is excessive in himself, and increases where there is any defect, bringing about an equality, according to the nature of the case, in his treatment of himself and others.

LITERAL TRANSLATION

Qian; Modesty is the way to success.

Six at the First line; modestly modest, the superior man can traverse the river and it will be auspicious.

Six at the Second line; A reputation for being modest is to be conserved and it will be auspicious.

Nine at the third line; The industrious and modest gentleman obtains good results and good luck.

Six at the fourth line; There is nothing against you, time to act in a modest way.

Six at the fifth line; Following a just cause your neighbour will join you and you can have success without boasting about it.

Six at the top line; Your reputation as a modest leader brings people to your cause. It is a good time to send out troops.

The image; Mountains under the earth. The great man does what needs to be done. Confidence in his skills, there no need to boast.

INTERPRETATION

In this hexagram, the upper part is Kun, indicating earth; the lower is Gen, meaning the mountain. The mountains are hidden under the ground, just like a person hiding strength, not showing it to people so quickly. Therefore, the sage called this humility and gave the most unreserved praise to the quality of modesty. From the six hexagrams with auspicious interpretation (no disadvantage), this is relatively easy to understand, we will take a look.

First; of all, the modest gentleman crosses the river. The modest gentleman always reminds me of Confucius' "The gentleman praises the humble", and the two-time Oscar-winning Chinese director An Lee, with a discrete smile, such a person can take heavy responsibility. Even for being modest he is too subtle, and I understand it.

Second line; that humility that stands out. With applied wisdom there will be good fortune. Everything should be modest, but humility alone does not have to be shy, just like in "yield to nobody when doing what is right'. As long as it is sincere and modest, rather than inviting praise, it is a good thing to have a name for being humble.

Third line; shows the superior man of acknowledged merit. He will maintain his success to the end and have good fortune. Being modest, by doing things industriously, everything will be accomplished.

Fourth line; one, whose action would be in every way advantageous, stirring up, even more, his humility. It would be beneficial to apply the concept of modesty to the processing of various matters. For example, there is room for everything, and this is a modest concept. Even in *The Book of Han*, the Taoist ideology is about modesty.

Fifth, if there is no resources available, use the neighbours' to no disadvantage. Modest people are easily helped by allies.

Sixth; the subject of it (of modesty) will with advantage put his hosts in motion; but he will only punish his towns and state. Modesty is actually a strategy, hiding power, letting the enemy relax its guard, and then suddenly, defeat him.

The book of documents is full of the benefits of modesty. This is some of the oldest Chinese wisdom. In reality, everyone likes modest people, and they often touch our hearts like a spring breeze. Humility belongs to a powerful person and has nothing to do with external strength. A person may be poor, but if he is still modest, he is not afraid of others, this is a strength, such people can get up sooner or later.

If the burden is too much, if his modesty is sincere, it must be based on deep awe and lust for life. Such people will not be defeated. Then, what does the sage mean in summing up "Qian": "The superior man, in accordance with this, diminishes what is excessive in himself", what does it mean? It should be based on the above-mentioned modesty. When dealing with others, we must cut an extra piece and even give it to the less fortunate; we must weigh something and distribute it according to uniform standards to other people. From a personal point of view, this is not to be snobbish, and it treats everyone equally: do not flatter dignitaries, nor have contempt for those who are not as good as yourself. From a social point of view, it is to maintain fairness, to be strong, to support the weak, and to maintain balanced development in all aspects of society. In the *Yellow Emperor's Four Classics*, there is a saying, "the way to change is to be balanced". Balance is the great wisdom of Taoist thought. I will make an in-depth interpretation in another book, *The Song* of Lao Tze and the *Yellow Emperor*. In addition, fairness and balance are the biggest problems facing

China today. But this is not a political book, so that I will not elaborate on that.

In short, "Qian" is modesty, the modest person, all things smooth, a lifetime of peace, everything will eventually fall in its right position.

Yu:

Yu: Are you happy?

CLASSICAL TEXT

Yu; Princes may be set up, and the hosts put in motion, with advantage.

Six at the First line; shows its subject proclaiming his pleasure and satisfaction. There will be evil.

Six at the Second line; one who is firm as a rock. He sees a thing without waiting until it has come to pass; with applied wisdom there will be good fortune.

Six at the third line; reflects one looking for favours, while he indulges in the feeling of pleasure and satisfaction. If he would only understand! If he be late in doing so, there will indeed be occasion for repentance.

Nine at the Fourth line; shows him from whom the harmony and satisfaction come. Great is the success which he obtains. Let him not allow suspicions to enter his mind, and thus friends will gather around him.

Six at the fifth line; one with a chronic complaint, but who lives on without dying.

Six at the top line; its subject with darkened mind devoted to the pleasure and satisfaction of the time; but if he change his course even when it may be considered as completed, there will be no error.

The image; The trigrams for the earth and thunder issuing from it with its crashing noise form Yu. The ancient king, in accordance with this, composed their music and did honour virtue, presenting it especially and most grandly to God, when they associated with Him at the service of their highest ancestor and fathers.

LITERAL TRANSLATION

Yu; Time for the prince to command the army into a campaign.

Six at the First line; Feeling too self-confident, there will be misfortune.

Six at the Second line; Do not wait until the next day to get things done, keep auspicious.

Six at the third line; Looking for complacent approval will bring remorse, slowness and more regret.

Nine at the Fourth line; A source of inspiration for others. Do not hesitate if friends gather in a hustle and bustle.

Six at the fifth line; Keep virtuous even through illness, you might be week, but not dead.

Six at the top line; There is no evil in light pleasures.

The image; Thunder over earth, Yu. The royal first born pays his respects to heaven and conducts the proper rites.

INTERPRETATION

In this hexagram, the upper part is Lei, indicating thunder; the lower is Kun, meaning the earth. The reverberation of thunder on the earth. What is this? It is like the sound of the celebration of the ancestors' drums. During Chinese New Year, the most lively and festive scene is knocking the drums and loud music. The drums shook loudly. Therefore, the sage named this hexagram "enthusiasm", which means pleasure and happiness.

The sage believes that happiness is good. Happiness means a healthy body and mind, which means the growth of confidence and the rise of morale. This is a good time to organise people to go to war, establish vassal states, and develop their careers.

And the sage emphasised a few points:

First; do not make your happiness known, because it may distract or even hurt some people.

Second; happiness should be moderate, not overwhelming, or to lose yourself. The sage said, "one who is firm as a rock sees a thing without waiting until it has come to pass", means to have strength in front of happiness, to keep it controllable.

The name of Chiang Kai-Shek was taken from this saying. Since ancient times, heroes have been lustful. When he was defeated, he also got syphilis, and he renamed himself to break with his misfortune.

Third; do not rely on people who seem too happy. That kind of happiness is too embarrassing and not long-lasting. People in love should pay attention to this point. You should look for someone's whole personality. In the end, someone can just leave you.

Fourth; is to be a source of happiness for everyone. Influence others with their joy and optimism to be good.

Use positive energy to convey positive action, smile to get closer to others and their hearts. Fan Zhongyan said, 'After the world is happy, be happy'. Once everyone in the world is happy, it is a real joy. When a family is happy, it is a real pleasure; when a team is happy, it is real happiness. With such a mentality, who would not want to join you?

Fifth; happy people get less sick. One smile makes you feel ten years younger.

Sixth; the pleasure of a happy life is a success.

In addition, two more profound points are included in the "The ancient king, in accordance with this, composed their music and did honour to virtue, presenting it especially and most grandly to God, when they associated with Him at the service their highest ancestor and their father".

"To compose music and do honour to virtue" can be understood as a leader who wants to guide people to enjoy good behaviour and high moral values. And "presenting it especially and most grandly to God, when they associated with Him at the service their highest ancestor and their father". This can be understood as, when you are happy, you should drink and thank God for this gift of heaven, and thank the ancestors for their blessing. This is especially important. You have to know that their happiness is not yours. How can you enjoy this? Gratefulness comes from awe and respect; only like this, we can cherish happiness, and it will not fly away like a bird. You know, some birds will never come back once they fly away.

Sui: Follow, follow, follow

CLASSICAL TEXT

Sui; There will be great progress and success. But it will be advantageous to be firm and correct. Then, there will be no error.

Nine at the First line; shows, one changing the object of his pursuit; but if he be firm and correct, there will be good fortune. Going beyond his own gate to find associates, he will achieve merit.

Six at the Second line; of one who cleaves to the little boy, must become the man of age and experience.

Six at the third line; offers us one who cleaves to the man of age and experience, and let go the little boy. Such following will get what it seeks; but it will be advantageous to adhere to what is firm and correct.

Nine at the Fourth line; shows us one followed by and obtaining adherents. Though he be firm and correct, there will be evil. If he is sincere in his course, and make that evident, into what error can he fall?

Nine at the Fifth line; the ruler sincere in fostering all that is excellent. There will be good fortune.

Six at the top line; shows us sincerity firmly held, clung to and bound fast. We see the king with it presenting his offerings on the western mountain.

The image; the trigram for the waters of a marsh and that for thunder hidden in the midst of it form Sui. The superior man in accordance with this, when it is getting towards darkness, enters his house and rests.

LITERAL TRANSLATION

Sui; Initiate, go smoothly, stick to righteousness and virtue, there will be no harm.

Nine at the First line; Change your mindset, keep watch for auspicious signs. Go out and find support and you will succeed.

Six at the Second line; Reluctant to leave the small one, but letting the big one go.

Six at the third line; Chase after the big one, let the small go. Everyone is eager to do so, which is the right way to proceed.

Nine at the Fourth line; after the harvest, everyone is trying to protect it. If chasing after fame, is there anything wrong?

Nine at the Fifth line; Integrity and honesty is what make people beautiful. Good fortune.

Six at the top line; Bound by loyalty or by rope, the sovereign can praise heaven by obligation or by devotion.

The image; Thunder within the lake. The sovereign rest at the fall of night.

INTERPRETATION

This hexagram is: on the top is [Dui], meaning the lake and marshes; below is [Lei] the thunder. A boulder is thrown into the lake, and a thunderous bang is heard. At the same time, the waves undulate in a circle, and the waves follow. Thus, the sage think of this as [Sui] "to follow", that is, consequences and similar meanings. The sage believes that the use of the character for "following," has the meaning that of what can be created, can be smooth, can be profitable, can be safe that has certainty, and no problem. The sage said a few things about this:

First; ideas should change at the right time, only then can it be successful.

Second; to follow is a choice. There is a cost for doing that. If you marry the wrong person, you will miss at least a year, and you may lose a lifetime of happiness.

Third; is to follow the right person, one smooth and good person.

Fourth; relying on imitation is to avoid risk, try to get it right.

Fifth; is that sincerity is good; it is the right way to go.

Sixth; the person who knows the right time is an outstanding person. Sometimes it may be painful. However, in the context of the long run, an individual is fragile and small. To survive, it must be resilient. Moreover, if flowers do not bloom in a garden, plant a willow tree, you might as well have a shadow, and this can be beneficial in time. I conclude that this is followed by three kinds of 'following': follow people, follow the trend, follow the path. There are three main aspects of following people: one is to learn from others, the other is to do with people, and the third is to listen to people.

Stay hungry. These three things must be done right. But if one fails, do not give up, can you be down for a lifetime? On the other hand, if you do not follow the right person, like the teacher who missed the student, the leader who is stuck by over-regulation, and the friend who had the best idea, you will not be sure until it has happened. Or, you have no teacher at all, no one to support, no friends to help, all rely on self-reliance, work hard in spite of the circumstances, then you are following the path, this is not an easy thing to do. Of course, these three aspects cannot be understood in a narrow sense. Teachers, leaders, and friends all include various forms. For example, a father may have both of these roles, and his opponents are sometimes teachers. In addition, this kind of attitude, being easy going, following, being good, feeling free, acting casual, is also conducive to winning the hearts of others and self-cultivation.

More about following the trend. The heaven is in motion, the universe is changing, a person cannot step into the same river twice, and everything changes with time, big or small. If you look at yesterday's things with today's ideas or analyse yesterday's situations, it will be misplaced. When we look twenty years ago, we find how the audience's clothes are rustic, but when they look twenty years ago, they feel fashionable. There is also an acceleration in the development of the times. Changes are getting faster and faster. If we do not read newspapers, do not watch TV, do not go online, do not use mobile phones, after seeing the world in a year or two, we will feel strange, like outsiders. The *Book of Change*s has a clear and profound understanding on this issue, continually reminding people that "the world is always changing" "advance with the times" and "keep up with the time," there can be no wrong in taking measures without regard to changes in circumstances.

More about following the trend. The trend is changing, and the road is unchanged. What is the path? The path is the truth, the law, the correct thoughts and values that have been proven by history. Where is the path? This seems difficult to answer, but I think the path is in the classics – including classic books and paradigms. The reason why it is a classic is that it is recognised by most people and benefits the most people. Therefore, following the path is to learn, practice, and study the classics.

The following thoughts have a profound impact on the entire East Asian culture. For example, the rise of Japan and China's economy, regardless of product or business model, relies mainly on copying, imitating, and following European and American companies. Therefore, it is criticised for lack of innovation, but development has the last word.

In short, whether you are a person or a company, follow up, and keeping up are things that bring success or failure. The people who adopt these principles "to be back at home to rest by dusk," follow the natural Taoist principle of inaction.

Maybe this is why Chinese people love to compare; it may also be related to this.

Gu:

Chaos is an opportunity

CLASSICAL TEXT

Gu; Indicates great progress and success to him who deals properly with the condition represented by it. There will be advantage in efforts like that of crossing a great stream. He should weigh well, however, the events of three days before the turning point, and those to be done three days after it.

Six at the First line; indicates a son dealing with the troubles caused by his father. If he be an able son, the father will escape the blame of having erred. The position is perilous, but there will be good fortune in the end.

Nine at the Second line; shows a son dealing with the troubles caused by his mother. He should not carry his dedication to the utmost.

Nine at the third line; suggests a son dealing with the troubles caused by his father. There may be some small occasion for remorse, but there will not be any great error.

Six at the fourth line; a son viewing indulgently the troubles caused by his father. If he goes forward, he will find cause to regret it.

Six at the fifth line; shows a son dealing with the troubles caused by his father. He obtains the praise of using the fit instrument for his work.

Nine at the top line; suggests one who does not serve either king or lord, but in a lofty spirit prefers to attend to his own affairs.

The image; The trigram for a mountain, and below it that for wind, form Gu. The superior man, in accordance with this, addresses himself to help the people and nourish his own virtue.

LITERAL TRANSLATION

Gu; it is time to try to cross the great river. Be careful of everything three days before and three days after.

Six at the First line; there are issues that need to be dealt with. The son helping the father is appropriate.

Nine at the Second line; the mother should not need the son's help, it is not the traditional way.

Nine at the third line; the father in need of the son's help, there is little regret, no harm done.

Six at the fourth line; Not amending old family matters will only make things worse if dealt in the wrong way.

Six at the fifth line; Helping your father even when there was problems in the past, small regret.

Nine at the top line; Serve not the lord because he is mighty, but because it serves a higher purpose.

The image; a tree under a mountain. The sovereign wants to instil virtue on to the people.

INTERPRETATION

This trigram contains: in the upper part is Gen (the mountain), indicating the mountain; in the lower part is Xun (the abysmal), meaning wind. The wind on the plains is unobstructed, blowing straight, either east, west, or southeast, and in some cases, there are tornadoes, but its rotation also has a direction. At the foot of the mountain, in the valley, and the mountain skirts, the wind is different. Because the mountain blocks it, the wind direction will follow the slope. In some land, the course is left, some land is right, in some places is down, in some others is up. It is a trap for the air, like a locust crawling inside a human stomach. Thus, the name of "Gu", which means internal disaster or accumulation. What should I do in the face of this situation? In this regard, the sages put forward a few points;

First; the issue of the overall situation must overcome all difficulties and resolutely bring order out of chaos.

Second; for issues that are irrelevant to the situation, but are more sensitive (such as emotional problems), there should be room for manoeuvring, flexible control, specific analysis of specific issues, and different appropriate solutions.

Third; is that the chaos must go up and down from the roots, and accomplish its fate; if you cannot find the roots, see the chaos on the surface, do not act rashly, avoid inadvertently alerting an enemy, or provide palliatives and become passive.

Fourth; treatment of illness cannot be dragged out, the more it is delayed, the more difficult it is to cure.

Fifth; is that if the chaos or the burden is accumulating, it should be open and aboveboard, so it increases public attention and mobilisation so all unite their thoughts, be convinced, and united. This process will help establish a new authority.

Sixth; there is merit in retreat, do not be greedy. Zeng Guofan calmed the Taiping Heavenly Kingdom (The Boxer Rebellion), but he plunged the Qing Dynasty into a dying dynasty. Then he did not know how to talk about it – a sage stresses that the gentleman should assume the responsibility of "help people nourish its virtue'.

The various businesses that have withered have been revitalised and restored, and the people and values that have suffered from these disasters have been re-established.

Since the Opium War, the Chinese nation has been bullied by Western powers and was almost conquered. Since the founding of New China, it has suffered many twists and turns. From the National Anthem, "Arise! People Who Are Unwilling to Be a Slave" to the Chinese Dream of General Secretary Xi, "Revival." This has become the theme of national development. This is the meaning of Gu" at the national level.

Political, economic, and cultural developments are all invigorating the people; vigorously promoting the national spirit of self-reliance and hard work, and promoting the return of traditional morals and values such as Confucianism and all virtues. We must pay special attention to the fact that the destruction of the economy in troubled times is not the most important. The most important thing is the destruction of the human heart. This is too difficult to recover from.

Behind the chaos, there is often the cost of suffering all kinds of pain. However, the sage believed that "When in a situation like [Gu] is, it is time to cross the great river, but be careful three days before and three days later". Chaos is temporary, and big chaos has big order; chaos is an opportunity and an opportunity for entrepreneurial development. For three years, there were no problems in the east bank, and for three years, there was a lot of trouble on the west bank.

There is a saying about a hero in trouble; If the world is peaceful, the hero is useless, Superman will be idly looking after crops, Spider-Man swinging everywhere, and they will not motivate anyone. Weekdays are then only for regular work, and everyone does the same. Only when there is a problem when a crisis occurs, the value of the outstanding person can be revealed, and the attention and respect of everyone will be won. The reason why Deng Xiaoping excelled was because he brought the country out of chaos and set it on the right path. Many great people in history have similarly been powerful at the right time. So, if you are good, when small trouble is in front of you, tell yourself that an opportunity is coming. However, do not be afraid that the world will not be chaotic, and deliberately ruin things, that would be too dark.

In business, the expansion of a company is inseparable from a large number of mergers.

This is the spirit of "Gu". Of course, heroes are not good from the start. Before you save others, you must be strong enough, and "nourish people's virtue" must be done in a gradual process. It is necessary to coordinate the process in stages and be careful during implementation. There must be patience and perseverance.

Lin: Leaders' four key words

CLASSICAL TEXT

Lin Indicates that under the conditions supposed in it, there will be progress and success, while it will be advantageous to be firmly correct. In the eighth month there will be evil.

Nine at the First line; suggests its subject advancing with the company of the subject in the second line. Through his applied wisdom there will be good fortune.

Nine at the Second line; shows its subject advancing in the company of the subject of the first line. There will be good fortune; advancing will be in every way advantageous.

Six at the third line; shows one well pleased advancing, but whose action will be in no way advantageous. If he is anxious about it, there will be no error.

Six at the fourth line; suggests one advancing in the highest mode. There will be no error.

Six at the fifth line; shows the advance of wisdom, such as befits the great ruler. There will be good fortune.

Six at the top line; reflects the advance of honesty and generosity. There will be good fortune, and no error.

The image; The trigram for the waters of a marsh and that for the earth above it form Lin. The superior man, in accordance with this, has his purpose of instruction that are inexhaustible, and nourishes and supports the people without limit.

LITERAL TRANSLATION

Lin; remain caution, there is good luck on being conservative. There is danger in the eighth month.

Nine at the First line; close to feelings, keep an eye out for lucky events.

Nine at the Second line; through observing fairness there shall be no harm.

Six at the third line; a reckless attitude will bring trouble, make amendments and avoid harm.

Six at the fourth line; you are in a position of influence, there is no harm.

Six at the fifth line; handle things with wisdom, with the superior man qualities there will be good fortune.

Six at the top line; through a sincere and honest attitude there will be good fortune and no harm.

The image; earth over the lake form Lin. The great man educates people and protects them.

INTERPRETATION

This hexagram is formed by [Kun] on top, meaning the earth; and [Dui] below, which is the lake. Standing on the ground, looking at the lake below in a condescending posture. Therefore, the sage named this as "Overlooking" [Lin] and extended the attitude and manner of the leader to the subordinates. In this regard, the sages put forward a few points;

First; follow your feelings. Zeng Guofan led the soldiers to pay attention to the importance of enlightenment. He believed in the importance of benevolence, as well. He had the mindset of a patriarch and preached to help others along, while striving to be successful themselves.

Second; is to observe fairness. It is necessary to treat all subordinates equally and not to divide each other. Otherwise, if the relatives are arrogant and distant, they will be prone to problems.

Third; is that you cannot rely on bad words to issue some empty promises; you cannot rely on money to maintain and drive people. In Si Ma's *Historical Records*, it is said that, 'Those who are united because of mere interests disband when the benefits are distributed'. You can only share your wealth, not your suffering.

Fourth; is to mingle with the subordinates, be approachable, and come to check the masses, learn from the masses. For example, when Liu Bang (founder of the Han Dynasty) was in front of the minister, he would act solemnly, but with the gatekeeper, he chattered.

Fifth; management is learning with wisdom. Especially in large organisations, it is necessary to form a scientific management system.

Sixth; the highest level of management should be honest and straightforward and deeply humane. Then the sage made a summary; he said that a leader should 'teach endlessly and protect the people'. There are key concepts a leader should always keep in mind: To teach, be an example.

The leader is first and foremost a teacher, just like educating students, he should conduct training, and guide subordinates to work. In reality, many leaders have a professional background behind them. Mao Zedong was a teacher; famous entrepreneurs such as Ma Yun and Yu Minhong, and many other officials were professional teachers. Ancient intellectuals generally had two options: sucked at the imperial examination and became an official and an unsuccessful teacher. To think, reasoning. A great leader must be a thinker, Lenin was like this, Mao Zedong was like this.

The height of thought determines the height of the person and determines the height of the career. Ning Gaoning, the CEO of COFCO, said that leaders must be thoughtful. Many grassroots leaders cannot talk well about ideas, but at least they must be good at thinking. They can come up with suitable solutions to all kinds of problems they face.

To be patient, tolerance. When we interpret the "teacher" as in the past, we have already begun to understand. The leaders must be broad enough, and the platform of the career should be broad enough to accommodate these people. Concerning tolerance, it is important to take the initiative and to ignore small problems. Because if the water is clear, there are no fish. Keep in mind a common saying: do not be afraid to be a master. The Eastern Han Dynasty's famous general, Ban Chao was over thirty years old when he ruled the Western Regions. He also taught his successor about his experience: big error needs short explanations.

To guarantee, provide protection. To ensure that the various needs of the people under our supervision are met, it is necessary to shield them from the wind and rain. But first, you need to have enough material wealth, and you have to be mentally happy. When employees do their work, but they want to kill themselves (literally, jump off a building). Such leadership is not humane.

Teaching and thinking, on the axis of time, is not exhaustive; there should be tolerance and security, on the axis of space, without boundaries. This is the responsibility of the leader. Can you handle it?

Guan: The way you see the world is the way you see other people

CLASSICAL TEXT

Guan; When making offerings you should wash your hands.

Six at the First line; about an unexpected child – not something unexpected in uneducated, but matter for regret to men in with bigger responsibilities.

Six at the Second line; suggests one peeping out from a door. It would be advantageous if it were the applied wisdom of a female.

Six at the third line; shows one looking at the course of his own life, to advance or recede accordingly.

Six at the fourth line; suggests one contemplating the glory of the kingdom. It will be advantageous for him, being such as he is, and to seek to be a guest of the king.

Nine at the Fifth line; shows its subject contemplating his own life. A superior man, he will fall into no error.

Nine at the top line; reflects its subject contemplating his character to see if it be indeed that of a superior man. He will not fall into error.

The image; The trigram representing the earth, and that for wind moving above it, form Guan. The ancient king, in accordance with this, examined the different regions of the kingdom, to see the ways of the people, and set forth their instructions.

LITERAL TRANSLATION

Guan; Rituals of sacrifices have to be made. By reflecting thoroughly making sure the mind is full of sincerity and respect.

Six at the First line; Observe the world like a child, there is no harm, the adult has many regrets.

Six at the Second line; Peeking through a half opened door, there is fortune in being conservative.

Six at the third line; Observe self-behaviour and choose whether to advance and retreat.

Six at the fourth line; Looking for the glory of the country is conducive to becoming someone important for the king.

Nine at the Fifth line; Observing oneself is the way to become impeccable.

Nine at the top line; Observing the behaviour of others will not harm a great man.

The image; A tree over earth form [Guan]. The king is out in the open inspecting the country.

INTERPRETATION

This hexagram is formed by Xun (The Gentle) in the upper part, indicating the wind; the lower is 'Kun,' meaning the earth. The wind swept through the ground, and the grass swayed in one direction. If you have always been a city man and have no idea about the wilderness, you can imagine all kinds of flags on a square being moved by the wind. The wind makes these things go in the same direction. This is similar to people in the same place. They also have the same characteristics in character and ideas. The concepts of folk customs, fashion, and local traditions are the result. Thus, the sage thinks of the meaning of observation, he observes:

First; the ignorant, only look at the surface and is shallow. Keen observers must have a wealth of knowledge and experience to see the truth through the stuff to see the real thing. For the same thing, different people often see different things. Zen has a famous saying: before meditation, verify the mountain is the mountain and the water is the water; during meditation, observe that the mountain is not the mountain and the water is not the water; after meditation, remember that the mountain is the mountain and the water is the water.

Second; the observations must be comprehensive, not one-sided, not blind. Be eye-catching, be careful everywhere, see problems inadvertently, and trust intuition.

Third; observation is not only outward, but also inward, to reflect on the self and jump out of yourself to see yourself.

Fourth; is that when it comes to insight, one should travel the world, know the general situation of the world and its mountains and rivers, it will be of great use. Observers must have a broad field of vision, depending on how big the field of view is; that is how high the level of this person is. People with a global perspective are international talents; those who only look at a few things around them may be good at work, but they will not develop much. Also, observation is not equal to picking faults. To discover truth, goodness, and beauty, to see the merits of others, this is a truth that can bring good things.

Fifth; is that you stand on the bridge to see the scenery, and the people watching the view look up to you. Each observer is also the object of observation. Can you stand the attention of others?

Sixth; others are their mirrors, and they must see themselves in others.

The sage sums up; and believes that it is important to derive a conclusion, not to be cluttered with a bunch of stuff.

Finally; the sage raised the level of observation and proposed that the leaders should "provide education to the people," and should extensively inspect and observe tradition, and then correctly educate the people.

The following layers of meaning should be emphasised here:

First, inspection. Leaders should do the following every day. It is said that Ma Yun has a habit of keeping a small stick every day in the company's various halls, then if there are problems at any time, he was ready to firmly solve.

Second; there are divinities. In the words of Inamori Kazuo; "Many problems are not visible. There is no emotional observation experience on the spot and you cannot think of a solution, when you arrive at a scene, feel for inspiration, such as the help of the gods".

Third; is to integrate problems and discover everyday things, to solve them all together.

Fourth; the observation is ultimately for education. A leader should not be only a person who solves specific problems. Instead, he should be a person who spreads common values, a teacher, a pastor, or even a father figure.

In "Guan," it also mentions, "push people toward virtue by the threat of final retribution", which is a fundamental idea. It is not fully explained here and will be discussed later.

Shi Ke: Violence and Punishment

CLASSICAL TEXT

Shi Ke; indicates successful progress in the condition of things, which it supposes. It will be advantageous to use legal constraints.

Nine at the First line; shows one with his feet in the stocks and deprived of his toes. There will be no error.

Six at the Second line; of one biting through the soft flesh, and going on to bite off the nose. There will be no error.

Six at the third line; suggests one gnawing dried flesh, and meeting with what is disagreeable. There will be occasion for some regret, but no great harm.

Nine at the Fourth line; indicates one gnawing the flesh dried on the bone, and getting the pledges of money and arrows. It will be advantageous to him to realise the difficulty of his task and be firm – in which case there will be good fortune.

Six at the fifth line; shows one gnawing at dried flesh, and finding yellow gold. Let him be firm and correct, realising the peril of his position. There will be no error.

Nine at the top line; one deprived of his ears. There will be evil.

The image; The trigrams representing thunder and lightning forms Shi He. The ancient king, in accordance with this, framed their penalties with intelligence, and promulgated their laws.

LITERAL TRANSLATION

Shi Ke; confront the situation, abide by all laws.

Nine at the First line; wearing a torture device on the foot, hurting the toes, no harm.

Six at the Second line; bite into the meat too deep, hurt the nose, no harm.

Six at the third line; bite into the meat, the meat is putrid; small regrets, no harm.

Nine at the Fourth line; the meat on the bones is bitten, and an arrow-head is obtained, which is good for the sake of being upright and auspicious.

Six at the fifth line; bite the meat and find some gold, keep from danger and no harm will come.

Nine at the top line; the neck is covered with a shackle, which hurts the ears and is dangerous.

The image; fire over thunder; the First king must be strict with punishment, and rectify the law.

INTERPRETATION

This hexagram is formed by [Li] (the clinging) on top, meaning lighting and [Zhen] (the arousing) underneath, meaning thunder. Thunder and lightning, together are like a bite, so the sage named the hexagram "the bite", which is the meaning of Shi Ke. There are very few people who can open a beer cap by hand, but there are many people who can bite it off with their teeth. The most powerful place on the human body is the jaw, and this can be aggressive. When the World Heavyweight, Tyson, beat others with his fists, he got up and bit the ear of an opponent. This is especially true for animals, tigers, lions, wolves, etc. Biting is their deadly attack. Therefore, the sages logically thought of this as punishment.

Then, the sages talked about the principle of applying punishment, such as the torture of toes, cut noses, and the relationship between punishment and confession. Everyone has seen war films like *The Message*, and similar scenes. Those are contrary to modern humanitarianism.

However, it can be determined that the *Book of Change*s has no warmth. It is cold, because reality itself is cruel, and some problems cannot be separated from violence. The essence of punishment is to use violence to meet violence, which is relatively far from the lives of today's ordinary people. Therefore, it is advisable to understand punishment from the perspective of violence:

First; the use of a bit of violence is no problem; this is more like being rough rather than violence.

Second; use force only on the right situation and distinguish each occasion.

Third; punch back only when defending from an aggressor.

Fourth; the spirit of confrontation must have a spirit of death and persistence until victory.

Fifth; Violence can be profiteering, but it can also be a disaster.

Sixth; bellicosity leads to death. Below, we return to the original ideas of the sage and analyse the emphasis of the sage in leadership for those who should be clearly punishable.

People should see punishment and understand what punishments will be imposed once they do something wrong.

It is said that Zhu Yuanzhang (founder of the Ming dynasty) was one of the best at this. As a county magistrate, he killed the previous county magistrate, and then peeled off his skin. This was filled with straw to make a straw man standing at the gate of the county government. Then whenever the new county magistrate went in and out, and he saw the scarecrow, he would not dare to be greedy.

Many local disciplinary committees conduct regular education on corruption and organise local officials to visit prisons to see the "happy life" of former officials who have been imprisoned for various problems. This is equally important in business management. For those things that are forbidden, those that should never be done; it is necessary to clearly emphasise to each employee how to navigate a clearly marked way around these minefields.

The law should be respected, and enforcement should be strict. Only in this way can the law make sense. In short, the severe punishment of "Shi Ke" is not only reflected in the spirit of the Legalist but also emphasised by Confucianism.

The commentary of Zuo records a section of a famous politician history. He said, 'The husband is fierce, the people look forward to it and fear it, so it is deadly. The water is weak, and the folks are happy in, but they are at more risk of drowning there'. "Where there is fire, people are afraid and run far away, so there are very few people who are burned to death by fire! There is nothing terrible in water, and there are many people who have been drowned by water". The Legalist has a famous saying: the sentence comes when the law has failed to prevent a crime. The purpose of using heavy punishment is to show everyone to respect the law and not be punished.

The ancients also had a saying, "in times of chaos, punishment is heavier. In troubled times, it is like a wild jungle. If human nature is evil, and human life is not worth anything, the people are arrogant, and conventional punishment cannot be used". During the Taiping Heavenly Kingdom, there were troubled times. Zeng Guofan used this idea to govern the people and was nicknamed "The Shaved Head". It was said of a child crying and being disobedient, that the mother would scare him by loudly saying, 'They'll shave your head!'

There are also some extraordinary moments, such as the loss of soldiers in battle. The American blockbuster *City under siege* has this a scene – the soldiers in the rear are armed with machine guns, and whoever tries to flee the battle, will be killed by the rear guard. All the victories of human society have a similar scene! This is the meaning of punishment.

Bi:

Beauty is productivity

CLASSICAL TEXT

Bi; indicates that there should be free course in what it denotes. There will be little advantage if it be allowed to advance and take the lead.

Nine at the First line; shows one adorning the way of his feet. He can discard a carriage and walk on foot.

Six at the Second line; suggests one adorning his beard.

Nine at the third line; shows its subject with the appearance of being adorned and bedewed with rich favours. But let him ever maintain his applied wisdom, and there will be good fortune.

Six at the fourth line; shows one looking as if adorned, but only in white. As if mounted on a white horse, and furnished with wings, he seeks union with the subject of the first line, while the intervening the first pursuer, not as a robber, but intent on a matrimonial alliance.

Six at the fifth line; reflects subject adorned by the occupants of the heights and gardens. He bares his roll of silk, small and slight. He may appear stingy; but there will be good fortune in the end.

Nine at the top line; suggests one with white as his only ornament. There will be no error.

The image; the trigram representing a mountain and that for fire under it forms Bi. The superior man, in accordance with this, exerts brilliancy around his various processes of government, but does not dare in a similar way to decide cases of criminal litigation.

LITERAL TRANSLATION

Bi; There is good fortune in going forward.

Nine at the First line; Leave the carriage and walk.
Six at the Second line; Trim your beard.
Nine at the third line; Clean and tidy, perfumed and pleasant, always prone to good fortune.
Six at the fourth line; Clean and tidy, clad in white, on a white horse, he is not a robber, he is here to propose marriage.
Six at the fifth line; The present roll of silk is not very big, but it is adorned with garden scenes, a little regret, but auspicious in the end.
Nine at the top line; Clad in all white. No harm shall come.
The image; There is fire under the mountain. The gentleman cultivates beauty and handling of governmental affairs, but cannot send anyone to prison.

INTERPRETATION

In this hexagram: the upper is Gen, indicating the mountain; the lower is Li, meaning the fire, and also the sun. When the sun sets behind the mountain, it gives the mountain a backlight. The mountain is set with golden edges and a sense of sorrow. Under the background of the clouds, it is soft and beautiful. Therefore, the sage named this as "Bi," which means modification and beautification.

In this regard, the sage has a few points:

First; people often struggle to pursue beauty. To show others that they are wearing a pair of beautiful shoes, they would rather walk instead of riding a car; this is vanity, not pragmatism.

Second; it is human nature to please the opposite sex by appearing attractive.

Third; external beauty, plus inner strength is perfection. You have, first to be gentle, and then you can be a gentleman. If there is no foundation, there cannot be a building. You need to have romance, and then true love will come.

Fourth; beauty is lucky. Good looking students, even when the marks are not good, they will still have a future.

Fifth; alcohol makes people not be afraid of a deep alley; beauty helps to succeed.

Sixth; nature is the most beautiful make-up, the decoration is better when it is not visible, simple, and elegance is the highest form of beauty. To exaggerate is fake, but when you laugh at it, it is counterproductive.

Everyone loves beauty. Not only people but also animals, male peacocks show their plumage to please the female to achieve mating. People suggested that Darwin's study of evolution was once plagued by the cumbersome big tail of peacocks, because according to Darwin's theory, this big tail is not suitable for survival, affecting his ability to camouflage and escape. In the end, he found that there is still a significant driving force for species evolution, which is to make it easier to find a partner, that makes evolution better!

This profound biological character shapes human sexual consciousness and broad social psychology and affects people's behaviour in various ways.

We look at many successful people. And those who look good are the majority. The people who are not are special cases, regardless of politics, business, or gender. Because of good looks, you can win people's hearts without trying, and thus have more resources and opportunities.

In the government's popular language, beauty is productivity. It is not difficult to understand the world's unusually large beauty industry, and it is not difficult to understand girls who have endured the hardships it offers.

Steve Jobs said that his success had benefited from the study of calligraphy, and the aesthetic ability cultivated in calligraphy has made his products look better than others. Sony and other electronics manufacturers attach importance to product design and strive to make products look better. The same product sells better when it looks good; it does not matter if the function is almost the same, as long as it looks good, it is still good to sell. It is reasonable to sell a piece of leather.

The image; wins over the essence, and the form wins over the content. The same is true for writing. If a text is not eloquent and explains with more words than needed, even if its truth is profound, there is no literary talent, it is written like a textbook, and it is difficult to spread it widely. I write "Chinese-style inspirational," which is not necessarily richer than Carnegie, but I believe it offers wisdom.

In short, we must strive to make ourselves look better, make our products look better, make our services look better, and make our company, team, and organisation look better so that it is easier to succeed. In business terms, it is to take care of the package.

Generally speaking, it is costly to look good. Every sixty-year-old woman wants to look like a young actress, but it can be too costly and not for everyone. However, sometimes, it does not cost much; it just needs awareness or habits or creativity.

Finally; returning to the sage, "the gentleman cannot send people to prison." It means that the government should also establish a good image so that it will benefit the people and win their favour. In addition to dealing with legal cases, there can be no sham, and in other respects, there are often significant gains. At this point, many of today's officials have gone out, image engineering, performance engineering, false reporting of GDP, etc., they will go to any length.

Bo: When the foundation is not firm, it is easily shaken

CLASSICAL TEXT

Bo; indicates that it will not be advantageous to make a movement in any direction whatsoever.

Six at the First line; shows one overturning the couch by injuring its legs. The injury will go on to destruct any applied wisdom, and there will be evil.

Six at the Second line; reflects one turning over the couch by injuring its frame. The injury will go on to the destruction of all applied wisdom, and there will be evil.

Six at the third line; reflects its subject among the over throwers; but there will be no error.

Six at the fourth line offers that its subject having turned over the couch, and going to injure the skin of him who lies on it. There will be evil.

Six at the fifth line; suggests its subject leading on the others like a school of fish, and obtaining for them the favour that lights on the inmates of the palace. There will be advantage in every way.

Nine at the top line; shows its subject as a great fruit, which has not been eaten, meaning great achievements. The superior man finds the people again as a chariot carrying him. The small men, by their course of action overthrow their own dwellings.

The image; The trigrams representing the earth, and above it, that for a mountain, which adheres to the earth, forms Bo. Superiors, in accordance with this, seek to strengthen those below them, to secure the peace and stability of their own position.

LITERAL TRANSLATION

Bo; It is not auspicious to move forward.

Six at the First line; the destruction of the bed begins with the foot of the bed, fix it and evil can be eliminated.

Six at the Second line; destruction has reached the bed, evil is present and the danger is near.

Six at the third line; time to peel off the outer layer, there will be no harm.

Six at the fourth line; destruction has reached the bed, and it is dangerous.

Six at the fifth line; moving forward in line, be thankful to your hosts, no disadvantage.

Nine at the top line; the fruit has not been eaten, the gentleman has to take advantage, the villain will suffer.

The image; mountain over the earth. The gentleman needs to erect broader foundations.

INTERPRETATION

In this hexagram, the upper part is Gen, indicating mountain; the lower is Kun, meaning the earth. The mountain is above the ground. This seems to be fine, but the sage thinks differently. He believes that if the mountain is really above the ground, it is equivalent to a rockery. It is stripped from the earth and is not strong. Sages may also have seen landslides or mudslides. If things are not strong enough, they are inevitably stripped and peeled off. So he named this as "peeling" to indicate a state without foundation and rootlessness. In this regard, the sage put forward a few points

First; a rootless drift is difficult to achieve. Many of my classmates went to Northern Shangguang after graduation. Ten years later, there are very few people who take root in the big cities. The overall quality of life is not as good as that of the third-tier cities in their hometowns.

Second; do not talk if you do not have roots. Confucius said, 'To gossip is to abandon virtue'. Do not pass on misleading information; many people in social media groups receive things they would do better to not distribute. Besides, you are as good as your word is – that I can promise. But do not make promises easily, let yourself be embarrassed by knowing when to say no.

Third; is that something is stable when it is rooted in the ground, but you must try it first with your feet before you can to catch the things above.

Fourth; if there is no foundation at all, it is too easy to rely on others, too passive. Whenever someone else kicks you off, you end up having nothing.

Fifth; when there is no foundation you can take advantage of the situation. If the foundation is relative, the soil is also relative.

Sixth; most people's lives are like peeling onions; they peel off layers, again and again, until this life is over. A few people's lives are like peeling walnuts, they peel off unbroken skin, and eat the core inside. In the end, the sage stressed that they should "be bold to be safer", and to do things to stabilise the foundation and lay a solid foundation.

There is a saying, the taller the building, the stronger its foundations. In fact, no construction is built on flat land. It takes a good one or two meters deep foundation for each story. This foundation usually accounts for a large part of the entire construction volume; otherwise, the building is shaken. Suddenly, I found that the sage and our way of thinking are striking close. This is also an excellent foundation — the sage uses "a house" as a metaphor. I use the building or to build a house, and the "foundation". Both derived from architectural terms.

About the basics, you can get them from three aspects:

First; basic skills. Chinese culture places particular emphasis on basic skills, no matter which line or industry.

These are the so-called basic skills that are the simplest and most commonly used techniques, also known as Kung Fu (the work of an advanced person). These basic skills are best mastered at a young age, like a child. The boy will turn a great man, if he grows up in training, and is easy to integrate into his body, mind, and life. After doing this effort, he will be able to take care of himself without issue. The basics are: the constant repetition of practice, the most time-consuming, and the treasure of childhood, the more impetuous, the more appropriate. I have been practicing calligraphy for nearly two decades and have not made great progress. The reason may be that I did not start as a child.

Second; is the foundation. No matter what you do, you have to draw your base area, grow a little bit, and develop a little bit. One point is one point, and one inch is one inch. It will prove successful, sooner or later. Be afraid of drifting, like duckweed. Over a century ago, in America, the media suggested, "Go and explore the north". And when they returned, between such coming and going, were not young anymore. For learning, you have to draw a circle for yourself. This circle can be small, but those things in the circle, you have to do well, and whoever is "killing it" outside, you should not be jealous. Keeping your circle is the foundation, and then think of ways to expand it.

Third; is the people base. In fact, it is still based on land, friends, and relatives; this group of people in the base. Without them, you are a fish out of the water. Also, the foundation of the plant is at the root system, the foundation of the river is at the source, and the foundation of culture are the classics.

In the case of reading, I do not read the major classics, including the major works of history. I do not mess with my foundation. I read many books, and it is also like grass without roots. Passive water is untenable. Traditional Chinese Medicine stresses roots and solid foundations over focusing on single problems.

Fu: The heart of Heaven and Earth

CLASSICAL TEXT

Fu; indicates that there will be a free course and progress. The subject finds no one to distress him in his exits and entrances; friends come to him, and no error is committed. He will return and repeat his proper course. In seven days comes his return. There will be an advantage in whatever direction movement is made.

Nine at the First line; The subject returning from an error of no great extent, which would not proceed to anything requiring repentance. There will be great fortune.

Six at the Second line; shows the admirable return of its subject. There will be good fortune.

Six at the third line; reflects one who has made repeated returns. The position is perilous, but there will be no error.

Six at the fourth line; the subject moves into the centre, among those represented by the other divided lines, and yet returning alone to his proper path.

Six at the fifth line; shows the noble return of its subject. There will be no ground for remorse.

Six at the top line; suggests its subject is astray on the subject of returning. There will be evil. There will be calamities and errors. If with his views, he put the hosts in motion, the end will be a massive defeat, whose issues will extend to the ruler of the state. Even in ten years, he will not be able to repair the disaster.

The image; The trigram representing the earth and that for thunder in the midst of it forms Fu. The ancient king, in accordance with this, on the day of the winter solstice, shut the gates to the people travelling, close the borders so the traveling merchants could not continue their journeys, nor the princes go on with the inspection of their states.

LITERAL TRANSLATION

Fu; prosperity. There is no disease, friends come to visit, and there is no harm in it. By sticking to the path, return once after seven days of traveling.

Nine at the First line; return as soon as something is not wrong, and there will not be regret, good fortune.

Six at the Second line; returning in good shape is auspicious.

Six at the third line; there is a risk in frequently going back and forth, but no harm.

Six at the fourth line; stay on the middle path, do it alone if necessary.

Six at the fifth line; be honest when returning to the right path, there should be no regrets.

Six at the top line; lost and unable to return, there is a danger. If the sovereign wages war, calamity will come, and no victory will come for a long time.

The image; thunder over earth forms Fu. The sovereign does not come close to the border during the solstice, and the nobles do not leave for business.

INTERPRETATION

In this hexagram, the upper part is Lei, indicating thunder; the lower is Kun, indicating the earth. Just as the lighting makes the depths of the earth tremble, it makes the power of growth wake up again. During the spring festival in the north, the earth is still covered with snow and ice, and we can read in the Spring Festival couplets pasted on the doors:

The restart, everything is fresh again. Yes, dark clouds cannot cover the sun, and the snow cannot lock the spring. What the saint sees from this image is the rebirth of the four seasons, and the will of Heaven behind it all. What is Heaven? It is complex. The sage said, "In Fu, where is the heart of heaven and earth?" In reciprocating, that is the law of heaven and earth. This concept has become a major principle of Chinese philosophy, especially the core of Taoist thinking. The so-called "Tao De Jing" is called the flow, the movement of the Tao.

In this regard, the sages have said a few things:

First; when it comes to "Fu" (the reconstruction), the sooner, the better. The Buddha said that the sea of suffering is boundless, and the way back to shore is to give up and let go.

When practicing out in the real world, the earlier you awake, the earlier you can become a Buddha.

Second; away from the body but close to the heart. Gu Cheng says in one of his poems: In the spring, you wave your handkerchief, is it to let me go or to welcome me go back?

Third; is that it is not good to turn over and over again, but it is not a bad thing to correct the course several times.

Fourth; is that things are always in opposition to something else; that is the way of heaven. The sun always declines after reaching its summit, and the full moon immediately begins waning. When you reach the top of the mountain, you should carefully plan your way back down.

Warren Buffett said, 'Fear when others are greedy, be greedy when others fear'.

Fifth; the way is always returning to the heart, returning to the homeland, returning to dullness, and even returning to the dust, this is the only way to warmth, enjoy this process, have no regrets.

Sixth; the lost one does not know the way, stick to obscurity, and you will not be saved. The four season's cycle because of the earth's motion, and the reciprocation of day and night is due to the earth's rotation. The moon turns around the earth, the earth rotates around the sun, the sun is turning around the centre of the Milky Way, the Milky Way is turning in the universe, and the entire universe is expanding. Rotation is allegedly a "complex" mode of operation: starting from a point, going around a circle, returning to that point, then starting all over, then returning, and so on. This is the "Heavenly Way" and the development of everything most likely.

If you go to work, you quite at the end of the shift; you leave work and return home; when you go up a mountain, you have to climb down; if you jump up, you will fall; if you take off, you have to land somewhere; if you go on stage, you have to step down at the end of the show; when you start something, you have to go stop at some point; In war, you have to fight for peace; and so on.

Such a sentence can be extended infinitely. In the end, there will be two points: when you are born, and when you die, if you move, you have to stop at some point.

The weakness of human nature is that the drill bit ignores the engine, it only wants to make progress, thinks about rushing up, fighting, calculating, and vying, but neglects to end at some point, to go back to be at ease, to return to silence. When we cast large stones into the lake, and a stone stirs a thousand waves, but the lake recovers it calm after a while. Relative to movement, being static is fundamental and normal. This is what the "Resurrection" (Fu) and Taoist thoughts remind us of it.

"During the solstice, the sovereign does not go near the border; the merchant does not travel; the noble does not look for power." This sentence shows an example of holidays in ancient times. During their festivals on the two days of the winter solstice and the summer solstice. Everything in the world stops, and the country was on holiday, resting quietly. Is there anything special about the winter solstice and the summer solstice? There is something quite special. Now we are used to thinking that the Spring Festival is the beginning of the year, while the ancients used the winter solstice as the beginning of the year. The winter solstice is the shortest day of the year and the longest night, that is, the weakest and most sinful moment of the year. After the winter solstice, the day gets longer, and longer; it is the raising of yang and the birth of the "Fu." Summer solstice. The sages emphasise this point, and it is intended to remind us that the heavens and the earth are all reciprocating, there is no stopping, we should seize these moments and adjust our status. If we do it, we will rest, and we will start all over later.

Of course, the cycle is different from the universal rotation. Still, a self-development method includes, taking a step back to advance two steps forward. Just like when there is a ditch in front, to jump over it, we have to take a few steps back and build up momentum. Therefore, in all fields, retro is always a strategy of innovation.

Wu Wang:

Abide by one's station in life

CLASSICAL TEXT

Wu Wang; great progress and success, while there will be an advantage in being firm and correct. If the subject and his actions are not correct, he will fall into error, and it will not be advantageous for him to move in any direction.

Nine at the First line; the subject free from all insincerity. His advance will be accompanied by good fortune.

Six at the Second line; shows one who reaps without having ploughed, and gathers the produce of his third year's fields without having cultivated them the first year for that end. To such a one, there will be an advantage in whatever direction he moves.

Six at the third line; reflects the calamity happening to one who is free from insincerity – as in the case of an ox that has been tied up. A passer-by finds it and carries it off, while the people in the neighbourhood suffer the calamity of being accused and apprehended.

Nine at the Fourth line; a case in which, if its subject can remain firm and correct, there will be no error.

Nine at the Fifth line; shows one who is free from insincerity, and yet has fallen ill. Let him not use the medicine, and he will have occasion for joy in his recovery.

Nine at the top line; when its subject is free from insincerity, yet sure to fall into error, if he takes action. His action will not be advantageous in any way.

The image; the thunder rolls under the sky, and to everything there is given its nature, free from all insincerity. The ancient king, in accordance with this, made their regulations in complete accordance with the seasons, thereby nourishing all things.

LITERAL TRANSLATION

Wu Wang; thunder in the sky. There is wholehearted sincerity without deceit. Acting without seeking reward.

Nine at the First line; go forward expecting nothing, and it will bring luck.

Six at the Second line; if you do not cultivate, you will have no harvest. If you do not work for them, you will have no good fields; if you do, they will help you to go forward.

Six at the third line; one gain is another's lost. A traveller takes the ox; it is the farmer's lost.

Nine at the Fourth line; carry on, there will come no harm.

Nine at the Fifth line; if you are not sick, you do not need medication. You will have to heal yourself from small illnesses.

Nine at the top line; do not act; action can bring disaster at this point.

The image; thunder under the sky; the old king, used the power of the weather to raise all.

INTERPRETATION

This hexagram is formed by Gan (The Creative) in the upper part, indicating the dry, and the lower is Zhen, indicating the thunder. Thunder in the world, deafening, dark clouds, lightning, wind, and rain, rainstorms, such weather is like the gods' wrath; who dares to sway outside? Better hide in the house, to be honest. This is not only about people; the birds, animals, insects, and living things in nature must also be hidden in caves and squatting in their nests. Everything that was arrogant does not dare to brag now, and it is beaten by lighting back to its original way of being. This kind of honesty was called "innocence" by the sage.

From the perspective of the rulers, if the people of the world are in this state, would it not be peaceful? Laozi taught, "The rule of the sages is to falsify their hearts, to be weak, to weaken their ambitions and to strengthen their bones". People are often ignorant and unwilling to do things by themselves so that the wise will not dare to do things for them. "Let the people be honest and innocent, and then they will know their place", the world will be quiet and stable.

But how can we make the people innocent? Laozi believed that the ruling class must first be innocent.

Laozi famous saying, 'Do not do'. This is consistent with the Confucian idea that "If you lead the people with correctness, who will dare not to be correct?" People will know who is up and who is down. However, the sage in The *Book of Change*s is not so optimistic. He emphasises that "the old king should take advantage of strength and authority to shock the world so that the people will be innocent and beneficial to themselves, and for the overall development of the country. Lee Kuan Yew said that the most effective mode of governance in Chinese society is the rule of enlightened autocracy. This point should be inspiring for business management and family education.

Let us take a look; There are two things that are innocent: one is wishful thinking, and the other is rushing to take action.

Not to overthink: I do not expect anything over just because you think you deserve it, I do not expect others to be kind to me without reason, do not think about how to get things at any cost.

There is no good in breaking the law and violating morality. No acting: do not behave improperly, do not heed ill words, do not utter false words, and do not commit foul deeds. If you find a synonym for innocence, it is "abide by one station's in life". This word is worthy of serious reflection. People must think about what their points are, what "self" is, and make an examination of consciousness.

In this regard, the sage added a few more profound points:

First; fear of doing things on behalf of other people, to make a good fortune fast, to be too cautious, not to doubt things.

Second; do not think that the sky will drop food into your mouth; you must believe that you will earn something.

Third; is that if you do not kill, you should not be killed. Lying after being gunned down in the street, or dying in your house, are small probability events.

Fourth; if you are faced with one of those situations, you should calmly respond, as long as you are not afraid of evil, they will pass, and ultimately there will be no danger.

Fifth; is that I have not done anything wrong; I do not need to be afraid of ghosts calling at the door. Do not be bothered by the brutality of life; everything will be fine in the end.

Sixth; if the timing is right or not, simply be honest, and you should know if there's a chance.

Taken one step further, "Inaction" is ultimately a question of how to face human desires. Being self-discipline is not a problem for just some people, but a problem for all human beings. Online, a female star was warning her husband by saying, 'I can get used to you, or I can also replace you with someone else'. When human arrogance exceeds the limits of tolerance in nature, can it be replaced?

Da Xu: Pointers for officials

CLASSICAL TEXT

Da Xu; Under the conditions of Da Xu, it will be advantageous to be firm and correct. If the subject does not seek to enjoy his revenues in his own family, there will be good fortune. It will be advantageous for him to cross the great stream.

Nine at the First line; shows its subject in a position of peril. It will be advantageous for him to stop his advance.

Nine at the Second line; a carriage with the strap under it removed.

Nine at the third line; suggests its subject urging his way with good horses. It will be advantageous for him to realise the difficulty of his course, and to be firm and correct, exercising himself daily in his charioteer and methods of defence; then, there will be an advantage in whatever direction he may advance.

Six at the fourth line; shows the young bull having the piece of wood over his horns. There will be good fortune.

Six at the fifth line; showing the teeth of a castrated hog. There will be good fortune.

Nine at the top line; the subject in command of the firmament of heaven. There will be progress.

The image; the trigram representing a mountain, and in the midst that represents heaven in the form Da Xu. The superior man, in accordance with this, stores largely in his memory the words and deeds of former men, to subserve the accumulation of his virtue.

LITERAL TRANSLATION

Da Xu; Taking the reins, time to take the bull by the horns and cross the river.

Nine at the First line; Danger is at hand, time to stop and consider.

Nine at the Second line; the cart's wheel fell off the axle. Time for repairs.

Nine at the third line; the good horses are rushing, which is conducive to hardship. Practice riding, which is good for travel.

Six at the fourth line; cover the horns of a calf, control bad habits so they do not control you.

Six at the fifth line; keep a castrated pig from harming others is good luck in finding the source of an error.

Nine at the top line; Walking the heavenly path, things are easier once they follow the right way.

The image; a mountain over the sky. The power of heaven is safely kept under the mountain's stability. The gentleman must remember the wisdom of his predecessors to accumulate virtues.

INTERPRETATION

In this hexagram, the upper part is Gen, indicating mountain; the lower is Qian, indicating the sky. There is an altogether different world under the mountains. According to all the stories in ancient and modern China and abroad, from Alibaba's (equivalent to Amazon) treasures to Jin Yong's martial arts novels. The sage is also a person, and he imagines the treasure on this image and thinks of the wealth coming from them, so he named it "big beast" (Da Xu). Compared with the previous talk about "abundance', the Da Xu has a deep hidden meaning. It emphasises the wealth in the strength accumulated in the long-term forbearance, including financial strength and ability. The people of the following Da Xu are low-key, restrained, deep and heavy, and have a city government, which is suitable for being a prominent official. How to achieve Da Xu? The sage said a few things about this:

First; when doing things for people do not keep a tally of good deeds, and do not show up because of it. During critical years of his reign, (Ming's founder) Zhu Yuanzhang's strategy was to "build tall walls, stock with grain, and slowly plan the crowning".

Second; is to strengthen inside and examine your mind. To make a truck, you have to use a high-powered engine, axles, tires, etc., you need to have a large model.

Third; is to strengthen skills training. Skill comes from practice, but also from a master and a book.

Fourth, you need to strap the reins tight on a calf, or else it will get tired faster. There should be an elderly person to help with guidance.

Fifth; is that if you have the strength, and you are arrogant, can such a person still be as successful? For those who have been grounded for a long time, the moment they fly, they will soar very high. The longer the gestation period of an animal, the longer its life. The hen will be able to lay eggs in half a year. It can live for up to ten years, which is no match for humans. So, do not worry, "lay off the eggs".

The small animals that realised the importance of capital accumulation were regarded as bourgeois. Big livestock has bets on large capital accumulation, and it is successful. At this time, it has enough strength to pursue higher goals and realise the value of life.

How to achieve life's potential? I understood this question when I read Confucius' *Great Learning*. What the *Great Learning* teaches is illustrious virtue is to raise people's standards, and to keep them and yourself virtuous. Give free rein to talents, do your best to benefit as many people as possible; that is how we achieve the potential of life.

How to benefit as many people as possible? Politics is the best way. In Liao-Fan's *Four Lessons*, Yuan Liao Fan is willing to do a thousand good things every year. If as little as one task is not completed, he became upset. A high-ranking sergeant told him that the good deeds he had done this year had already exceeded the standard because he had implemented a burden-reduction policy as a county magistrate this year, which benefited tens of thousands of farmers in the county, and that is equivalent to doing tens of thousands of good deeds.

Many of the wealthiest people in the West have moved into politics because earnings are immense. It is said that Schwarzenegger, the actor, earnt many millions when he was governor of California. He did this for several years. What was he thinking? This is what he was probably planning.

Regarding this, the sage said in the *Da Xu* that 'not eating at home is auspicious'. Not eating at home then meant to be out to become an official, or engaging in other careers that benefit the world, this is an opportunity when you can act disinterred and still get benefits.

How to be an official? The sage believes that it is necessary to "store largely in his memory the words and deeds of former men in order to honour and preserve their moral values". This is to have knowledge. Having money may not mean you are knowledgeable; it is only earning experience; it does not make you a good public servant.

To be an official, you must know about public service. Where do these insights come from? History books offer all kinds of anecdotes in this respect. The historical texts such as *Historical Records* and Sima's *Comprehensive Mirror in Aid of Governance* are all about the knowledge of the past, especially the kings and officials' affairs. What do you do? What do you say? How do you get it? How do you lose it? How do you die? In thousands of cases, you can find examples that correspond to real-world problems, so that you can understand the benefits and gain in many situations. They are references. Bacon said that reading history makes people wise. This is reasonable. However, the history books are separated by something. Those doing the real work may give you more experiential lessons. Therefore, it is necessary to consult with seniors.

Nurturing virtue makes me think of Mencius's famous saying, 'I understand words. I am skilful in nourishing my vast, flowing passionate nature'. If people only like to put things in their stomachs and show off their own homes to others, they will be like a leaky ball, and they will never be full. Men have the same issue – when it is released, it gets soft, immediately. Accumulating strength without being exposed, just like in this hexagram, hiding the sky in the mountains, enhances the content without reluctance, and continuously increases the internal accumulation by means modest progress so that people can become bigger and stronger, and they can rise and stand as officials.

Yi: How's it going?

CLASSICAL TEXT

Yi; indicates that with applied wisdom, there will be good fortune. We must look at what we are seeking to nourish, and by the exercise of our thoughts, seek for proper aliment.

Nine at the First line; you leave your efficacious tortoise, and look at me until your lower jaw hangs down. There will be evil.

Six at the Second line; This shows one is looking downwards for nourishment, which is contrary to what is proper, or seeking it from the heights above, advance towards it will lead to evil.

Six at the third line; one acting contrary to the method of nourishing. However firm he might be there will be evil. For ten years, let him not take any action, it will not be in any way advantageous.

Six at the fourth line; shows one looking downwards for the power to nourish. There will be good fortune. Looking with a tiger's downward unwavering glare, and with his desire that impels him to spring after spring, he will fall into no error.

Six at the fifth line; one acting contrary to what is regular and proper; but if he abides in firmness, there will be good fortune. He should not try to cross the great stream.

Nine at the top line; showing him from whom comes the nourishing. His position is perilous, but there will be good fortune. It will be advantageous to cross the great stream.

The image; the trigram representing a mountain and under it that for thunder forms Yi. The superior man, in accordance with this, enjoins watchfulness over our words, and the temperate regulation of our eating and drinking.

LITERAL TRANSLATION

Yi; we are what we eat. Looking after the ones that look after us.

Nine at the First line; disregard of your turtle stew to watch me eat something different is dangerous.

Six at the Second line; upturning the order of rank, or to violate the common sense of seeking support from high-level people leads to danger.

Six at the third line; Neglecting the maintenance of roads, keeping resources unused, not using something for ten years, cannot expect it to work properly.

Six at the fourth line; Now can the ranking order be upturned, the tiger (desires and passion) is close, but there is no harm.

Six at the fifth line; going against common sense, keep living in a safe and auspicious manner, do not get involved in crossing greater rivers.

Nine at the top line; People dependent on high risk might be dangerous, but they are good for the risking crossing the river.

The image; mountain above and thunder below form Yi (Feedback and nourishment). The superior man observes temperance when eating and drinking.

INTERPRETATION

In this hexagram, the upper part is Gen, indicating mountain; the lower is Lei, indicating the thunder. Thunder is under the mountain, and the sage named this as "Yi", which means the mouth. The mountain and the thunder. In the eyes of sages, the big universe of nature and the small universe of human beings is analogous. The mountain corresponds to the head, and the mountain to the mouth; the mouth emits various sounds, such as the voice, singing, the sound of eating, etc. It is no exception, and these are like thunder. If you put your ears next to a chewing mouth, it feels obvious.

The most basic function of the mouth is to eat, so the meaning of "Yi" is also extended to feeding and health.

In this regard, the sage offered a few points:

First; it means that if the family is not full, then each mouth will not be either. Whoever is looking at others eating, but forget that they are actually holding their bowl of food, is stupid.

Second; to eat to live? Or to live to eat? The old raise the young, or the young raise the old? Such problems should be clarified.

Third; is that if you do not understand how to eat healthily, you will surely have trouble. Many geriatric diseases develop during youth.

Fourth; human beings die in pursuit of wealth, and birds die for food. With ambition and desire, you can enjoy more exciting things, but you may also lose your life.

Fifth; health care is precious, but let nature take its course.

Sixth; the more people you nurture, the more achievements you will get. Whether people can be nurtured or not depends on success or failure. In general terms, the masses regard food as their prime want. Feeding the people has been a test for any ruler for thousands of years. Every change of the dynasty happens when people have not enough to eat; if they do not have anything else to lose and starve to death, this will undoubtedly lead to rebellion. Between death and revolution, the answer is simply rebelling. Vast famine has wreaked havoc countless times. Eating has become part of many common concepts in the Chinese people's bones, so that countless words are marked with "eat", such as saying, 'how is it going? Have you eaten yet?' The Chinese words for "population" includes the character for mouth; be "well-received" means "smell delicious"; have a "steady job" is "to hold an iron rice bowl"; something unbearable is "unable to be eaten", and so on. Unfortunately, today, this issue is still not completely solved! In short, the chief responsibility of a leader of a company or organisation is to let everyone earn enough money to live a good life. This should be the main thing.

If a man cannot support his family, he will have no dignity. People have a mouth, so eating and talking are linked. When the baby is hungry and wants to eat, it will cry.

When you go to work, and the person in charge of the matter said that something is not doable, or that it is not available, and gives all kinds of excuses. If you treat him a meal, he will stuff his mouth. People often talk because they have needs, but when they are full and do not need to eat, they will be silent.

The mouth is the gateway to the human body. What is the path? It is the security door, too, which is usually locked, and no thief can open it. The sage said, 'The superior man, in accordance with this, enjoins watchfulness over our words, and the temperate regulation of our eating and drinking'. Keep your mouth shut, close your mouth, talk less, eat less (30 to 40% less), and avoid misfortunes and illnesses. There are many idioms and proverbs related, such as silence is gold, loud calling birds have no food, pipe mouth, and so on. Whether it is for health or protection, it is vital to keep your mouth shut.

If a person cannot control his mouth, what can he control?

Da Guo: The Lone Wolf is a hidden Dragon

CLASSICAL TEXT

Da Guo; suggests to us a weak beam. There will be advantage in moving under its influence in any direction whatsoever; there will be success.

Six at the First line; shows one placing mats of Cogon grass under things set on the ground. There will be no error.
Nine at the Second line; a decayed willow producing shoots, or an old husband in possession of his young wife. There will be advantage in every way.
Nine at the third line; if a weak beam. There will be evil.
Nine at the Fourth line; shows a beam curving upwards. There will be good fortune. If the subject of it looks for other's help, there will be cause for regret.
Nine at the Fifth line; a decayed willow producing flowers or an old wife in possession of her young husband. There will be occasion neither for blame nor for praise.
Six at the top line; shows its subject with extraordinary boldness wading through a stream, until the water hides the crown of his head. There will be evil, but no grounds for blame.
The image; the trigram representing trees hidden beneath that for the waters of a marsh forms Da Guo. The superior man, in accordance with this, stands up, alone, and has no fear, and keeps retired from the world without regret.

LITERAL TRANSLATION

Da Guo; The beams are crooked; it is time to move on.

Six at the First line; Spread grass tatamis to prepare for a big burden, no harm should come.

Nine at the Second line; the dried poplars grow new branches, and an older man married a young woman, which is not bad.

Nine at the third line; the beam is crooked and cracking.

Nine at the Fourth line; the roof beam is strong, but do not add any extra weight.

Nine at the Fifth line; a withered poplar grows new flowers. The older woman marries a younger man, not a good omen.

Six at the top line; water is overflowing its course, there is a risk, but no danger.

The image; the tree under water, the weight on top, is too heavy.

INTERPRETATION

In this trigram, the top of is Dui (the lake), and below is Xun (the tree), though sometimes it means Wind, here is the tree. The grove growing in low places will be submerged. So the sage saw that and called it "The big mistake".

While in a crowd of people, are we not each of us a tree that is submerged? Why does someone feel lonely in the middle of a crowd?

You are only one among eight billion human beings. Compared to humanity, you are just a dust speckle. You may be the sun in the eyes of your parents, but they may not know that well. The warmth of the family cannot dissolve the loneliness of the soul. In fact, the closer you are, the more the negative is visible. Denying this is no less stressful than the ridicule of outsiders. Lu Xun said that life has to know himself well, then you realise there is no such thing as intimacy. You have privacy when no one knows who you are, how do you know what is worthy of respect? People can only measure you based on wealth, power, family, and other external things. But that is not you, even if you have no wealth, no power, no family, and no one, that is enough to win the favour of the world. You may have good reasons but unfortunately for what use? You do not have to explain it; it can only attract more doubt and disdain. How do you face this?

The sage said:

First; be careful and settle down.

Second; there is no shortage of people in the world.

Third; if the spirit does not fall, then the belief does not fall.

Fourth; persistence is a victory.

Fifth; do not give up opportunities because of morality.

Sixth; hope is always there, never despair.

Finally; the sage said that there must be a spirit of "do not be afraid of loneliness; there is no sorrow in the world". Even if everyone rejects me, I still insist on myself, not afraid at all; even if the whole world forgets me, or never cares about me, I am still happy to live the life I want.

Mencius said that, 'I will go forward against thousands and tens of thousand!'

It is quite challenging to do this. Human nature desires to be respected, naturally inclined to live for vanity, to live in the eyes of others, to determine their state from the opinion of others. Whoever does not care about other people's opinions, can be called anti-social. The sage did not teach us how to fight against the sky. He only used two metaphors: one was the old husband who had a younger wife, and the other was the dry poplar (the dead tree blossoms). His meaning is clear, endure loneliness, persist in dreams, listen to the fate of people, and always have a clear mind to think about things. Even if the tree is dry, it might still bloom. For example, Van Gogh, Gu Zhun, Wang Fuzhi, Bada Shanren, Xu Wei, and many other great people are all late bloomers. However, rest assured, you are not so powerful, the flowers that bloom from a dry tree are all too few, and you may be, in the best scenario, just one of those great minds that mature slowly.

When the sage interprets the "a capable person biding his time" in the hexagram "Qian", there is a wonderful time, which can be used as a footnote: "There he is, with the powers of the dragon, and yet lying hidden". The influence of the world would make no change in him; he would do nothing merely to secure his fame. He can live, withdrawn from the world, without regret; he can experience disapproval without a troubled mind. Rejoicing in opportunity, he carries his principles into action, sorrowing for want of opportunity, he keeps with them in retirement. The meaning of this passage is: the loner is a dragon hidden underwater.

Kan: Doom

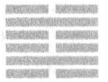

CLASSICAL TEXT

Kan; here it is repeated, and shows sincerity, through which the mind is penetrating. Action in accordance with this will be of high value.

Six at the First line shows its subject in danger and going under. There will be evil.

Nine at the Second line; its subject is in peril of the defile. He will however, derive some benefit from that he seeks.

Six at the third line; shows its subject, whether he comes or goes, confronted by a defile. All is a peril to him and unrest. His endeavours will lead him into the cavern of the pit. There should be no action in such a case.

Six at the fourth line; its subject is feasting, with a bottles of spirit, and a subsidiary basket of rice, while the cups and bowls are earthenware. He introduces his important lessons as his ruler's intelligence admits. There will, in the end, be no error.

Nine at the Fifth line; shows the water of the defile not yet full so that it might flow away, but the order will soon be brought about. There will be no error.

Six at the top line; This shows its subject bound with cords of two or three strands, and placed in a thicket of thorns. But in three years, if he does not learn the course for him to pursue. There will be evil.

The image; the representation of water flowing, forms the repeated Kan. The superior man, in accordance with this, constantly maintains virtue of his heart and the integrity of his conduct, and practices the business of principles.

LITERAL TRANSLATION

Kan; Falling to a pit, upholding convictions can let the heart prosper, a truly admirable behaviour.

Six at the First line; heavy falls into a deep pit, danger.

Nine at the Second line; safe but surrounded by pits, time to be careful.

Six at the third line; whatever you do, the fall is imminent; there no use in doing anything about it.

Six at the fourth line; a bottle of wine and two scoops of fresh food, you have received some help, act carefully, and there will come no harm.

Nine at the Fifth line; the pit has not yet been filled with dirt, so the prisoner is safe.

Six at the top line; tied up with ropes and thrown into thorn bushes, you cannot be released, and any attempt to escape is dangerous.

The image; water is flooding the place, doom can be foreseen. The superior man trusts his heart to get through.

INTERPRETATION

In this hexagram is a ridge above and below, Kan means pit, and it usually implies water in a hexagram. Potholes on the ground are connected one to another. When the floods come, they become dangerous, so the sage named this hexagram "Xi Kan" (Xi means overlapping), and thought of the various risks and crises that are faced continuously in life.

Regarding these risks and crises, the sage shares the following points:

First; there are two pits in life, which are destiny and robberies; neither can be avoided.

Second; is that there is some necessarily risk. Risk and opportunity coexist. In the process of dealing with uncertainty, as long as it is handled properly, there are often unexpected gains and blessings caused by a disaster.

Third; when you really fall into a pit, you should not panic and fumble. Think calmly and save your energy, wait for an opportunity.

Fourth; under the eaves, people have to bow their heads. They must understand how to compromise and avoid debacle, and must know how to suffer unexpected financial losses but forestall calamity.

Fifth; take precautions; it is raining in the spring breeze, pave the roads in advance to prevent problems before they occur.

Sixth; when a turnaround occurs, we must dare to stake everything on one attempt and counter any incoming offense. Once an opportunity is missed, you do not know when the next will come.

Generally speaking, the sage believes that in the face of a crisis, you need to maintain constant virtue (in your heart) and integrity of your conduct, and practices the art of teaching it. Virtue, or "moral action" here means to adhere to the right path in the midst of difficulties and crises, and adhere to moral actions, such as the pillar of Confucianism: benevolence, righteousness, courtesy, wisdom, and faith.

It is said that people's poverty chills ambition. When in a difficult situation common people will try to get out of that situation as fast as possible. In the film *1942*, a girl was spotted by a trafficker and wanted to take her as a prostitute. The family was very happy because she would not starve to death in the famine. For the vast majority of ordinary people, if their lives cannot be maintained, the four cardinal virtues (humanity, justice, propriety, and wisdom) are nonsense. However, as Confucius said, "the gentleman is strong, the villain is poor". Ordinary people can think like this, but gentlemen cannot. As far as a gentlemen is concerned, the more difficult the situations are, the more they must adhere to moral action, even if they give up their lives for justice and sacrifice themselves, this is an opportunity to show the value of their lives!

"Principle" is to use what we have learned in times of trouble and crisis. After practicing self-defence techniques for a long time, I was overwhelmed when I met a real hooligan. If I had not use what I learned, I would have been doomed. After studying for a few years in any professional field, it is often the case when it comes to working that things are different. This is also a problem. No matter what you learn, if you do persevere, it will always be insufficient. *The Doctrine of the Mean* speaks of "knowing what is difficult", so then overcoming difficulties and resolving crises becomes an opportunity to test what you have learned, to improve what you have learned, try what you know, and confirm what you are capable of doing. Therefore, do not be afraid, do not complain, calm yourself down as soon as possible, and cautiously show what you have learned in your daily life and what you have learned on weekdays. You will definitely survive most of the things. Adversity test the strength of character. This is where the truth comes about.

The truth is that it is hard when things really turn bad. 2014 is my Chinese horoscope birth year. I have learned what "Living Kan" is. It is difficult. My mother was seriously ill. My wife and I were not healthy. The company's yield was not good. The children were going through a critical stage. The pressure was huge. What to do? When you feel the water getting high, the walls closing in, be well prepared to meet any onslaught, there is not any insurmountable problem. Yet when my mother was gone, she was never coming back!

Li: Leaving the original turf

CLASSICAL TEXT

Li; indicates that it will be advantageous to be firm and correct and thus there will be free range and success. Let its subject also nourish a docility like that of the cow, and there will be good fortune.

Nine at the First line; of one who is ready to move with confused steps. But he treads at the same time cautiously, and there will be no mistake.

Six at the Second line; suggests its subject in his place in yellow (yellow is an auspicious colour). There will be good fortune.

Nine at the third line; shows its subject in a position like that of the declining sun. Instead of playing on his instrument of earthenware, and singing to it, he utters the groans of an old man. There will be evil.

Nine at the Fourth line; shows the manner of its subject's coming. How abrupt it is, as with fire, with death, to be rejected by all.

Six at the fifth line; shows its subject as one with tears flowing in torrents, and groaning in sorrow. There will be good fortune.

Nine at the top line; suggests the king employing his subject in his punitive expeditions. Achieving admirable merit, he breaks only the chiefs of the rebels. Where his prisoners were not their associates, he does not punish. There will be no error.

The image; the trigram for brightness, repeated, forms Li. The great man, in accordance with this, cultivates more and more his high virtue and diffuses its brightness over the four quarters of the land.

LITERAL TRANSLATION

Li; Time for being protective, raising cattle is good and auspicious.

Nine at the First line; the implementation of affairs is done the right way, by respecting people and dedication, without blame.

Six at the Second line; A golden glow brings luck.

Nine at the third line; As the sun sets, beat the drums or hear the laments of the old.

Nine at the Fourth line; Fire flare up, burns strong, then dies away, it is gone soon after.

Six at the fifth line; weeping is a good sign when it is with real sadness.

Nine at the top line; the king sent troops to conquer, there will be rewards, cut off the enemies head, capture the principal offender, no harm will come.

The image; Fire over fire form Li, mutual support. A flare that shines in all directions.

INTERPRETATION

This hexagram is separated in the top and bottom. Li represents Fire and Lighting. In the hexagram, there is a sun above and another sun below. Two suns cannot appear at the same time, only moving separately, in continuity: the sun that rises today, is the sun that rises again tomorrow, and the sun that rises the day after tomorrow. Soon enough, the spring breeze is blowing again. An ancient poem cuts into the beauty of the "Li" hexagram.

The sage describes the process of the presentation of the hexagram "Li" in terms of the process of human life:

First; work hard and diligently;

Second; then, it reaches the peak of the day;

Third; when this cycle comes to an end, you should prepare for the next cycle;

Four; when the new cycle comes quickly, it is going to be very long, and it will end soon;

Five; then, in the cycle of renewal, experience the pain of renewal and gradually gain benefits.

Six; finally, at a given cycle, it will achieve good success. The sage, therefore, thinks that "great people will continue to shine on to their mature age", the great people will continuously emit light and heat, illuminating people's eyes, dreams, and hearts. Is it possible for the vast majority of people? Of course, it is impossible, and they have not emitted any light throughout their lives; or maybe there is some glory, but people die like a lamp, and with the demise of life, all their flowers will disappear.

But it is different for great people, as in *The Commentary of Zuo* "there are high ethics, followed by merits, and then there are philosophies, which are not immortal, but long-lasting." Confucius died, Lao Tzu died, Socrates died, Shakyamuni died, Jesus died, Yue Fei died, Wen Tianxiang died, Zeng Guofan died, Lei Feng died, etc.. However, their light still shines and enlighten us, when we still touch their light.

Of course, this is an ultimate ideal. If we cannot do it, let us try it while we are alive. How to do it? Try the following:

First; we can "pass the torch", and pass down the light of Confucius.

Second; is to find that your light may be small. Still, a small smile is enough to illuminate your family and those around you, enough to give them positive energy.

Third; from the perspective of utilitarianism, if you want to create glory, you cannot be just a comet that flashes by. Goodness is not enough to become famous. Even if you write a book that makes people stand out, and people soon forget it. You have to write a second, a third, and a fourth book, each better than the others, and eventually, people will remember you! Zhao Benshan performed a sketch for the Spring Festival Gala twenty years ago, and he still performs in Spring Festival Gala every year. In addition, he also makes TV dramas and has gained great status. Some advertisements are still being run year after year. In the Internet era, there was a hot topic every two days, and a new person every ten days. My fellow internet celebrity Yanshen Master is well aware of this. He said, 'a flare is not called a fire; a continuous fire is called fire'. So he insisted on posting on Weibo every day and suddenly became the king of streaming in

China. However, I have to remind him that people will get tired of new products if they do not have any new ideas. They keep insisting on production.

Intel 286, 386, 486, 586, and so on; Windows 95, 98, 2000, 2003, and so on; iPhone 1, 2, 3, 4, 4S, 5, 5S and so on.

Or learn online this, get a car today, be like Lei Feng tomorrow. No wonder the old Chen Fa Cai is a marketing genius!

Jackie Chan had one or two movies every year, and Feng Xiaogang, too, those who stop suddenly will go out of fashion soon. Without success once and for all, in whatever you are successful now, will only indicate that the next big thing is around the corner.

Xian: Moving with the feeling

CLASSICAL TEXT

Xian; indicates that, on the fulfilment of the conditions implied in it, there will be free course and success. It is advantageousness will depend on being firm and correct, as in marrying a young lady. There will be good fortune.

Sixth at the first line; shows one moving his great toes.

Six at the Second line; shows one moving the calves of his leg. There will be evil. If he abides quietly in his place, there will be good fortune.

Nine at the third line; one moving his thighs, and keeping a close hold of those whom he follows. Going forward in this way will cause regret.

Nine at the Fourth line; that applied wisdom, which will lead to good fortune, and prevent all occasion for remorse. If its subject is unsettled in his movements, only his friends will follow his purpose.

Nine at the Fifth line; offers, one moving the flesh along the spine above the heart. There will be no occasion for remorse.

Six at the top line; gives one moving his jaws and tongue.

The image; the trigram representing a mountain, and above it that the waters of a marsh forms Xian. The superior man, in accordance with this, keeps his mind free from pre-occupation, and open to receive the influences of others.

LITERAL TRANSLATION

Xian; Remain cautious; there is good luck on marrying.

Six at the First line; Wiggling the toes.

Six at the Second line; moving the calf, there is a risk. Do not be restless.

Nine at the third line; starting to walk while being grabbed by the ankle. Remain calm, or you will trip over.

Nine at the Fourth line; you are confused and busy, remain focused and alert, friends will come to your aid.

Nine at the Fifth line; pain in the back, there will be no regrets.

Six at the top line; using your mouth.

The image; a mountain and a lake on top. Xian, the sovereign must be tolerant and receptive.

INTERPRETATION

In this hexagram for the lake (Dui) is over the one for the mountain (Gen). The reference to "getting a partner" in the hexagram shows that this hexagram is related to marriage and gender. We might as well understand this hexagram boldly: The mountain represents the male genitalia, the lake represents the female genitalia, and the entire hexagram is a copulating scene. Therefore, the sage thinks of the kind of interaction, touch, and feelings between men and women. He named this hexagram as "Xian" (equivalent to a similar word in Chinese for "feeling"). This describes the relationship between men and women that the sage understands as natural:

First; feelings begin with a slight movement in the deepest part of the heart or a slight touch of a finger.

Second; you fall in love at first sight, do not be impulsive at first sight, first calm down and appreciate the sweet difficulties of courting.

Third; the result of emotion over reason is mostly remorse and sorrow.

Fourth; the emotions once within the intellectual framework are perfected over the years.

Fifth; the feeling buried deep in a heart is like a gem buried deep underground.

Sixth; do not believe in sweet words, do not take women's hard words seriously, men can be trusted, sows can climb up a tree!

The Doctrine of the Mean, says, 'The way of a gentleman starts as a husband to his wife, and extends to the world'. The matter between men and women, in fact, contains the principle of heaven and earth.

A paragraph said that of man's younger brother, who was the world's best battlefield commander: he was good at attacking the opponent, and it made him happy, good at creating friction and exciting everyone, but always keeping a low profile after victory. In reality, when we want to enter other people's fields and occupy other people's resources, we are usually rejected. Obviously, sexual intercourse is also a process of entering into other people's fields and employing other people's resources. Instead of confrontation, it is welcomed, and a close cooperative relationship is achieved. This is very subtle. In fact, sexual intercourse does not just happen between the actual bodies. It exists in a variety of mutual interaction processes between people. Such as thought. When other people's thoughts enter your brain, many times you are not rejecting, but happy. Of course, the more obvious is emotion. When someone's emotion surrounds your heart, you are not rejected, but you are moved, you can do all kinds of things with this kind of momentum, and act from your heart.

Here, the sage says that, 'The superior man, in accordance with this, keeps his mind free from pre-occupation, and opens to receive the influences of others'. To put it plainly, this is to use emotions to deal with others, instead of using actual force, material influence, and power to subdue others, make a deal.

We must be good at relations with family members, leaders, colleagues, subordinates, and customers; China is a collectivist society. If you live in this kind of environment, you must be a successful person if you handle family, friendship, love, and human relationships well.

So, how to practice emotional affection? The sage has a secret in this hexagram: Communicate closely, talk, and chat every day, and people will yield what you think. The same is true for a leader. If you go to him every day, he should not be bothered? It must be a bit annoying at first, but in time, he will feel close to you. This is human nature. Many similar statements, such as aggression and sincerity, are all worthy of reflection and have some hands-on sense.

However, the sage also reminds us that there is a problem with complete emotional affairs. It is impossible to rely on words to move others or the emotions expressed by others in words.

Heng: No change, no shake, no stop

CLASSICAL TEXT

Heng; indicates successful progress and no error in what it denotes. But the advantage will come from being firm and correct, and movement in any direction whatever will be advantageous.

Six at the First line; shows its subject deeply desirous of long continuance. Even with applied wisdom, there will be evil; there will be no advantage in any way.

Nine at the Second line; reflects on all occasion the need for repentance disappearing.

Nine at the third line; one who does not continuously maintain his virtue – there are those who will impute this to him as a disgrace. However firm he may be, there will be grounds for regret.

Nine at the Fourth line; a field where there is no game.

Six at the fifth line; shows its subject continuously maintaining the virtue indicated by it. In a wife, this will be fortunate; in a husband, evil.

Six at the top line; shows its subject exciting himself to the long continuance. There will be evil.

The image; the trigram representing thunder and that for wind forms Heng. The superior man, in accordance with this, stands firm and does not change his method of operation.

LITERAL TRANSLATION

Heng; continuing without fault is blessed and will bring good fortune.

Six at the First line; being persistent but impatient is not good.

Nine at the Second line; no more regrets.

Nine at the third line; not keeping to your place will lead to suffering and humiliation.

Nine at the Fourth line; no luck in the hunt.

Six at the fifth line; attaching to the virtue of obedience and chastity, is auspicious for women, but not for men.

Six at the top line; conservation is disturbed by vibration, and it is dangerous.

The image; thunderstorm; the gentleman must stand firm, and not easily change direction.

INTERPRETATION

In this hexagram, the upper part is Lei, indicating thunder; the lower is Xun, indicating the wind. Whenever thunder strikes, the wind must be blowing, just like you always get up at six o'clock every day to run, you must read a book for an hour at night after dinner, you must wash your feet before going to bed every night, you must visit your parents at least one weekend a month, and you must deposit some dollars into your bank account monthly, and so on. Everyone is faced with a huge number of people and things in their life, the world is complicated, but certain things are regularly done, you are doing the same thing, which is constant. What is this called? Heng is perseverance.

In this regard, the sage offered the following:

First; everything is not expensive and constant at the beginning, but it is costly to change your direction.

Second; when you are uneasy about the ambiguity and uncertain of the future, it is better to stick to it than to be impetuous.

Third; that being capricious is a lack of character and will achieve nothing, and you be looked down upon.

Fourth; perseverance is a road that can go to the dark side, and will take you far from the middle path. This of course is risky and has a huge opportunity cost. But has there been any success without any risk in the world?

Fifth; soft is easy; being firm is hard.

Sixth; perseverance should also conform to temperament and not be overly forced. The sage said, 'A gentleman cannot make things the easy way', we must stand firm and hold ourselves in order to set ourselves up and to do what we have to do.

The essence of perseverance lies in not changing direction, not shaking the mind, and not stopping. Do not change direction.

There are three points: one is finding a direction, the second is that it must be correct, and the third is not to change it. The right direction is of the utmost importance. Confucius said, 'The study of strange doctrines is injurious indeed'. The smarter you are, the easier it is to go wrong. How to make sure the direction is right? Generally speaking, for things that are common sense, legal, and moral, it should not be a problem. Otherwise, the more persistent, the more trouble. Do not shake your mind.

There are two points: one is to have a set intention, and to have this understanding of life, worldview, values, morals, methodologies, etc. Of course, the sage certainly wants you to base this on Confucianism; the Second is to wish for nothing, those things that are destined not to be, do not look at them again. Do not stop. Do not be afraid to travel thousands of miles, be afraid of stopping half-way; do not be afraid if you are not slow, be afraid of not making progress every day. Why worry?

Why has China's corruption, and the many systemic problems been criticised when it has developed so rapidly over the last thirty years? Many foreign scholars are puzzled by this. In fact, the secret lies in "Heng", being persistent. Over the past three decades China has not changed its direction, has not shaken its mind, has not stopped its pace and has ensured its development with a steady sense of stability. According to the *Tao Te Ching*, to rule a large country is like cooking a small fish, it is not possible to turn the fish frequently when frying it or the fish will fall apart. Only by not tossing and turning can we develop. The rule of Han Emperors Wen and Jing (179–143 B.C.) also benefited from this, and left a famous political allusion: slavishly follow precedent. Cao Shen succeeded Xiao He as prime minister. All the policies made by Xiao He were continually unchanged, maintained, and unwavering. Therefore, the rule was eased. Many local governments today do not do well in this regard. The mayors changed too often. The new officials come up with new ideas to show off their ability. As a result, there was no continuity in policies. A lot of work and investment were abolished before they were effective, and all previous achievements were abandoned.

The story of the turtle and rabbit race reflects a reality: the person with the highest I.Q. is not the most successful, and most of the successful people are people with an average I.Q. and a low starting point. These people choose to persist because they had no other way to go. They braced themselves and finally succeeded. A smart-start person is too flexible, and can easily turn to another road when encountering difficulties. Then, when he encounters a bump on that road and turns again, he gives up and finally does nothing.

Zeng Guofan talked about three qualities of success: ambition, insight, and perseverance. Ambition means having goals and directions; insight means having methods and abilities; consistency means integrating the first two items to ensure that skills are used to achieve this goal in the same direction.

Dun:

Take a step back

CLASSICAL TEXT

Dun; indicates successful progress in its circumstances. To a small extent, it will still be advantageous to be firm and correct.

Six at the First line; shows a retiring tail. The position is perilous. No movement in any direction should be made.

Six at the Second line; suggests its subject holds his purpose fast, as if by a thong made from the hide of a yellow ox, which cannot be broken.

Nine at the third line; of one retiring but bound to his distress and peril. If that person was retrained in a similar way as a servant or concubine, it would be fortunate for him.

Nine at the Fourth line; its subject is retiring, notwithstanding his liking. In a superior man. This will lead to good fortune; a small man cannot attain to this.

Nine at the Fifth line; suggests its subject retiring in an admirable way. With applied wisdom, there will be good fortune.

Nine at the top line; shows its subject retiring in a noble way. It will be advantageous in every respect.

The image; the trigram representing the sky, and underneath the mountain form Dun. The superior man, in accordance with this, keeps small men at a distance, not by showing that he hates them, but by his dignified gravity.

LITERAL TRANSLATION

Dun; in order to survive, the weaker needs to retreat.

Six at the First line; retreat when it is all over. It is dangerous to remain there. Leave!

Six at the Second line; tie with a rope made of yellow leather, no one can undo it.

Nine at the third line; if there is a relationship, and cannot retreat, there will be illness and danger, keep your little piglets tied up.

Nine at the Fourth line; there are some options, but you need to concentrate on a single goal.

Nine at the Fifth line; there is a reward when seeing through a matter until the end.

Nine at the top line; going far and finding an enclave to retreat without any disadvantage.

The image; mountains under the sky; a gentleman should stay away from villains, so they can plot without engendering evil

INTERPRETATION

In this hexagram, the upper part is Qian, indicating the sky; the lower is Gen, indicating the mountain. Someone looking at the horizon, the mountains are undulating, beyond the reach of authorities, whilst the autumn wind is gradually rising. The person who leans against the wind will inevitably develop a "defeated look" of tiredness, and at the same time, a feeling of longing for the distance and fantasies of freedom. Let us go, move on, escape this troubled and complicated place, and live a quiet and leisurely life.

I cannot blame myself for attempting poetry. Similar stories have such beautiful themes. The two most famous stories happened in the Wei and Jin era, where Lao Zhuang's thoughts prevailed. One is of Zhang Jiying. *Zhang Jiying appointed by prince Qi as superior official of the Eastern region of Luo. Feeling the autumn wind, he said, "Life is so valuable, how can you constrain yourself thousands of miles away just to get the title?"* He then returned home.

The other story; *Tao Yuanming (365–427), a scholar, famous for his distaste of official life. Come back! The fields and garden will be overgrown with weeds, shall you not go back? Not only do you force your heart to servitude, but aren't you sad?* I cannot admonish this, knowing that doing so can be traced back to my state. Going the wrong way gets you further away, that is how one can realise that one has been wrong in the past.

Alas, the original meaning is to escape, concede, and retreat. Generally speaking, these meanings fit well with Taoist thinking.

Lao Tzu said, 'That when he became famous, he retired to follow the way of heaven'. History is constantly evolving. The Yangtze River's back waves push the old ones, and so the new push the old. Once you are successful, it is time to step down and let someone else succeed. If you do not take the initiative, others will push you down. This is the way of heaven. Therefore, after Zeng Guofan laid down Nanjing City, he immediately withdrew the Xiang Army, letting his brother lead for the opportunity to show his talent. Fan Ye did the same. After the kingdom of Wu was annihilated, he immediately brought Xi Shi to become a hermit; Wen Zhong was greedy for the fruits of victory and died miserably in the end. Zhang Liang also went back home immediately after helping Liu Bang save the (known) world. At the peak of one's success, resolutely retire from one's career; this is what the sage called a "Good Retreat".

What is it called, when retiring in times of crisis? It is called "follow all the possible schemes to find the way out", Zhang Jiying mentioned it was, and it was the case at his time.

What is it called, when you are placed in an awkward position when there is no meat to eat and nothing to give up? It's called "retreat in order to advance", and the so-called "shortcut to official-doom", that is what it means. To be hopeless and with no hope to be promoted. He quit and retreated to the south. Then, the king summoned him and returned him to the Third rank. Although Tao Yuanming was not recalled as an official, he became a great celebrity through the ages, and this hexagram also influenced him.

The sage also said a few things about Dun:

First; when it is time to retreat, retreat, sooner rather than later.

Second; if you avoid it, you will suffer.

Third; is that too much care, emotional affection, and indulgence will be exhausting physically and mentally. However, it is worth to do so for family and true friends.

Fourth; there is no endless feast. No matter how happy you are, you must be prepared to leave.

Fifth; retreating from time to time is like selling vegetables when they are fresh, you can sell them for a good price. Resolutely retire at the peak of one's career for the satisfaction of everyone.

Sixth; if you want to flee, you can only go so far, if you are to retreat, you will have to be clean, do not argue this point.

The sage believed that the most fundamental benefit of this is to keep "far from the villain and evil". Stay away from villains, but even if you hate them, you will not show it, to avoid the villain from hurting.

In short, if you take a step back straying from the subject, at least you will protect yourself, and you may have unexpected gains.

Da Zhuang:

In the prime of life people often despair

CLASSICAL TEXT

Da Zhuang; indicates that under the conditions, which it symbolises, it will be advantageous to be firm and correct.

Nine at the First line; shows its subject manifesting his strength in his toes. But advance will lead to evil most certainly.

Nine at the Second line; suggests that with applied wisdom there will be good fortune.

Nine at the third line; in the case of a small man, one using all his strength; and in the case of a superior man, one whose rule is not to do so. Even with applied wisdom, the position would be perilous. The exercise of strength in it might be compared to the case of a ram butting against a fence, and getting its horns entangled.

Nine at the Fourth line; shows a case in which applied wisdom leads to good fortune, and occasion for remorse disappears. We see the fence opened without the horns being entangled. The strength is like that in the wheel-spokes of a large wagon.

Six at the fifth line; one who loses his ram-like strength in the ease of his position. But there will be no occasion for remorse.

Six at the top line; suggests one who may be compared to a ram butting against a fence, unable to either retreat or advance as he should. There will not be an advantage in any respect, but if he realises the difficulty of his position, there will be good fortune.

The image; the trigram representing heaven and above is that for thunder form Da Zhuang. The superior man, in accordance with this, does not take a step, which is not according to propriety.

LITERAL TRANSLATION

Dazhuang; Great strength correctly applied.

Nine at the First line; evil forces are still operating, not strong enough. Fidgety feet and bad luck ahead.

Nine at the Second line; loyal and persevering, auspicious.

Nine at the third line; evil forces are still operating, not strong enough. The ram hits the fence, and the horns get entangled

Nine at the Fourth line; keep good fortune on your side, a ram butts the fence and breaks free, the wheel of the cart is strong and can roll far.

Six at the fifth line; lost ram at the border of the field, let them go free.

Six at the top line; the ram butted the fence and got stuck. It is a difficult situation, but auspicious.

The image; thunder over the sky forms Da Zhuang. The gentlemen must break the norms.

INTERPRETATION

This hexagram is formed by Lei in the upper part, indicating the thunder, and the lower is Gan, indicating the sky. Above the blue sky, thunder rang throughout the world. This reminds me of the crazy character in *Transformers Megatron*. This hexagram has a strong and magnificent feeling, so the sage named it Da Zhuang.

Here we will find a problem. From the first hexagram to "Da Zhuang", there are more than thirty hexagrams. And there are actually "Da You," "Da Chu" and "Da Zhuang," all three containing "Da" (Big). What does this mean? It shows that the main target of The *Book of Change*s at that time was the highest class of aristocracy, and most of them were in this state.

The sage pointed out that when you are strong, you should pay attention to the following points:

First; you must not rush into it.

Second; is to take the right path.

Third; that a wise person will not rely on his strength, or on acting arrogantly, because then, even if others are helpless, they will get hurt themselves. Zeng Guofan said, 'When you are prosperous, think about when you were not and those who are still there'.

Fourth; if you do not do the first thing, you will never finish the second. Once we have chosen a distant place to be, we only care about wind and rain.

Fifth; you do not need to pay too much attention to some harmless losses.

Sixth; no matter what level a person is, he or she may always face an involuntary situation. At this time, we must keep in mind, difficulty has its upside.

China's richest man, Zong Qinghou, when appointing his daughter to take over his business, told her, 'Maintain a hard-working ethos'. Zeng Guofan said, 'Children of a family holding financial rank, live and eat the same as those of a poor family; hopefully, they will become outstanding talents; but if they are contaminated with lofty habits, they can hardly be successful'. Mao Zedong, Deng Xiaoping, Jiang Zemin, Hu Jintao, and Xi Jinping also all emphasised that the ruling party must fully understand this point. The stronger you are, the more you cannot relax, and you cannot do all you fancy.

In the end, the sage's summary was, 'do not go against politeness'. How to understand this? Let us review a little story first: After Liu Bang (founder of the Han dynasty) consolidated his domain, Lu Jia talked to him every day about the benefits of *The Book of Songs* and *The Book of Shang* for the country. Liu Bang was one who hated Confucianism deeply.

When he heard someone speaking some kind words of righteousness and morality, he would take off that person's hat and get angry, so fed up was Liu Bang with Confucianism. Lao Tzu came to illustrate the relationship with these poems and etiquette? Lu Jia had already prepared for this; he said to Liu Bang, 'You took over the world by storm, which is not wrong, but do you still think that will work to govern it?' The Shang Dynasty and the Zhou Wu emperor of the Zhou Dynasty. Both can be passed on to their descendants for hundreds of years, as relying on loyalty and obedience. Both civil and military are useful skills in the long-term.

When rebelling against the old powers, they had bare feet but not afraid to wear shoes; by hook or by crook they will go to any length to achieve what they wanted. But after taking over the world, it was different: First, their role changed, from rebels to rulers; then, the main problems they faced changed, from military issues to economic issues. Therefore, it is necessary to change your mindset from entrepreneurship to business-oriented. When conducting business, do not be impolite and do everything in accordance with the rules, play your cards in accordance with the rules, step by step, and being honest and prudent. This is the most robust and the least risky way. But if you follow the rules when you are small and weak, you may not have a chance to rise.

In addition, in terms of personal cultivation, gaining self-control makes you strong. People with a high degree of restraint are free from the influence of desires and emotions, self-denial and revenge, and have a clear mind when doing things. Such people are also called "Da Zhuang" (The strong ones).

Jin: It's not easy coming forward

CLASSICAL TEXT

Jin; In Jin, we see a prince who secures the tranquillity of the people presented on that account with numerous horses by the king, and three times in a day received at interviews.

Six at the First line; shows one wishing to advance, and at the same time, kept back. Let him be firm and correct, and there will be good fortune. If trust is not reposed in him, let him maintain a large and generous mind, and there will be no error.

Six at the Second line; the appearance of advancing, and yet of being sorrowful. If he is firm and correct, there will be good fortune. He will receive this great blessing from his grandmother.

Six at the third line; suggests the subject is trusted by all around him. All occasion for remorse will disappear.

Nine at the Fourth line; this subject with the appearance of advancing, but like a marmot. However, firm and correct he may be, the position is one of peril.

Six at the fifth line; regret to die, to have nothing to lose, go to good luck.

Nine at the top line; one advancing his horns. But he only uses them to punish the rebellious people of his city. The position is perilous, but there will be good fortune. However firm and correct he may be, there will be an occasion for regret.

The image; the trigram representing the earth and that for the bright sun coming forth above it form Jin. The superior man, according to this, gives himself to make more brilliant his bright virtue.

LITERAL TRANSLATION

Jin; the marquis was received three times by the king and was rewarded.

Six at the First line; the efforts to be promoted did not bear fruit, remain calm and generous, there is no blame.

Six at the Second line; strived hard to be promoted, but now feel sad, luck will come. You might receive a great blessing from the Queen Mother.

Six at the third line; everyone approves of you; do not doubt yourself.

Nine at the Fourth line; moving forward like a rat, be careful.

Six at the fifth line; recover your losses, do not worry about what you lost, follow your heart, it will be auspicious.

Nine at the top line; you have been promoted and can now command troops to the offensive. Although it is dangerous, it is auspicious, and there is no blame in it, you might have a chance to make amends later.

The image; the sun over the earth, the gentleman's virtue comes to light.

INTERPRETATION

In this hexagram: the upper part is Li, indicating a fire or the sun; the lower is Kun, indicating the earth. A fiery sun rises from the horizon. The sage, feeling motivated, named this "Jin", which means promotion, enterprising, outstanding, superior. People get promoted, no matter whether in public service or in a company, everyone wants to climb up: the clerk wants to be the section chief, the section chief wants to be the chief authority; Seniors want to be masters, and masters want to be professors.

For this, the sage summed up a few ideas:

First; for each gain, the skin will peel. Competition is brutal, and winning comes at a price. This is a purgatory process that helps people mature. When you first start, you should have patience. After all, you are not known by others, and others do not know how much you matter.

Second; is that noble people can help you to win the top position and gain success! Do not be complacent when you go up. Be extra careful.

Third; is that winning people's respect and recognition is the real success. However, in most cases, the winner is the prince and the loser a bandit; people only respect the winner, regardless of how he wins.

Fourth; is that without diamonds, do not discard the porcelain work. It is not necessarily a good thing to squeeze into a certain class or position without the corresponding strength and ability. If your ability is suitable for being an engineer, and you have to be an officer and do management, be sure you will not make a fool of yourself. Many people, like Julian Sorel in Stendhal's novel *Red and Black*. Trying to quickly ascend by drilling right on top of your head might seem the fastest way, but in the end, it will be a tragedy.

Fifth; if you struggle upward, you will get a lot of things, and you will undoubtedly lose a lot of things. Do not look back, walk boldly, forget the past, and look to the future.

Sixth; the high place or name is not the purpose. What we want is to unleash our full potential with richer resources. The office is risky, but the officer makes it worth it. Otherwise, it is holding down a job without doing a stroke of work, do it right or get out of there.

When you achieve a new level, the people will feel that their status has been challenged and threatened, and they will step on you. And then people around you will be like crabs in a basket. When a crab tries to climb up, the other crabs will drag it down. Unless you greatly exceed the original person holding your new position or push the other crabs away.

The same is true of the rise of a country. Therefore, in this upward struggle, we must first rely on ourselves, develop self-confidence, and show our strengths, talents, and virtues so that leaders, colleagues, and subordinates can see them too. Then they might help you. You can volunteer to serve, but without showing off. Keep it low-profile, or it will be counterproductive. It is best to show people by doing and facts, than by saying. Do not complain about having a frustrated talent if people do not see your talents at all. Who is it to blame? Use your brains and let them see! Remember, your positive aura is only lit by yourself!

Ming Yi: Facing darkness

CLASSICAL TEXT

Ming Yi; indicates that in the circumstances, which it denotes, it will be advantageous to realise the difficulty of the position, and maintain applied wisdom.

Nine at the First line; the subject, in the condition indicated by Ming Yi, flying, but with drooping wings. When the superior man is in turmoil, he will go away, he may be without food for three days. Wherever he goes, the people there may speak derisively of him.

Six at the Second line; shows its subject, in the condition indicated by Ming Yi, wounded in the left thigh. He saves himself by the strength of a swift horse and is fortunate.

Nine at the third line; suggests, in the condition indicated by Ming Yi, hunting in the south, and taking the great chief of the darkness. He should not be eager to make all correct at once.

Six at the fourth line; shows its subject just entered into the left side of the belly of the dark land. But he is able to carry out the mind appropriate in the condition indicated by Ming Yi, quitting the gate and courtyard of the lord of darkness.

Six at the fifth line; is how the count fulfilled the condition indicated by Ming Yi. It will be advantageous to be firm and correct.

Six at the top line; shows the case where there is no light, but only obscurity. Its subject had at first ascended to the top of the sky; his future shall be to go into the earth.

The image; the trigram representing the earth and that for the setting sun, forms Ming Yi. The superior man, in accordance with this, conducts his management of men; he shows his intelligence by keeping it obscured.

LITERAL TRANSLATION

Ming Yi; a light at the end of the tunnel

Nine at the First line; damaged in flight, not eating for three days.

Six at the Second line; wounded in the left leg while roaming in the light, then rescued with a strong horse.

Nine at the third line; darkness is coming to an end; the leader of a rebellion can turn things in the right way.

Six at the fourth line; you can be aware of problems while being in the dark; if you remain uncorrupted, you can escape from it.

Six at the Fifth line; a light in the dark, it is important to keep shinning while everything seems dark.

Six at the top line; it was not bright and gloomy, you reached to the sky, and finally fell underground.

The image; a light after a tunnel, the gentleman knows he needs to keep going.

INTERPRETATION

In this hexagram, the upper part is Kun, indicating earth; the lower is Li, indicating fire and light. The light is hiding beneath the ground; the sage called it "Mingyi". Yyi" is, raise to the ground, meaning to level and destroy. The light has been buried, that is, darkness is everywhere, in official matters, political matters, social matters, or future matters. Confucius mentioned this issue many times in The *Analects*, such as, "When bad government prevails, he can roll his principles up, and keep them in his breast". When corrupt government prevails, irreproachable conduct that exposes the coming generations to danger. When corrupt government prevails, the refined and valuable fall in disgrace. We do not need to delve into the meaning of these words. At least we can see that the dark problem of "statelessness" was often faced by people at the time. So, what should we do? The sage shares his experience:

First; it is important to save your life. Do not be decent when you run away.

Second; there must be a road to the front of the mountain, and a boat that goes straight to the other shore. When topography is too complicated and the way not clear, a village seems like a gleam of hope in a desperate situation.

Third; there is an opportunity in the midst of danger and great opportunities.

Fourth; if you do not enter the tiger's lair, can you hunt a tiger? When it is time to take a shot, take a shot.

Fifth; if something is difficult, it is probably worth it.

Sixth; everything will pass, just like a strong wind does.

To sum up, there are only three options: One is to escape. Just like when the King of Shang was politically in the darkness, it was useless for ministers and nobles to say anything, loyal ministers were either tortured or chased away. So King Zhou Wu had to constantly fight, and the nobles had to escape, it is said that they fled to North Korea and brought the culture and blood of the Shang Dynasty.

Whilst escaping, a great man's downfall becomes like a master-less dog. It is normal for people to reject them. You do not have to flee to another place; you can also stay in place and act crazy, even eat faeces if you must. Such people are by no means rare.

Second; is deliverance. Do not be rushed by external forces.

Third; is to endure. Although the sun goes down, it will rise sooner or later. There are countless dark periods in history. What fatuous and self-indulgent monarchs, evil ministers ruling the state, the chaos of war, and epidemic; those who are in it are like in purgatory, but as Lao Tzu said, 'The wind does blow all day, rain does not fall forever'. This kind of extraordinary period will not last long, hold on!

The sage's thoughts do not stop there. He can always see the positive from the negative. He said that 'The gentleman comes to the public with both obscurity and clarity'. This has several meanings:

First; like in the dark, when you light a match, it will be dazzling. Leaders should seize the opportunity to light the match.

Second; leaders should hide their wisdom. This has many benefits. First of all, if you are too wise, and you are too careful about everything, subordinates' ingenuity and subjects initiative will not be exerted. Zhuge Liang (181–234 BC) encountered this problem, not only exhausted himself but also did not use his full potential.

Third; when you show your wisdom, you will inevitably expose your blind spots. This will let your subordinates see through you and come up with a way to trick you. In the end you will be controlled by others. Once again, one should not be too fault finding, without purpose. The so-called ignorance is bliss, do not hear, do not talk, do not see, have a deep truth. Both Taoists and Legalists exerted this kind of thinking.

Jia Ren: Learning to live

CLASSICAL TEXT

Jia Ren; For the realisation of what is taught in Jia Ren, or for the regulation of the family, what is most advantageous is that the wife is firm and correct.

Nine at the First line; shows its subject establishing restrictive regulations in his household. An occasion for remorse will disappear.

Six at the Second line; shows its subject taking nothing on herself, but in her central place attending to the preparation of the food. Through her applied wisdom, there will be good fortune.

Nine at the third line; showing its subject treating the members of the household with severity. There will be an occasion for remorse, there will be peril, but there will also be a good fortune. If the wife and children were to be smirking and chattering, in the end, there would be an occasion for regret.

Six at the fourth line; showing its subject enriching the family. There will be good fortune.

Nine at the Fifth line; the influence of the king extending to his family. There need be no anxiety; there will be good fortune.

Nine at the top line; its subject possessed of sincerity and arrayed in majesty. In the end, there will be good fortune.

The image; the trigram representing fire, and that for wind coming forth from it, forms Jia Ren. The superior man, in accordance with this, orders his words according to the truth of things, and his conduct so that it is consistent.

LITERAL TRANSLATION

Jia Ren; Domestic qualities are an advantage.

Nine at the First line; stay home and lock your doors, or there will be regret.

Six at the Second line; stay home and prepare food, it will prove auspicious.

Nine at the third line; better to be strict than get humiliated for being frivolous. There is a risk but will prove auspiciousness.

Six at the fourth line; this shows its subject enriching the family. There will be great good fortune.

Nine at the Fifth line; the king is in the castle, his virtues are safe.

Nine at the top line; integrity and majesty are earned, the result is auspicious.

The image; wind over a fire, the gentleman talks and acts upon those words with perseverance.

INTERPRETATION

In this hexagram, the upper part is Xun, indicating fire; the lower is Li, indicating fire. In the evening, everyone in the village starts a fire to cook. Above the roof, the smoke drifts upwind. Teresa Teng's affectionate song *Seeing the smoke again* is a picture of this scene, who would not want to be home? Therefore, the sage named this hexagram "family" (Jia Ren) and believed that "the wife must be firm and correct", in which the woman determines the quality of the family, and the true face of the family:

First; they need to teach the children, and women should learn this and how to set up house rules.

Second; wives who can cook can make a household prosper. As the saying goes, to get to a man's heart, first get to the man's stomach.

What is home? Home is not merely a house. Houses are everywhere. The home where we fulfil all daily necessities, it is a family eating around a table with at least two mouths together. Therefore, it is important that women can cook.

Third; is that couples are not enemies, though they do fight. This is what people have summarised through countless family cases for thousands of years. There is no reason. The truth is this. Loving couples, who have never had really bad arguments in their lives, either leave an old lady alone for many years or leave an old man alone in his old age. There is an old couple in our village. At the age of ninety, they quarrelled for decades. Those who advised him shouted, 'You still fight, who cares if you kill your wife? The old man stopped on the spot, but his wife did not cook for three days. Couples that hit each other for a lifetime indicate that they are relatively stubborn people. At least there is a tough wife, and such a wife is generally of a prosperous family. For example, Liu Bang's wife was powerful, and there are many big-name wives who were powerful. Many of the company bosses I know are husbands and wives, and their other "better halves" are all known as "board chairmen." Of course, you have to fight smartly. Even after a fight, or bedside quarrels; you cannot fight your heart off, no matter who is doing it, it is not easy to lose your head together.

Fourth; poor couples are sad. Many quarrels are due to tight schedules, and while slowly getting wealthier, there is less worry and fighting. There is a saying: the tenderness of his wife is directly proportional to the talent of men. Try Harder!

Fifth; the home is a place of emotion, not a place of reason. Have a little more trust, leave some privacy and space for each other, do not go through each other's chat conversations!

Sixth; run the house strictly. There are filial sons raised by the stick. To the child, the more you hit him and control him strictly, the more he respects you in the future. Thinking back to our student days, those teachers who controlled us strictly left deep impressions. After being beaten by them, we rarely remembered hatred but were more grateful. Moreover, it is necessary to establish rules early. Zeng Guofan once said, 'Teach a child to behave, teach a wife to come first', educate a child from a very young age, and teach a daughter-in-law to start from the moment of marriage.

However, for the family, what the sage emphasised in the end was this, "A gentleman should act upon his words, and be constant with his actions". This is the finishing touch! For family members, "acting upon one's words" embodies mutual respect. Naturally, husbands and wives must use tender words. Still, in general, they should have something else to say, tell the truth, and live a real life. Be constant in your actions. What needs more long-term business commitment than a family? Home is a lifelong career. Even after seven years of itching and painstaking efforts, we must support a family. As a man in the family, it is not easy to achieve what you say and what you want. It takes effort and improvement. This is self-cultivation. Once you have cultivated your body, you will be able to teach, and it will be easier to run a family. You will be able to deal with all kinds of relationships and affairs in society. Starting from this sentence, the Confucian observes, 'Cultivate one's moral character, govern family, administer a country, and peace will be on earth' – this is the core of Confucianism.

Kui

Same same but different

CLASSICAL TEXT

Kui; indicates that, notwithstanding the condition of things, which it denotes, in small matters, there will still be a success.

Nine at the First line; that to its subject occasion for remorse will disappear. He has lost his horses, but let him not look for them – they will return. Should he meet with bad men, he will not err in communicating with them.

Nine at the Second line; shows its subject happening to meet with his lord in a bye-passage. There will be no error.

Six at the third line; we see one whose carriage is dragged back, while the oxen in it are pulled back, and he is himself subjected to the shaving of his head and the cutting off of his nose. There is no good beginning, but there will be a good end.

Nine at the Fourth line; its subject solitary amidst the prevailing disunion. But he meets with the good man represented by the first line, and they blend their sincere desires together. The position is one of peril, but there will be no mistake.

Six at the fifth line; shows that to its subject occasion for remorse will disappear. With his relative and minister, he unites closely and readily as if he were biting through a piece of skin. When he goes forward with this help, what error can there be?

Nine at the top line; reflects its subject, solitary amidst the prevailing disunion. In the subject of the third line, he seems to see a pig bearing on its back a load of mud, or fancies there is a carriage full of ghosts. He first bends his bow against him, and afterward unbends it, for he discovers that he is not an assailant to injure, but a near relative. Going forward, he shall meet with congenial rain, and there will be good fortune.

The image; the trigram representing fire above, and that for the waters of a marsh below, forms Kui. The superior man, in accordance with this, where there is a general agreement, admits diversity.

LITERAL TRANSLATION

Kui; estranged can only do small things.

Nine at the First line; bad luck is not your fault, your horse returns of its own accord. Meeting with the wicked will not make you one.

Nine at the Second line; there is no blame on meetings in the alleyway.

Six at the third line; it is difficult to haul a large cart. When the cart and oxen halted, it is not good at first, but the results will be good.

Nine at the Fourth line; while in isolation, encountering her eldest husband, intersect of good faith, dangerous but harmless.

Six at the fifth line; joining in the feast the ancestral temple. What harm can come from it?

Nine at the top line; feelings of guilt, loneliness, and scepticism when seeing a pig's back full of mud. Facing an archer who wanted to shoot, but then lowered his bow. Not a robber, but to someone coming to propose something auspicious.

The image; the trigram representing fire above, and that for the waters of a marsh below, forms Kui. The superior man, in accordance with this, looks for common ground while accepting the differences.

INTERPRETATION

This hexagram is formed by [Li] on top, meaning the fire, and [Dui] below, which is the lake. The fire is burning upwards, while the lake is below, seemingly together, but yet apart. So the sage named the hexagram "Kui", and the word was explained in the first Chinese dictionary (compiled by Xu Shen in 121 A.D.) as "eyes cannot look at each other". Two persons were passing each other on the road, ignoring each other. There is a good pun in Chinese that cannot really be translated into English coming from the above definition and the modern word for perverse. "Kui" nowadays in understood as some sort of bad person.

In life, if there is someone who likes you, there must be someone who does not. Everyone likes you only if you are a golden coin. The reverse is also true. Some people fall in love at first sight, smile at each other, never have opposing views, and interact with each other like clouds and rivers, naturally close to the warmth, but there are also some people who look at you awkwardly, avoid them. So, how do you deal with people who are bad to you?

In this regard, the sage has the following insights:

First; the reason why you hate someone is often because of something that makes you prejudiced against him. You should try to forget the unpleasant things, eliminate this prejudice, and then look at it with your usual heart; you will find that he or she may not be bad, and is still a good person.

Second; is that with those who you once hated, you must be able to get along. Through some indirect communication, you can improve the relationship. Private communication is important, especially if it is sensitive, do not gossip with others.

Third; is that you hate this and hate that, in the end, it can only be that you bother the world and the world bothers you, and you become a lonely person. To block the way of others is to block your way.

Fourth; is that people's hearts are all big, and frank exchanges of hearts can feel vulnerable, but they are more likely to win the trust and favour of the other party and strive to open their minds.

Fifth; is to find a way to have a meal together.

Sixth; suspicion is when there is tension and opposition between people. Suspicion is a disease that makes people distrust and lose objective judgment. When you start to hate someone, see if you happen to have prejudice.

Finally, the sage held a strong proposition: the same, but different. In this regard, a more recent understanding is: seek common ground while shelving differences. In The *Book of Change*s commentaries, it is said that know how to act in unison, birds of a feather flock together. Everyone likes people who are the same or similar to themselves. All fans of Li Yuchun are close to each other; they are bothered by the same thing, and they are sympathetic to each other; they all like Huang Shangu's calligraphy, they are happy to talk to each other; if they hold the same view on a problem, they feel that they are supporting each other, etc. Therefore, in dealing with people, we must be good at emphasising the same aspects of each other, shelving or ignoring differences in other aspects.

A deeper understanding is: harmony comes from different sounds. On the one hand, there is also an attraction between different people, repulsion of the same sex, the attraction of the opposite sex, heaven attracts the earth, and women attract men. People have different fears of rejection caused by strangeness, but also curiosity and even yearning for people who are different from themselves. Conversely, people who are surrounded by people alike will lose their creativity. A diverse, complementary, and even contradictory ecosystem is best for survival and development.

Jian: The difficulties of the journey

CLASSICAL TEXT

Jian; in the state indicated by Jian, the advantage will be found in the south-west, and the contrary in the north-east. It will be advantageous to meet with the great man. In these circumstances, with firmness and correctness, there will be good fortune.

Six at the First line; we learn that advance on the part of its subject will lead to greater difficulties while remaining stationary will afford ground for praise.

Six at the Second line; the minister of the king struggling with difficulty, and not with a view to his own advantage.

Nine at the third line; its subject advancing, but only to greater difficulties. He remains stationary and returns to his former associates.

Six at the fourth line; shows its subject advancing, but only to greater difficulties. He remains stationary and unites with the subject of the line above.

Nine at the Fifth line; offers, its subject struggling with the greatest difficulties, while friends are coming to help him.

Six at the top line; the subject going forward, only to increase the difficulties, while his remaining stationary will be productive of great merit. There will be good fortune, and it will be advantageous to meet with the great man.

The image; the trigram representing a mountain, and above it that for water, forms Jian. The superior man, in accordance with this, turns around and examines himself, and cultivates his virtue.

LITERAL TRANSLATION

Jian; It is favourable to retreat; it is not to advance. Look for wise man's advice.

Six at the First line; going forward is difficult, retreating will gain a good reputation.

Six at the Second line; kings and ministers work hard, not solving a problem of their own

Nine at the third line; the way forward is blocked, go back to safety.

Six at the fourth line; it is difficult to go forward, so it is to retreat, but it can be done with help.

Nine at the Fifth line; moving is difficult. Friends come to help.

Six at the top line; going forward is difficult, and returning can be fruitful and successful; it is good to seek wise advice.

The image; water over the mountain; the gentleman will turn back to cultivate virtue.

INTERPRETATION

This hexagram contains: in the upper part is Kan (the abysmal), indicating the water; in the lower part is Gen (Stillness), indicating the mountain. For a traveller, it is not easy to travel through mountains on winding roads. If there is a river above the mountain, you cannot carry a boat up, and this river is impossible to navigate. Therefore, the sage named this hexagram as "Jian", which means, cannot get through.

In life, there are always many ways to go; many things are uncertain; there are always many people who cannot change his heart. What to do?

The sage believed that different people and different situations should have different approaches:

First; is that moving a step forward will get you to the end of your rope, while retreating you stray from the goal. Now that there is a dead-end in front of you, simply move back and change to another road.

Second; is that great people do not avoid difficulties, regardless of success or failure, knowing that they cannot do it, knowing that there are tigers in the mountains, they still will go to the mountains. Just like Premier Zhu Ji's famous saying, 'No matter whether it is a minefield or a mighty abyss, I will always go forward, without hesitation, bow down and die.

Third; the road ahead is difficult, not the normal way. People will always want to return to a bland life. After pacifying the Taiping rebellion, Zeng Guofan gifted a couplet to his brother, who was the first general of the Hunan Army: In the years of fiery flames, do not forget to keep a calm heart and read books to cultivate yourself. To renounce the pen for the sword is an unusual choice; the essential characteristic of a scholar is to read.

Fourth; the way comes out of people's hearts. If the heart is dead, wherever he will go will be lost.

Fifth; if you are tenacious and unyielding in the face of difficulties, you will definitely get help from your friends.

Sixth; those who have experienced hardships, whether on the battlefield or in the markets, once they work their way up to officialdom, can make achievements. However, the sage believes that for most people, when facing the difficulties of the road ahead, they should "turn to their morals."

This sentence can be understood as follows: refining and cultivating, then facing the challenge. Why not? There are many reasons, but the root cause must be the core problem. This is the attitude of the Confucian school. When facing a problem, we must first reflect on ourselves! Introspection is divided into two aspects: First, is the skill – is there true power and true ability? The second is in the aspect of being a good person, first needs to have a clear conscience. Can that person be patient enough? Introspection is not difficult. The difficulty is to implement it. The problems introspected must be resolved immediately, and immediate action must be taken. If you could not get through the road, you have to find a way, how can you not lose something on the way? It is time-consuming and painful to return to the origin for refining, but as long as you persist, you will be reborn! Or, to do the opposite. If a road does not work, does not take you where you want to be, well, all roads lead to Rome, find another way. If you are unsure about something, it means that you are not good at it, not suitable, and simply should do something else. People cannot change their minds, might as well replace the person altogether. Without that person, we can still make it. Where in the world, have you not see the grass grow? God closed a door for you, and of course, opened another at the same time. In fact, more than one door, the whole world is open to you. If you lose a tree, you get the whole forest. Planting flowers intentionally without success might inadvertently plant willows with good shade. When you cannot get through, you must make a comprehensive reflection, change your mind, think, and change your mood. The world is so big! The sea is wide; the sky is high where birds fly. You will suddenly be cheerful.

Therefore, there is no big deal if you cannot get through. If the above two points are fully understood, then as the hexagram indicates, "good fortune" belongs to you. Brother, do not worry, take your time!

Jie: Enmity should not endure, is better to squash enmity rather than keeping it alive

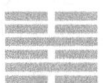

CLASSICAL TEXT

Jie; Here, the advantage will be found in the south-west. If no further operations are called for, there will be good fortune in coming back to the old conditions. If some operations are called for, there will be good fortune in the early conducting of them.

Six at the First line; reflect the subject will commit no error.

Nine at the Second line; its subject catch, in hunting, three foxes, and obtain the golden arrows. With applied wisdom, there will be good fortune.

Six at the third line; a porter with his burden, yet riding in a carriage. He will only tempt robbers to attack him. However firm and correct he may try to be, there will be cause for regret.

Nine at the Fourth line; Put one foot forward. Friends will then come, between you and whom there will be mutual confidence.

Six at the fifth line; its subject, the ruler, executing his function of removing whatever is injurious to the idea of the hexagram, in which case there will be good fortune, and confidence in him will be shown even by small men.

Six at the top line; here we see a feudal prince with his bow shooting at a falcon on the top of a high wall, and hitting it. The effect of his action will be in every way advantageous.

The image; the trigram representing thunder and that for rain, with these phenomena in a state of manifestation, forms Jie. The superior man, in accordance with this, forgives errors and deals gently with crimes.

LITERAL TRANSLATION

Jie; retreat if necessary; follow the path of least resistance.

Six at the First line; if you must, do it now, there is no blame.

Nine at the Second line; the hunter gets three foxes and is rewarded with a golden arrow.

Six at the third line; carrying baggage on top of a carriage invites bandits to rob. Beware of regret.

Nine at the Fourth line; take the first step, friends will come to help.

Six at the fifth line; the gentleman should be free and in doing so, inspires others.

Six at the top line; the prince shot a hawk on the high wall.

The image; thunder over water. Forgive yourself and others; free yourself from sin.

INTERPRETATION

This hexagram contains: in the upper part is Zhen (the arousing), meaning thunderstorm; the lower is Kan (the abysmal), indicating water and rain. In the long dry season, a thunderstorm is like a stalemate between heaven and earth being resolved. Therefore, the sage named this hexagram as "Jie". Many Chinese words contain this character: relax, unwind, solve, resolve, liberate, and reconcile. The extension to personnel matters is to "forgive sins," to forgive faults, and tolerate crimes to resolve opposition or hostility.

In this regard, the sage said a few things:

First; reconciliation should come sooner rather than later.

Second; reconciliation generally benefits multiple parties, and previous conflicting experiences will also become a valuable experience after reconciliation. For example, when a couple is divorcing, as an outsider, people should advise. Reconciliation means that they will find the best solution. Rather demolish ten temples than to destroy a marriage.

Third; is that catching contradictions, problems, or small braids and letting go, often cause accidents. Especially among relatives and friends, it is the least worthwhile to hold a grudge because of a dispute over money, interpersonal resource are wasted, health is affected by anger, and the loss will be much greater than that.

Fourth; is that the enemy should eventually be forgiven. You did not do him any good, but by letting him go you can let him know your feelings, it is definitively worth the price you might have to pay because of it. During the Warring States Period, Meng Tajun had a little boy, and he was left to die because there were already over forty children. Meng Tajun, however, was raised by his mother in secret. A few years later, Meng Tiajun was rescued, and he proved to be a very intelligent asset.

Fifth; we must be flexible in doing things, be able to make appropriate compromises, and be gentle with people who oppose us so that they do not make trouble for themselves.

Sixth; reconciliation is a brilliant art, and it is a great wisdom that can resolve embarrassment or stalemate and crisis. With this ability, there is no way to be defeated.

The sage also said that your thoughts complicate things. Some people only find themselves problems. Just be honest and do not need to overthink things.

This is a world full of contradictions, opposites, and conflicts. Darwin's findings are interesting: On the one hand, he saw the cruel nature of natural selection, the battle of the weak and the strong; and on the other hand, he discovered that this cruelty promotes the progress of species!

The wolf on the prairie is the natural enemy of sheep, but if the wolf is completely eliminated, it is not good for the sheep either. Therefore, for the cruel things we have experienced in life, the schemes of evil people, the attacks of enemies, the bullying of the wicked, the bragging of the strong, the betrayal of friends, all of these, the moment when we experience them is, of course painful. Yes, but at this experience from a more detached and higher level, you can find that it is normal, almost necessary, and this is the way of life, and all this is more experience for you, the most experience you have the more powerful you become! Therefore, in the process, people who stand on the opposite side should be taken lightly. They are just the equivalent of an extra in a movie, who inadvertently plays a role in your life. Buddhism has studied this. It refers to these people as "retrograde Buddhas" in your life.

Think of it this way; you no longer need to carry the burden of that painful memory; you can easily reach out to that person and shake hands and talk. This is not only reconciliation but also a liberation of the soul.

Lu Xun has a famous poem: Brother's who cross paths as enemies, they meet each other with smiles. Japan invaded China and killed tens of millions of people. How much hatred is this? How could it be possible to re-establish diplomatic relations? Germany also brought a terrible disaster to Europe. How could it be pardoned? Can everyone with scars forget the pain? Maybe, but if we look at history, there are too many situations like this: during the Warring States Period, one day was peaceful, the next will be overwhelming; in the late Han Dynasty, the Sun and Liu Alliance defeated Cao Cao (155 – 220) today; later they would share spoils of war together. There are no eternal friends, only eternal interests. Reconciliation is usually good for everyone, and peace and development are the mainstream. But today's reconciliation means tomorrow's conflict, and all we have to do is make this "tomorrow" come later rather than sooner.

Of course, in daily life, it is not so heavy. People are not sages, and who can live without them? Small frictions between colleagues, small misunderstandings between friends, and small misunderstandings between husband and wife, we are all a bit dramatic; think about each other's goodness, take the initiative to break the deadlock, apologise, and take responsibility. If you do not have this kind of spirit, you do not deserve to learn about the *Book of Change*s, haha. In addition, it is a contradiction to look down with your head up. What it was originally a laughing matter escalates when you make it bigger than it is.

There is also another problem mentioned in the hexagram of Jie: it is often the villain's provocation that then turns into conciliation. This is what we should pay attention to, especially not to be such a villain yourself.

Sun: Life should be minimalistic

CLASSICAL TEXT

Sun; Here, if there be sincerity in him who employs it, there will be great good fortune: freedom from error; firmness and correctness that can be maintained; and advantage in every movement that shall be made. In what shall this sincerity in the exercise of "Sun" be employed? Even in sacrifice, two baskets of grain, though there be nothing else, maybe presented.

Nine at the First line; shows its subject suspending his affairs, and hurrying away to help the subject of the fourth line. He will commit no error but let him consider how far he should contribute to what is his own for the other.

Nine at the Second line; that it will be advantageous for its subject to maintain applied wisdom, and that action on his part will be evil. He can give an increase to his correlate without taking from himself.

Six at the third line; this shows how three men walking together, the number is diminished by one, and how one, walking, finds his friend.

Six at the fourth line; this shows its subject diminishing the ailment under which he labours by making the subject of the first line hasten to his help, and make him glad. There will be no error.

Six at the fifth line; parties adding to the stores of its subject ten pairs of tortoise shells, and accepting no refusal. There will be good fortune.

Nine at the top line; shows its subject giving increase to others without taking from himself. There will be no error. With applied wisdom, there will be good fortune. There will be advantage in every movement that shall be made. He will find ministers more than can be counted by their clans.

The image; the trigram representing a mountain and beneath it that for the waters of a marsh forms Sun. The superior man, in accordance with this, restrains his wrath and represses his desires.

LITERAL TRANSLATION

Sun; There is no blame in having only the basics; it is good to simplify. Two bowls of rice are enough.

Nine at the First line; do what you need to do and move on quickly, do not overextend matters.

Nine at the Second line; advance but not all the way to the front, for your duties without looking for higher gains.

Six at the third line; one person gains support, and three people move together, they should act as one person.

Six at the fourth line; let the fever diminish, do not rush to get things done.

Six at the fifth line; a gift of valuable tortoiseshells is a great help from friends.

Nine at the top line; simplification is accomplished, you can now go after good fortune without looking to take from others.

The image; mountain over a lake, the gentleman does more with less.

INTERPRETATION

This Hexagram is formed by [Gen] on top, meaning the mountain, and [Dui] below, which is the lake. The lake slaps at the foot of the mountain, eroding the mountain day after day, year after year, and damaging the mountain. Therefore, the sage named this hexagram "Sun" (loss), which means to reduce, to lose, and to reduce. Human nature is good or bad, and the first impression of "loss" will feel negative, but in the eyes of a sage, there will be great good fortune – freedom from error, firmness, and correctness that can be maintained, which are all good things. This is also the main idea of Taoism. Lao Tzu said: For practicing the Tao every day, let go until you have nothing to do, and things will just be. Life is good in minimalism. A simple heart and simple matters are enough to live a noble life, such as Zhuangzi. Zhu Geliang called, "Frugality helps to develop simple and diligent moral conduct".

In this regard, the sage has several opinions: First, leave room for everything, do not be too full, do not seek perfection, and do not add more stuff to the bucket list.

First; for everything there should always some space for improvement. The first rule of weight loss is, do not put on weight.

Second; is that everything, whether profit or loss, increase or decrease, all has an intrinsic cost and should not be forced blindly. This is how one can lose weight, just as a company cuts jobs.

Third; is that there is plenty to lose for getting to heaven and less to make up for it. (I deeply doubt about this heaven. Oh!)

Fourth; is that happiness is the real wisdom of life.

Fifth; what is reduced today, will secretly return. For example, if you do good, the more you donate, the more you will earn. This is divine law.

Same as rewards, the more you reward, the more the employees earn back for you.

Sixth; some things are not lost by giving them to others. Why are you not happy? Like laughter and love!

Then; the sage looks further at how the mountain was eroded from the lake water in the Hexagram and thought of the infringement of human emotions and desires on the body, so he reminded people to "curb one's temper and desires", meaning, to suppress anger and control sexual desire. This captures the key to health and mind, and is also the root of self-cultivation. Zeng Guofan attaches great importance to this Hexagram. He often educates his children to "beware of the inner dragon and tiger, conquer one's passions and be careful of losing one's temper". Here, the "dragon" and "tiger" also refer to the spirit and desire.

People get sick mainly because of anger and lack of desire. When angry, the energy in the body is not smooth, as if something is always pressing on the heart, the blood flow seems to have slowed down, and we can feel the whole body functioning differently. As time goes on, you are likely to develop a slow chronic disease or a tumour.

Desire is insatiable, and indulgence of sexual desire will certainly not last long. Many emperors died on it, like Ximen Qing in The Gold Vase Plum novel, who also died because of it.

From the perspective of traditional Chinese medicine, anger is a liver problem, and sexual desire is a kidney problem. Modern people's problems occur mostly in these two organs.

When something happens, it is often because you cannot control the fire (excess yang energy) and cannot control your "lower mind". A young man with a strong temperament fights without thinking and may destroy his life and that of others. Be patient, save your energy. The more you can save it, the more you have for self-development. Han Xin could not tolerate His Majesty's insults, while Chiang Kai-Shek reminded himself, "be patient" every day.

Heroes have problems when it comes to beauty; they have a hard time enduring it, so beautiful spies are always the most efficient. The Buddhists spoke of precepts. It was said that when the gods tried to test Shakyamuni, they sent a group of beauties to entice him. He said that these beauties were just "skins and blood", and nothing more, human skins with bones and only flesh and blood. Ah, how horrible! As the saying goes, lust is the poison of life. Think of these words of horror. I hope you can stop and remember that at the hour of truth.

Furthermore, besides lust and desire, there are many things that may damage our bodies and minds, and some of them are not even easy to detect. The significance of the Hexagram is to remind us that in life, we must learn to reduce and to throw away and minimise all those bad things and burdens.

Yi: Life shall provide

CLASSICAL TEXT

Yi; indicates that in the state which it denotes there will be advantage in every movement which shall be undertaken, that it will be advantageous even to cross the great stream.

Nine at the First line; suggests that it will be advantageous for its subject in his position to make a great movement. If it is fortunate, no blame will be imputed to him.

Six at the Second line; shows parties adding to the stores of its subject, ten pairs of tortoise shells whose oracles cannot be opposed. Let him persevere in being firm and correct, and there will be good fortune. Let the king, having the virtues thus distinguished, employ them in presenting his offerings to God, and there will be good fortune.

Six at the third line; shows increase given to its subject by means of what is evil so that he shall be led to good, and be without blame. Let him be sincere and pursue the path of the mean, so shall he secure the recognition of the ruler, like an officer who announces himself to his prince by the symbol of his rank.

Six at the fourth line; its subject pursuing the due course. His advice to his prince is followed. He can, with advantage, be relied on in such a movement as that of removing the capital.

Nine at the Fifth line; its subject with a sincere heart seeking to benefit all below. There need be no question about it; the result will be good fortune. All below will, with a sincere heart, acknowledge his goodness.

Nine at the top line; here we see one to whose increase none will contribute, while many will seek to assail him. He observes no regular rule in the ordering of his heart. There will be evil.

The image; the trigram representing wind, and that for thunder form Yi. The superior man, in accordance with this, when he sees what is good, he will move towards it; and when he sees his errors, he turns from them.

LITERAL TRANSLATION

Yi; It is good to follow your plans, it is better if there is a river crossing involved.

Nine at the First line; time to pursue big things, there no regret in it.

Six at the Second line; someone sent a treasure of tortoiseshells, you cannot refuse it, it is a good thing. The king makes offerings to the goods and it was auspicious.

Six at the third line; gain something through misfortune, the sincerity of the jade seal (the official authority) will grant it.

Six at the fourth line; you have done your duty, now have the authority to participate in moving the capital of the kingdom.

Nine at the Fifth line; honesty is the right path, do not ask for gains, virtue is its own reward; it will make people treat you with good faith and goodwill.

Nine at the top line; constantly expanding is an invitation to get attacked. Get yourself straight and then help others.

The image; thunder below the tree or the wind. The gentleman recognises the right moment for action.

INTERPRETATION

In this hexagram, the upper part is Xun, indicating wind; the lower is Zhen, indicating thunder. Wind produces thunder, thunder alters wind; they benefit each other. Therefore, the sage named this hexagram as "benefit", which means gain, growth, and increase.

If I ask you, 'Is it better to increase or decrease?' You probably are not able to answer because, depending on what it is, of course, it might be good or bad; a salary increase is good, and an increase in the degree of myopia is bad. The sage saw the hexagram of "Yi" and was entangled with similar issues. He offered a few points:

First; if people want to make a big difference, they must strengthen their skills, increase their resources, and improve their tools.

Second; access to wealth and other resources mainly depends on the blessing of heaven.

Third; avoiding loss is a basic means of increase. One point saved is one point earned. It is necessary to work hard where possible.

Fourth; that everyone has higher ambitions, and it is necessary to mobilise as many people as possible to work for a certain gain.

Fifth; is to give a token of affection to beauty in the form of beautiful words. Emotion is the same as material. The more you give, the more you gain, to high input, high output, no input, no output.

Sixth; when there is nothing to gain, be calm and persistent. There is a bottleneck period for everything. It will stay there for a long time. If you stick to it, you will finally arrive at a new level. In addition, insatiable greed must suffer.

From the perspective of the ruling class, the sage warned: increasing may not be a good thing. The ruler and the ruled are often playing a zero-sum game. There are only so many benefits. When you increase the number of opponents, the number of enemies decreases. Imperceptibly, people's hearts are lost. On the other hand, when there is no harm to the people, the people are happy, when the ruler voluntarily gives up some interests, and does not compete with the people for profit, and hides wealth from the people, only then will the people will be happy and support him. Of course, it is not the ruler's problem only; it has been replaced by "the nation". As far as the country is concerned, it is better to use tax leverage less. Regardless of everything, if it is regulated through tax increases. In the end, it is bound to hurt the interests of those at the bottom. At present, the biggest burden on Chinese people is rising house prices. The root of this problem lies in the fact that the country's tax-sharing system concentrates taxes on the central government. Local governments can only increase their income by selling land, thereby pushing up land and house prices.

However, when the sage summed up the hexagram of "Yi", he focused on cultivation. "A gentleman changes for good, and changes one's life first." Life must be constantly changed and evolving. Increasing might be good, but decreasing might also benefit.

The simpler the truth, the harder it will be. Generally speaking, the distinction between good and evil, right and wrong, good and bad is a conscience instinct, and everyone can do it. Such as hard work is good, laziness is not good; helping others is good, harming people is evil; loyalty is right, cheating is wrong; smoking is bad, gambling is bad, masturbation is bad, and so on. But often, we know exactly what is right, but we do not follow through. This is really the biggest problem in life.

What "Curbs one's temper and desires" is in the "Sun" hexagram, "change one's evil ways and reform" is in the "Yi" hexagram. Both are important for self-cultivation.

The curbing of one's temper and desires is something you do from within, and on the outside, where the body and mind are cultivated, decreasing of "evil ways" applies. Increase within, decrease outside; that is the way of self-cultivation. The reason is simple and clear, do your best.

Guai:

About stress

CLASSICAL TEXT

Guai; requires in him who would fulfil its meaning the exhibition of the culprit's guilt in the royal court, and a sincere and earnest appeal for sympathy and support, with a consciousness of the peril involved in cutting off the criminal. He should also make an announcement in his city, and show that it will not be well to have recourse at once to arms. In this way, there will be an advantage in whatever he shall go forward to.

Nine at the First line; shows its subject in the pride of strength advancing determination. He goes forward, but will not succeed. There will be grounds for blame.

Nine at the Second line; offers its subject full of apprehension and appealing for sympathy and help. Late at night, hostile measures may be taken against him, but he need not be anxious about them.

Nine at the third line; suggests its subject is about to advance with strong and determined looks. There will be evil. But the superior man, bent on cutting off (the criminal), will walk alone and encounter the rain, until he is hated by his proper associates as if he were contaminated by the others. In the end, there will be no blame against him.

Nine at the Fourth line; shows one from whose buttocks the skin has been stripped, and who walks slowly and with difficulty. If he could act like a sheep following its companions, an occasion for remorse would disappear. But though he hears these words, he will not believe them.

Nine at the Fifth line; the small men like a bed of porcelain, which ought to be uprooted with the utmost determination. The subject of the line having such determination, his action, in harmony with his central position, will lead to no error or blame.

Six at the top line; shows its subject without any helpers on whom to call. His end will be evil.

The image; the trigram representing heaven and that for the waters of a marsh mounting above it form Guai. The superior man, in accordance with this, bestows emolument on those below him, but dislikes allowing his gifts to accumulate because of lack of use.

LITERAL TRANSLATION

Guai; Have courage in your convictions, take the matter up with the king's court.

Nine at the First line; stumbling forward in a rush to get ahead.

Nine at the Second line; be alert to call signs, there are soldiers placed on guard in the twilight, so do not worry.

Nine at the third line; struck on the cheek and walking under the rain, danger. The gentleman was determined to walk alone and wetting his clothes in the rain. Pride and anger should not compromise your commitment.

Nine at the Fourth line; lead sheep to surrender, you should listen and not disobey.

Nine at the Fifth line; dealing with lower tasks, do not have bad influence, and there should be no regret.

Six at the top line; without warning, evil is removed, be prepared for an unexpected disaster.

The image; lake over the sky. It is about to rain, the gentleman prepares for disclosing his intentions, self-righteousness is counterproductive.

INTERPRETATION

This hexagram is formed by Dui (The Joyous) in the upper part, indicating the lake, and the lower is Qian (The creative), indicating the sky. When the lake reaches the sky, it is unstoppable and must fall. The sage living near the Yellow River may have a thought of a terrifying scene of a Yellow River flood, like a lake falling from the sky, so he named this hexagram "Guai" (the Break-through).

There is a sense of tension in the Chinese words containing this character: duel, split, prognosis, decisiveness, decision. The hexagram "Guai" is about this tension.

The sage emphasised the following:

First; one should be decisive but not arbitrary.

Second; is to be fearful when it comes to serious situations and get through them.

Third; mood and anger are invisible, do not let others notice your determination and thoughts.

Fourth; is that when you are mature, you must dare to stand by the crowd, or stand-alone, overcome difficulties and have the courage to stick firm to the end.

Fifth; decisions must be made according to your word.

Sixth; take responsibility. Yes, if something is inevitable, even if you win, you will pay the price.

Above all, when you decide to take various decisive actions to break the status quo, such as breaking up, divorcing, tearing up an agreement, betrayal, dissident, etc., think about it.

The sage does not encourage people to take extreme measures in tension. Instead, they believe that leaders should work hard to eliminate tensions, to avoid sharpening conflicts, and to prevent problems before they occur. The relationship is tense, mostly because of interests. Therefore, leaders should "dislike allowing his gifts to accumulate unutilised".

Water is the main source of wealth, and a hexagram with water ascending seems like money being poured into the pocket of the person above. And partaking, do not think of it as a favour you do to others, that is also sharing the risk. You should look at it with your usual heart; your sharing is justified! Wealthy people, famous officials of all generations, or the founders of corporations, all understand this. The so-called heroes, do you think they are stingy in terms of money? In short, if you can take the initiative to share benefits, relationships will not be too tense. Of course, benefits come in various forms. In addition to money, there are all kinds of things that people like, such as influence and reputation. Be a hog, and you will be the target of public criticism; when you share, you will be a good friend.

Gou: Life is just like a First meeting

CLASSICAL TEXT

Gou; shows a female who is bold and strong. It will not be good to marry such a female.

Six at the First line; shows how its subject should be kept like a carriage tied and fastened to a metal drag, in which case with applied wisdom there will be good fortune. But if he moves in any direction, evil will appear. He will be like a lean pig, which is sure to keep jumping about.

Nine at the Second line; the subject with a wallet (treasury) of fish. There will be no error. But it will not be well to let the subject of the First line go forward to the guests.

Nine at the third line; suggests one from whose buttocks skin has been stripped so that he walks with difficulty. The position is perilous, but there will be no great error.

Nine at the Fourth line; the subject with his wallet, but no fish in it. This will give rise to evil.

Nine at the Fifth line; the subject seems as a medlar tree with fruit on it. If he keeps his good qualities concealed, a good issue will descend as from Heaven.

Nine at the top line; the subject receiving others on his horns. There will be an occasion for regret, but there will be no error.

The image; the trigram representing wind, and that for the sky above it forms Gou. The sovereign, in accordance with this, delivers his charges and promulgates his announcements throughout the four quarters of the kingdom.

LITERAL TRANSLATION

Gou; the woman is too powerful, do not marry her.

Six at the First line; stopped with a brake of iron, like a free ranging swine that needs to be reign in.

Nine at the Second line; there are still fish in the kitchen, do not give them away to guests.

Nine at the third line; you are injured and staggering from weakness, it is dangerous to move forward, but there is no major blame.

Nine at the Fourth line; there are no more fish in the kitchen, a dangerous situation arose.

Nine at the Fifth line; a melon wrapped with wolfberry leaves, which has a subtle beauty and is like it fell from the sky.

Nine at the top line; locking horns, regrettable, but not your fault.

The image; tree under the sky; the king is about to issue an order.

INTERPRETATION

In this hexagram, the bottom line is Yin, and the top are five Yang lines, so countless researchers from ancient to modern times have interpreted them in unison: one woman with five men. A woman has relations with five men. Is this group sex? In my opinion, this is the typical otaku thinking. Based on this, how can it penetrate the mind of the sage? The sage is a hermit. What he sees in this hexagram is "there is wind in the world": the upper part is Qian, which means heaven; the lower part is Xun, which means wind. Under the vast sky, the wind blows, buffeting the branches of the willow, buffeting the grass, buffeting eyelashes, and buffeting your soul, like a random encounter. Therefore, the sage named this hexagram as "Gou", meaning "meeting", to meet people, or to meet opportunities.

The most beautiful moment in life is to meet someone you love. Like in the movie *Love in a Puf* (A Chinese chick-flick), or *Finding Mr. Right*, or the classic *Dream of the Red Chamber*... In countless movies and novels, the moment when a man and a woman first met or reunite, those were the ones that most moved the audience. Of course, it does not have to be the encounter of men and women. When Sun Wukong met Tang Seng, and then met Zhu Bajie, when Zhou Wenwang met Jiang Ziya, when Zhang Liang met Huang Shigong, and when Yu Boya met Zhong Ziqi, it was equally promising. Just as the sage said, "that the heavens and the earth meet, they produce all that is valuable". The poet Qin Guan (1049–1100) said that, 'When the autumn winds blows dewdrops, it happens everywhere without people noticing". Of course, not all encounters are so beautiful. When Pan Jinlian met Simon Qing, when Dongfan Bubai met Lingwu Chong, when the beautiful woman met the satyr, those were tragedies. In addition, the sage made it clear that "strong women", vixens, adulteress, and such women, should not marry.

Whether it is tragedy or comedy, all stories begin with encounters. In this regard, the sage has several views:

First; love at first sight cannot be trusted, so be careful. When you see a good person or opportunity at first, you will be excited. You will not have room for thinking in your head. At this time, remind yourself to hold back a little.

Second; is that opportunities favour only prepared minds. Before you meet, you have to convince yourself that you hope or want to avoid something, you will eventually meet that, so you must prepare in advance.

Third; there are many hardships and many opportunities in challenges.

Fourth; is that good craftsmen do not show simplicity. If you are not ready, do not rush into it. If the product is not ready, the more successful the marketing, the worst it will fail.

Fifth; natural talents will be useful. With whatever talent you have, there will be opportunities. It is gold that will shine, sooner or later.

Sixth; a wife is not like a mistress, a mistress is not like a prostitute, a prostitute is not like thief, a robber is not like a hiding thief. There is a time before you are married, flowers bloom and decay. Do not be afraid to go out because you are afraid to meet a ghost. Only by going out, meeting more people, and meeting more things can life be richer and more exciting, and there will be unlimited possibilities for development. It is okay if you cannot get out. The sage said, 'The king delivers his charges, and promulgates his announcements throughout all directions'. You may not be able to travel around the world in person, but you can let your thoughts spread infinitely, and you can meet with countless people. For business, the Gua hexagram should give a lot of inspiration: no matter what medium you use – the Internet, TV, newspapers, as long as you try to "meet" with as many people as possible, you may make the most money. There are also modern marketing masters who call this "networking".

For men, the most beautiful encounter is to begin casually and to end in romance. Therefore, the end of this section must be romantic. The song of Liu Ruoying in the movie *A World Without Thieves* is similar to this hexagram: "the wind is blowing, where have you been? When I think of you, I look up and smile, you know why…"

Cui: Avoid crowded places

CLASSICAL TEXT

Cui; here, the king will repair to his ancestral temple. It will be advantageous to meet with the great man, and then there will be progress and success, though the advantage must come through applied wisdom. The use of great victims will be conducive to good fortune, and in whatever direction movement is made, it will be advantageous.

Six at the First line; shows its subject with a sincere desire for union, but unable to carry it out, so that disorder is brought into the sphere of his union. If he cries out for help to the right people, all at once, his tears will give place to smiles. He need not mind the temporary difficulty; as he goes forward, there will be no error.

Six at the Second line; its subject led forward by his correlate. There will be good fortune and freedom from error. There is sincerity, and in that case, even the small offerings of the vernal sacrifice are acceptable.

Six at the third line; suggests its subject striving after the union and seeming to sigh, yet nowhere finding any advantage. If he goes forward, he will not err, though there may be some small cause for regret.

Nine at the Fourth line; shows its subject in such a state that, if he is greatly fortunate, he will receive no blame.

Nine at the Fifth line; the union of all under its subject in the place of dignity. There will be no error. If any do not have confidence in him, let him see to it that his virtue be great, long-continued, and firmly correct, and all occasion for remorse will disappear.

Six at the top line; shows its subject sighing and weeping, but there will be no error.

The image; the trigram representing the earth and that for the waters of a marsh raised above it form Cui. The superior man, in accordance with this, has his weapons of war in good repair, to be prepared against unforeseen contingencies.

LITERAL TRANSLATION

Cui; A place for offerings, the virtues of the king is shown. Keeping the ancestral temple is conducive to meeting important people. Assemble around the shrine and make offerings.

Six at the First line; uncertain about joining in the offerings, no need to be afraid. Decent people will not laugh at you when you ask for help to get out of your confusion.

Six at the Second line; gaining guidance, present your offerings with sincerity.

Six at the third line; in a gathering, feeling rejected, no blame to leave, and go somewhere else.

Nine at the Fourth line; great auspiciousness, no blame.

Nine at the Fifth line; gathered with high people, there is no blame. Not everyone will follow; some will go their own way.

Six at the top line; weeping and wailing is not your fault.

The image; the lake resting on the earth; the gentlemen should repair weapons and guard against accidents.

INTERPRETATION

This hexagram is formed by Dui (The Joyous) in the upper part, indicating the lake, and the lower is Kun (The receptive), indicating the earth. Above the earth, ditches and rivers converge into rivers and lakes. Among the rivers and lakes, there is lush vegetation with birds and beasts roaming by the water. The sage, therefore, saw the image of the congregation, so he named this hexagram "gathering together", which means gathering, gathering, coming together, etc., that is, many people come together or a lot of wealth. In this regard, the sage considers:

First; people should have a shared conviction or a commonly recognised authority to maintain balance, or else they will be disorderly, and gang formation will occur.

Second; when the hearts of the people are aligned, something of great importance happens. Unity is a strength.

Third; people must be able to tolerate and compromise with each other and maintain a balance between various interests.

Fourth; there are many people, and some are powerful, but everyone must gather firewood for the pyre.

Fifth; find out where you are in the crowd and put a clear label on yourself. Success will not be far behind.

Sixth; people sympathise with the vulnerable, so showing vulnerability is a kind of wisdom. Liu Bei (founder of the Han Kingdom) could not beat people into supporting him.

The sage has anxiety in his mind. He believes that no matter whether people gather and wealth gathers, they may face many contradictions and threats, internal or external. Therefore, on the one hand, he emphasised that "the king will repair to his ancestral temple". And that means that religion should be used to educate people's hearts; on the other hand, it is necessary to "be prepared against unforeseen contingencies". Meaning to prepare war weapons to guard against unexpected dangers.

If the country gathers a large population and wealth, it must have an army. In Sun Tzu's *Art of War* he states that, "The art of war is of vital importance to the State. It is a matter of life and death, a road either to safety or to ruin". Strong soldiers must protect rich countries.

Personally, we should be inspired: first, the more money we have, the more we need to strengthen self-protection measures. Wherever wealth is, that is where the people go; when you have money, someone will remember you and try to figure you out.

Li Ka-Shing's son was abducted, and it took 1 billion to pay his ransom. One year later, the kidnapper did another hit, and a rich man in Hong Kong paid 600 million in ransom.

Do not stand in crowded places. There is a joke: I was at a crowded bar the other day. Suddenly a man fell and stopped breathing. The waitress yelled out, "does anybody know CPR?" I yelled back, "I do! I know the entire alphabet!" We all laughed. Well, except for that one guy. Because there are many people in crowded places, there are more dangers, more benefits, more guns and fires, more pickpockets, more perverts, more scammers, more stomping feet, more vehicles; bad things can happen, and so on. In addition, when many people gather together, they will be affected by the emotions of the mass on the one hand, and feel invincible on the other hand.

Violent checks and balances are necessary. The United States cannot help but shoot. Guns are banned in China, but ordinary homes still have anti-thief systems.

In short, in the face of "Cui" (Gather together), we must strive to keep ourselves safe and avoid being harmed. Gathering and scattering are big problems in life. There is "Cui" that is about getting together, but is there any hexagram that talks about scattering? Yes, of course, there is, in the "Huan" hexagram, please take a look.

Sheng: The two cruxes of growing up

CLASSICAL TEXT

Sheng; indicates that under its conditions, there will be great progress and success. Seeking by qualities implied, to meet with the great man, its subject need have no anxiety. Advance to the south will be fortunate.

Six at the First line; shows its subject advancing upwards with the welcome of those above him. There will be good fortune.

Nine at the Second line; its subject with that sincerity, which will make even the small offerings of the vernal sacrifice acceptable. There will be no error.

Nine at the third line; suggests its subject ascending upwards as into an empty city.

Six at the fourth line; shows its subject employed by the king to present his offerings on mount Qi. There will be good fortune; there will be no mistake.

Six at the fifth line; its subject is firmly correct, and therefore enjoying good fortune. He ascends the stairs with all due ceremony.

Six at the top line; shows its subject advancing upwards blindly. Advantage will be found in ceaseless maintenance of applied wisdom.

The image; the trigram representing wood and that for the earth with the wood growing in the midst of it forms Sheng. The superior man, in accordance with this, pays careful attention to his virtue and accumulates the small developments of it until it is high and great.

LITERAL TRANSLATION

Sheng; do not fear to meet with an important person.

Six at the First line; good fortune coming early.

Six at the Second line; sincerity is good for sacrifice, there will come no harm.

Nine at the third line; taking over of an empty city.

Six at the fourth line; the king is worshipped at the sacred mountain, it is a hard climb, there is no blame.

Six at the fifth line; one step at a time, keep ascending.

Six at the top line; climbing into the darkness, keep moving and keep virtuous.

The image; tree under the earth. The gentleman's accomplishments are small, but he remains virtuous.

INTERPRETATION

This hexagram is formed by Kun (The Receptive) in the upper part, indicating the earth; the lower is Xun (The Penetrating), indicating the wind. Trees grow from the ground; they keep growing and keep rising. Therefore, the sage named this hexagram as "Sheng," which means to increase and grow.

Regarding growth, the sage made a few points:

First; when everything is just beginning, growth is the most obvious. From birth to puberty, the child grows taller within a few days. Learning from everything, from knowing nothing to half-knowledge, is the most noticeable improvement. The so-called "law of diminishing returns" in economics is also the reason.

Second; is that sincerity in spirit, confidence, and belief are conducive to growth.

Third; there will be an accelerated period of growth after achieving an accumulation of the initial capital when learning the basics of a new skill.

Fourth; is to create an environment conducive to growth and to win the support of the gods and people.

Fifth; strive for progress while maintaining stability.

Sixth; by forming a good habit and a good growth system, life and career can be like planting a tree. Without deliberate management, it will still grow. The sage pointed out that the key to growth lies in "the virtue docility, accumulation of small steps", this applies to both the growth of people and the growth of careers. Virtue docility is the first two sentences in *The Doctrine of the Mean*, "What Heaven has conferred is called Nature; an accordance with this nature is called The Path of Destiny Duty". Growth must conform to a gifted personality and bring it into play naturally. You get what you sow. Melons will always grow like melons, and beans will always grow like beans. When the seeds of melon are grown into a big and sweet melon, this is the virtue docility. But if more people like beans and the seeds of a melon want to grow into beans, this is not virtue docility. Obama said that, 'The significance of primary and secondary education is to let children discover what they really like and where their strengths are. Mathematics? Languages? Physical education? Management? Technology? Of course, finding your talents and strengths is not easy, and you may never give it a chance to make it seem less obvious'. How to do it? I have heard lectures from many people, including Steve Jobs, and their approach is, "Listen to your inner voice and trust your intuition".

In terms of children's education, it is possible to do more with less. The same is true for enterprise development. We must carefully evaluate our core competitiveness to organise operations and conduct business; then, we are more likely to win over the competition.

Accumulation from small to large is steady accumulation. To accumulate over a long period, you know what you have, do not spend mindlessly, do not hoard, do not save the pennies and waste the dollars. From these idioms, you can see the ancients paid much attention to "accumulation". Chinese people work hard and focus on savings are aligned on this concept.

This sage's sentence also has two meanings:

First; is a belief that persists in accumulation, no matter how small it is now, it can still grow big!

Second; power does not come out of thin air; it does not happen overnight; it is heartfelt daily input. There is no qualitative change without quantitative changes.

Kun: The six plights of life

CLASSICAL TEXT

Kun; There may yet be progress and success. For the firm and correct, the really great man, there will be good fortune. He will fall into no error. If he makes speeches, his words cannot be made right.

Six at the First line; shows its subject with bare buttocks straitened under the stump of a tree. He enters a dark valley, and for three years, has no prospect of deliverance.

Nine at the Second line; seeing its subject straitened amidst his wine and viands. There come to him anon the red knee-covers of the ruler. It will be well for him to maintain his sincerity as in sacrificing. Active operations on his part will lead to evil, but he will be free from blame.

Six at the third line; its subject straitened before a frowning rock and being tortured. He enters his palace and does not see his wife. There will be evil.

Nine at the Fourth line shows its subject proceeding slowly to help the subject of the first line, who is straitened by the carriage adorned with metal in front of him. There will be an occasion for regret, but the end will be good.

Nine at the Fifth line; the subject with his nose and feet cut off. He is straitened by his ministers in their scarlet aprons. He is leisurely in his movements, however, and is satisfied. It will be well for him to be as sincere as in sacrificing to spiritual beings.

Six at the top line; shows its subject straitened as if bound with creepers, or in a high and dangerous position, and saying to himself, 'If I move, I shall repent it'. If he does repent of former errors, there will be good fortune in his going forward.

The image; the trigram representing a marsh, and below it that for a defile, which has drained the other dry so that there is no water in it, form Kun. The superior man, in accordance with this, will sacrifice his life in order to carry out his purpose.

LITERAL TRANSLATION

Kun; hold on to your convictions, and there should be no blame, what you say is not believed.

Six at the First line; trapped in a dark valley and beaten with sticks for three years.

Nine at the Second line; trapped in drinking and eating, the official has just arrived, which could help you out of the situation. Accepting is risky, but there is no harm to it.

Six at the third line; trapped in the rubble, holding onto thorns, even if at home with your wife, there is danger.

Nine at the Fourth line; crawling along in a bronze carriage, there is regret, but also good results.

Nine at the Fifth line; burdened with official duties, look for ways to cooperate, so conditions improve.

Six at the top line; entangled in vines, there is risk and regret. If there is remorse, it might be auspicious.

The image; water is below the lake. It should be in the lake. The gentleman must sacrifice to realise his aspirations.

INTERPRETATION

This hexagram is formed by Dui (The Joyous) in the upper part, indicating the lake, and the lower is Kan (The abysmal), meaning the water. Under the lake, the water can only be groundwater, indicating that the lake has dried up. This situation has occurred in Sichuan, Guizhou, and other places in recent years. The bottom of the lake cracked, just as a wound on the floor. What happened? A severe drought that happens once in decades, crops were lost, people and livestock did not have enough water, and the people face hardship. Therefore, the sage named this dilemma "Oppression" (Kun) and pointed out six dilemmas in life:

First; when stuck in a position. There is no career, no position, no opportunity, and you are ignored.

Second; is stuck with no money. A penny can stump a great man.

Third; is trapped in all sorts of difficulties, repression, emotion, feelings, or disease.

Fourth; trapped in wealth. If you have money, you will have no time. When you have money, you worry about others hankering after your money.

The daughter of a wealthy man sees greed in the eyes of a suitor and does not see love.

Fifth; stuck in power. Spend a lifetime in power struggles.

Sixth; trapped in the impermanence of fate. We worry about the vines we are hanging onto whilst crossing between the cliffs, and this is up to destiny.

How to face these difficulties? First, you have to accept your fate, and then you have to work hard. During a lifetime, we will inevitably encounter one or two dilemmas, but the refusal of this leads to ineffectiveness. Fortunately, I have not faced such a test so far, perhaps because I'm still a nobody.

Great men must undergo the baptism of life and death, and like the Phoenix, be born again. Just like Sun Wukong (The Monkey King) was trapped in the alchemy furnace of Taishang Laojun, he was also pressed under the five-finger mountain of Rugao Buddha, and after numerous disasters, he finally succeeded in understanding the Buddha. The sage's *Book of Change*s has two characteristics, which are particularly obvious: First, a sense of anxiety. All the promising and peaceful hexagrams, remind people of the risks that may be encountered. The second is optimism. Almost all the hexagrams include light and hope. In terms of this "Kun" hexagram, the sage still believes in "for the firm and correct great man, there will be good fortune." This means that the situation will eventually calm down, and overcoming difficulties will be accompanied by a good reputation. There are two meanings to "making speeches and making no good"; First, when you are in a difficult situation, what you say will not be believed by others, people might think that your promises can no longer be fulfilled; second, when you are in a difficult situation, do not believe what other people say, do not expect others to help you, you have to be firm and rely on yourself! In short, when you are in trouble, it is not helpful to say much, it depends on how you act.

So, how to protect this state of peace? The sage said, 'The superior man, in accordance with this, will sacrifice his life in order to carry out his purpose'. When the mountains and the rivers are exhausted, people must have the courage to let go of their houses, give themselves to fate, and fight for their ideals! The so-called dying for a just cause has historically been done by too many people. Maybe you have to ask if I lost my life in the end, what else can it be "Auspicious" and "Lucky"? If you think of it this way, you will limit your life to seven or eighty years. Life in the eyes of a wise man is "the big life". Living is only a part of life as an eternal precious thing. Wen Tianxiang died but lived forever in posthumous.

From a practical point of view, in a difficult situation, the determination of "to die or succeed" is often the only hope to get out of a difficult situation. Sun Tzu's *Art of War* states that, "there is a life after a certain dead" in a desperate situation, the human potential will be maximised and capable of surpassing the ordinary. Zeng Guofan also believes that many people's success is forced out of either dying or succeeding situations, and finally succeeding. Modern game theory also supports this view. In competition, if you are afraid of dying, everyone will be frightened of you and will make way for you.

Rowling, a single mother in the UK, is the wealthiest writer in the world. However, she had suffered a lot before the publication of her *Harry Potter* series. She said, 'That you never truly understand your potential or your relationship with others without the test of hardship. Being desperate means you can strip away irrelevant things and start using all your strengths for what you consider essential. The lowest point in life is a solid foundation for rebuilding a life. No matter how bad it is, where can you always go? Just let it go!'

Jing

The three virtues of a leader

CLASSICAL TEXT

Jing; Here, we know how a town may be changed, while the fashion of its wells undergoes no change. The water of a well never disappears and never receives any great increase, and those who come and those who go can draw and enjoy the benefit. If the drawing has nearly been accomplished, but, before the rope has quite reached the water, the bucket is broken, this is evil.

Six at the First line; shows a well so muddy that men will not drink of it, or an old well to which neither birds nor other creatures resort.

Nine at the Second line; a well from which by a hole the water escapes and flows away, reaching to shrimps and other small creatures on the grass, or one where the water leaks away from a broken bucket.

Nine at the third line; a well, which has been cleared out, but is not used. Our hearts are sorry for this, for the water might be drawn out and used. If the king were only intelligent, both he and we might receive the benefit of it.

Six at the fourth line; a well, the lining of which is well laid. There will be no error.

Nine at the Fifth line; a clear, limpid well, the waters from whose cold spring are freely drunk.

Six at the top line; the water from the well brought to the top, which is not allowed to be covered, suggests sincerity. There will be good fortune.

The image; the trigram representing wood, and above it, the one representing water forms Jing. The superior man, in accordance with this, comforts people and encourages them to help each other.

LITERAL TRANSLATION

Jing; the village can be relocated, but the well cannot be moved. There is no loss and no gain. Water will need to be transported; it might be dangerous.

Six at the First line; nobody likes to drink from a muddy well, and there are no animals to be caught there.

Nine at the Second line; shooting fish in a well, the bucket is leaking.

Nine at the third line; the well water is clear but is not being drunk. Regret. If the king is wise, people are blessed.

Six at the fourth line; the well is repaired, no misfortune.

Nine at the Fifth line; the well water is clear, everybody can drink from it.

Six at the top line; the well is left uncovered, this is auspicious.

The image; water over wood. The gentlemen should work for the people and encourage people to help each other.

INTERPRETATION

This hexagram is formed by Kan (The Abysmal) in the upper part, indicating water; the lower is Xun (The Penetrating), indicating the wind. Water over wood, how can it become a "well"? The ancient scholars had a lot of trouble reading it, and it was curious. For example, Zhu Xi said, 'that the water in the trees ascends to the leaves through the trunk and leaches into water drops like dewdrops', which is similar to water being drawn from a well, so this hexagram represents a well. It is also said that there were wooden boards at the bottom of ancient wells to separate water from the mud below. That wood at the bottom and water above formed the "well" image. How does the sage think of a "well" from this hexagram? Let us speculate. Here we look at what a well looks like in the eyes of the sage. The sage said that there are three virtues:

First; loyalty, and obedience. "Change the village instead of the well," the village can be relocated to another place, but the well cannot be moved. Where the well is dug, is where it will stay.

Second; dedication and diligence. "No pain, no gain", no one refills the well, and people take water from the well, but the well water is not diminished, and never overflows.

Third; is politeness among equals. "The well comers", a village lives around a well, the well is a bonding spot, all families live separately, and they meet at the well. The well brings people and people's feelings closer.

The sage further said that, 'a gentleman persuades people to work, and works with the people'. Officials should serve the people with the spirit and virtue of the well and promote these virtues among the people to improve the livelihood and promote harmonious development.

If you are an official, you can reflect on this: when you are sent as an official, do you want to take root there or use it as a springboard? Are you willing to give without asking in return or complaining? Do you bring people together?

In addition to these three kinds of "virtues", the sage believes that there are still some problems to which officials must pay attention:

First' there must be no blaming; ideas and practices must not be outdated. It is difficult to be a good person, it is not easy to do good things, and if there is a flaw, it is easy to be smeared and nagged. Alas, this is human nature.

Second; is that if you are talented, capable, and resourceful, you cannot afford to waste your potential; you should win your place for people's sake.

Third; sometimes good intentions are treated as evil intent.

Fourth; be self-cultivation and continuously improve yourself.

Fifth; serve the people with integrity, be upright and just.

Sixth; be bright and clear, hold firm to your beliefs.

Of course, you do not have to be an official. Being an ordinary person, you should also have this spirit, especially "no pain, no gain". When in love, no pain, no gain. Have devotion; it does not cause you to lose anything, so why not?

Ge: Change

CLASSICAL TEXT

Ge; For this hexagram, it is believed in only after it has been accomplished. There will be great progress and success. Advantage will come from being firm and correct. In that case, the occasion for remorse will disappear.

Nine at the First line; shows its subject as if he were bound with the skin of a yellow ox.

Six at the Second line; this subject making his changes after some time has passed. Action taken will be fortunate. There will be no error.

Nine at the third line; that action taken by its subject will be evil. Though if he is firm and correct, his position is dangerous. If the change he contemplates has been three times fully discussed, he will be believed in.

Nine at the Fourth line; shows occasion for remorse disappearing from its subject. Let him be believed in, and though he changes existing ordinances, there will be good fortune.

Nine at the Fifth line; the great man producing his changes as the tiger does when he changes his stripes. Before he divines and proceeds to action, faith has reposed in him.

Six at the top line; the superior man producing his changes as the leopard does when he changes his spots, while small men change their faces and show their obedience. To go forward now would lead to evil, but there will be good fortune in abiding firm and correct.

The image; the trigram representing the waters of a marsh and that for fire in the midst of them forms Ge. The superior man in accordance with this, regulates his astronomical calculations and makes clear the seasons and times.

LITERAL TRANSLATION

Ge; You will be believed when the day comes. With a good cause, the right time, willpower, and a desire to help others, there will be no regret.

Nine at the First line; tied tight with yellow leather rope.

Six at the Second line; the time for a change will come one day, and it will be auspicious and free from blame.

Nine at the third line; discussion about change is dangerous, beware of risk, and prevent danger. Many changes take shape in the hearts of people when acting with integrity.

Nine at the Fourth line; the doubt is gone, it is time for a change, it will be auspicious.

Nine at the Fifth line; great people change as well as ferocious tigers, and they can act virtuously without the guide of an oracle.

Six at the top line; gentleman change as leopards do, they use their camouflage to hunt, and this is dangerous. Remaining calm is auspicious.

The image; fire below the lake. Great men must adjust the calendar and make clear the division in the day and the hour.

INTERPRETATION

This hexagram is formed by Dui (The Joyous) in the upper part, indicating the lake, and the lower is Li (The Clinging), meaning fire. In the middle of winter the lake is covered with thick ice. In the centre of the lake, clusters of withered reeds were lit and soon burned out. The old reeds are burned, and new reeds grow next year. The sage, therefore, thinks of "Ge" (revolution), which means extermination, innovation, change, transformation, and reform, in a word: change. At the national level, there are two variations: reform and revolution. Reform first. If reform does not work or is uncertain, it will instil the revolution — for example, the Reform Movement of 1898. But the kung remained the king, and the Qing Dynasty remained the ruling dynasty. If this reform were successful, Chinese history would inevitably be different, and it would have likely followed a path similar to Japan's constitutional monarchy. The heroes of modern times would have never been what they are, and the suffering or glory encountered would have been different. However, there is no "if" in history. More than ten years after the failure of the reform, the Revolution of 1911 toppled the Qing Dynasty.

The Qing Dynasty and China changed dramatically. Change means breaking a stable state. Can it return to a higher level of stability after breaking? This is risky, so there are always tens of millions of reasons for a counter-reaction. When Shang Yang changed the law, some ministers said, "The benefits are not good enough, and the law is not changed enough; the rule is not completely legitimised, the machinery is not simple". How eloquent. The motivation of the anti-reformer derived mostly from the fact that change is a redistribution of interests that hurt his privilege. Li Keqiang said that it is harder to touch the privilege of someone than their soul. Therefore, reforms of all ages have been difficult, all at the cost of blood. However, the cost of change is relatively small. Be alert!

How to change? The sage believes that:

First; the pursuit of change must not be disclosed, and it must be thoughtful and careful.

Second; it is important to grasp the right timing of the change. If it is too early, everyone has not felt the crisis yet, definitely, do not go on without support; though by the time everyone understands the necessity for a change, it will be too late to move. Nor sooner, nor later, when the time, geography, and harmony are all there, changes occur.

Third; to promote change, we must strive for popular support, and do not be radical. There needs to be stability. The "shock therapy" in the former Soviet Union was too radical and doomed to failure.

Fourth; the change will ultimately require a more profound transformation in the soul and a new faith.

Fifth; change requires a strong iron hand. Dare to do it, stay away from superstitions.

Sixth; change is endless, but it should be done in moderation. It is okay to get talented people, make good people better, and reform bad people. At the personal level, the "three changes" mentioned by the sage are interesting: the villain changes, the gentleman changes to camouflage (like a leopard changes), and the great man becomes like a tiger. The ancients interpreted these three changes in a strange way. I think it can be understood as three levels of change:

> **First**; is that it change is right in our face and will happen. The villain is the most changeable, like Sichuan opera's performance of the face-changer, you will feel like a spring breeze, and tomorrow you will turn ruthless; today you are happy, and tomorrow you will be sad; there is no master in your heart, see how the wind blows.

Second; is that change is in both words and deeds. The knight devotes himself to something for three days to make a change noticeable. The most famous story is Lu Meng, a famous Soochow general in the Three Kingdoms, who was a veteran general. With the persuasion of Sun Quan, he studied earnestly and made progress.

Then, he was astounded by Lu Su's words, 'Do not go back to being a fool'.

Third; is to change the mental structure. Originally an unknown, after studying and practicing for several years, he then became a king. The most fickle in the world are not chameleons, but humans. A little man who, after hard work and being shackled by fate, can turn into a man worthy of worship and accomplish great things.

A great man may also turn around and become a prisoner. Good people will become bad people, and bad people will become good people.

Changing is unpredictable and unsteady; how can we grasp it? In this regard, the sage said that, 'The superior man, in accordance with this, regulates his astronomical calculations, and makes clear the seasons and times'. The calendar must be revised to make clear the solar terms. In this way, people can plan according to the same time. At the right season does the right thing, sowing, harvesting, and offerings; changing then can have a clear trajectory. If we have such a set keeping of seasons in our life, we will be able to understand the right time for development and take the initiative.

However, most of us are too dull and unchanging. When friends from afar call to ask: How are things going? We often answer with a bitter smile, "same old, same old".

Ding: Holding on

CLASSICAL TEXT

Ding; gives the intimation of great progress and success.

Six at the First line; shows the caldron overturned, and its feet turned up. But there will be an advantage in its getting rid of what was bad in it. Or it shows us the concubine whose position is improved by means of her son. There will be no error.

Six at the Second line; this caldron with the things to be cooked in it – if its subject can say, 'My enemy dislikes me, but he cannot approach me', there will be good fortune.

Nine at the third line; the caldron with the places of its ears changed. The progress of its subject is thus stopped. The fat flesh of the pheasant, which is in the cauldron, will not be eaten. But the genial rain will come, and the grounds for remorse will disappear. There will be good fortune in the end.

Nine at the Fourth line; the cauldron with its feet broken, and its contents, designed for the ruler's use, overturned and spilled. Its Subject will be made to blush with shame. There will be evil.

Six at the fifth line; the cauldron with yellow ears and rings of metal in them. There will be an advantage through being firm and correct.

Nine at the top line; the caldron with rings of jade. There will be great good fortune, and all action taken will be in every way advantageous.

The image; the trigram representing wood and above it, that for fire forms Ding. The superior man, in accordance with this, keeps his every position correct and maintains secure the appointment of Heaven.

LITERAL TRANSLATION

Ding; The cauldron, good fortune, and success.

Six at the First line; the cauldron reverses its content, which is suitable for pouring out bad things. No regret.

Nine at the Second line; the cauldron is full; an ill spouse cannot approach me, but it is auspicious.

Nine at the third line; the handles of the cauldron are broken, and it is difficult to move it. The food inside is burning. Rain washes regret away. Eventually, it will be auspicious.

Nine at the Fourth line; the cauldron leg is broken, the king's beautiful food spilled all over, it is now wet and dangerous.

Six at the fifth line; the cauldron has bronze handles, which is good for keeping it upright.

Nine at the top line; the cauldron has a jade carrying rod, which is auspicious and prevents all harm.

The image; the trigram representing wood under the fire forms Ding. The sovereign, in accordance with this, keeps his every position correct and secures the appointment of Heaven.

INTERPRETATION

This hexagram is formed by Li (The Clinging) in the upper part, indicating fire; the lower is Xun (The Penetrating), meaning the wind. A pile of firewood on the fire. Is it a bonfire? Did the sage see people singing and dancing around a campfire? No, the fire that the sage saw was for boiling soup. The ancients' soup was not like today's cooked on a gas stove, but a large cauldron, with large pieces of meat and many ingredients, and cooked on a lower rack. Ding is not only a meal but also part of a ritual for sacrifices. During the time of Yu the Great and the Nine States (The ancient name for China), he had cast nine cauldrons to symbolise the unification of the nine states under his rule. The cauldron became a symbol of power. The sage's mind was thinking about a problem at the national level every day, so he naturally named this hexagram "Ding".

The reason why Ding became a symbol of state power is certainly not accidental. On the one hand, the concept of "food supports the heaven" is implied; on the other hand, the shape of the character for Ding means solemnity, majesty, solidness, stability, atmosphere, and other qualities. Also, Ding is the means for cooking and reflects the ability to produce and advance, which is in line with the Chinese ideal of the characteristics of state power.

The value carried by Ding can be easily transferred to the spiritual level. The sage said, 'The superior man keeps his every position correct, and maintains secure the appointment of Heaven'. This means that people, like a cauldron, should stay put and be upright, have the invincible spirit, and be meticulous and strictly abide by their duty. In terms of being an official, it means being honourable, honest, and diligent. In terms of ordinary people's work, it is necessary to clarify their responsibilities and duties, remain focused, and stick to them.

It is easy to reform, but difficult to be innovative, and most difficult to defend change.

In this regard, the sage emphasised several points:

First; a stable state is the result of constant adjustment. Put the cauldron in its place. It will not move. This may not be stable. You always have to push, shake, move and adjust it, or find a stepping stone, or even have a spare. This is called stability.

Second; is that it is important to take responsibility, not to act rashly, and this is inseparable from sharing and assistance of relatives and colleagues.

Third, the internal and external environment is not stable and may encounter problems of its own. Unfavourable factors can occur, and there is no other way than to be patient.

Fourth; there are fixed numbers in life and career. Just as the monks and apprentices from the Tang Dynasty that went on pilgrimage to the Western Paradise (India). They had to fall to realise the difficulties of their journey. In life, there is bound to be a danger and a great crisis, and it will be miserable. When this time arrives, do not despair, tell yourself this is nirvana, a great baptism.

Fifth; people who stand up again, like hardened metal, are tempered.

Sixth; after great difficulties, you can become a Buddha. A finless eel swims across nine rivers to become a dragon.

Difficulty makes a person tough, flexible, and gentle, able to stand up again, and ready to bend and stretch. Safe and secure great deeds come to pass.

Zeng Guofan educated his children to take this hexagram seriously. The things in the world that scare you the most are the ones to take seriously. Stick to it earnestly, go all out to carry responsibilities, and stand up for yourself. You must have the spirit of standing upright, the perseverance of bearing humiliation, and endless perseverance.

Zhen: The greatest enemy

CLASSICAL TEXT

Zhen gives the intimation of ease and development. When the time of movement, which it indicates comes, the subject of the hexagram will be found looking out with apprehension, and yet smiling and talking cheerfully. When the movement, like a crash of thunder, terrifies all within a hundred Li (about a kilometre), he will be like the sincere worshipper who is not startled into letting go of his ladle and cup of sacrificial spirits.

Nine at the First line; shows its subject, when the movement approaches, looking out and around with apprehension, and afterward smiling and talking cheerfully. There will be good fortune.

Six at the Second line; the subject, when the movement approaches, is in a position of peril. He judges it better to let go of the articles in his possession, and to ascend a lofty height. There is no occasion for him to pursue after the things he has let go; in seven days, he will find them.

Six at the third line; its subject distraught amid the startling movements going on. If those movements excite him to the right action, there will be no mistake.

Nine at the Fourth line; shows its subject, amid the startling movements, supinely sinking deeper in the mud.

Nine at the Fifth line; its subject going and coming amidst the startling movements of the time, and always in peril, but perhaps he will not incur a loss, and find a business, which he can accomplish.

Six at the top line; amidst the startling movements of the time, in breathless dismay and looking round him with trembling apprehension. If he takes action, there will be evil. If, while the startling movements have not reached his person and his neighbourhood, he were to take precautions, there would be no error. However, his relatives might still speak against him.

The image; the trigram representing thunder, being repeated, forms Zhen. The superior man, in accordance with this, is fear and apprehension, cultivates his virtue, and examines his faults.

LITERAL TRANSLATION

Zhen; a sudden thunder in the night, people become apprehensive, then they laugh. Politics and religion can be shocking, but there is a sacrifice to get there.

Nine at the First line; when the thunder strikes, people become apprehensive, but then laugh, that is auspicious.

Six at the Second line; there is danger in the thunderstorm, and a large amount of coins will be lost. Take refuge in the hills, and do not worry about them. They can be regained later.

Six at the third line; the sound of thunder shakes you up.

Nine at the Fourth line; earthquake struck, and you fell in the mud.

Six at the fifth line; earthquakes are dangerous, they can be costly, but without much loss.

Six at the top line; thunder trailing away, but striking your neighbour.

The image; thunder over trembling; gentleman should know fear and cultivate morality.

INTERPRETATION

In this hexagram, thunder is up and is down. In actress Song Dandan's words, 'It is quite scary'. The sage warned the world with this hexagram, 'Be afraid of examining your conscience seeking for perfection'. In this regard, the sage said a few things:

One; is that people can smile calmly if they know awe. Li-An said, 'I'm afraid, therefore I'm strong'. Because of the tiger, the young boy returned safely from the wreckage.

Second; when the calamity is approaching, we must give up our fortune and save our lives, leaving the green hills in the back, not afraid that there is no wood to burn.

Third; is that, with awe and trembling, even if you are close to the abyss, or if you walk on thin ice, you can be safe.

Fourth; being too scared and nervous will cause abnormal behaviour; if you are too cluttered with emotion, you will achieve nothing.

Fifth; do not panic when disaster strikes, as long as you deal with it properly, you will usually avoid danger.

Sixth; disasters are not terrible. What is terrible is not being prepared for disasters. How to prepare? Be good at learning from the lessons of others.

Disasters that happen to others will happen to you sooner or later. Therefore, caring for others is often caring for yourself. Showing sympathy is caring and learning. Friends are the breakwaters of fate.

Fear is a survival instinct formed after a long-term evolution process. When you feel that your survival is facing threat, your body and mind enter a state of readiness, which is meant for avoiding danger. However, getting too nervous can cause computer crashes, electrical shorts, weak hands and feet, and loss of mobility. It is said that if a donkey encounters a tiger, it immediately paralyses, waiting for the tiger to come and eat it. This is the case for many animals on the food chain, one thing at a time. The escape of some animals from near-deaths is also be caused by fear. Fear, like animal instinct, has many psychological reactions in humans, including anxiety, feelings of defeat, and so on, which are all caused at different levels when we worry about survival.

The greatest enemies of life are in two extremes: one is not knowing fear, and the other is the endless desire. To cope with fear, we should consider the following aspects: On the one hand, maintaining proper fear on your own is conducive to avoiding harm and but also to gain profit. Confucius said, 'That there are some things we should always respect with fear. In everyday life, we must stand in awe of the ordinances of Heaven. Stands in awe of great men. Stands in awe of the words of sages. We must be awed by religious beliefs, laws, regulations, and moral principles in order to survive. On the other hand, even monks carry an umbrella. Yet those who defy the laws of the human and the divine, the unscrupulous, such people live not far from bad luck. As the saying goes, "whoever God wants dead, he will first him drive mad".

We should remember that fear is also an important lever for regulating human behaviour. Utilising people's fear is a clever psychological stratagem. For example, in almost all ancient wars, slaughtering cities appeared to disintegrate the moral of the enemy. Punishment is an essential thing in all management, including corporal punishment in education. In this regard, you can refer to the hexagram "Wu Wang" (Truth and Honesty).

Moreover, excessive fear often puts people at greater risk or at least a stumbling block to success. If you do not dare to do it, do not dare to say, do not dare to change, do not dare to act, then you are just waiting for death. How to do it? There are two ways: one is psychological cues and self-regulation. For example, failure is the mother of success. Inspirational quotes are often among these lines. It is okay to beat yourself up. The second is to take medicine. Some people are timid, that is not simple. Psychological problems are related to physiology and genes. It is said that U.S. soldiers take stimulants, and Chinese medicine has been used for thousands of years. Or, the simplest, alcohol, the social lubricant. One of the favourite phrases that Chinese people use for successful people is: he's courageous and knowledgeable. The former richest man, Wang Jianlin, said that Tsinghua University and Peeking University are not as bold. If people are bold, the land is productive. There are many similar sayings, but they might sound rough, but some of them make sense. In short, if there are no guts to overcome fear, do not get overambitious, just be honest.

Gen: Self control

CLASSICAL TEXT

Gen: When one is lying down resting, we should be like our backsides, hidden from the world, and without consciousness of self; when he walks in his courtyard and does not see any of the persons in it – there will be no error.

Six at the First line; shows its subject keeping his toes at rest. There will be no error, but it will be advantageous for him to be persistently firm and correct.
Six at the Second line; the subject keeping the calves of his legs at rest. He cannot help the subject of the line above whom he follows, and is dissatisfied in his mind.
Nine at the third line; its subject keeping his loins at rest, and separating the ribs from the body below. The situation is perilous, and the heart glows with suppressed excitement.
Six at the fourth line; its subject keeping his trunk at rest. There will be no error.
Six at the fifth line; the subject keeping his jawbones at rest so that his words are all orderly. The occasion for repentance will disappear.
Nine at the top line; its subject devotedly maintaining his restfulness. There will be good fortune.
The image; two trigrams representing a mountain, one over the other, forms Gen. The superior man, in accordance with this, does not allow his thoughts beyond the duties of his position.

LITERAL TRANSLATION

Gua; stop and look carefully, the passer by does not see you in your courtyard, no hurry, no harm.

Six at the First line; keep your feet still, it is conducive to integrity.

Six at the Second line; keep your legs still; you might want to act to prevent someone else's action from harming that person, resist.

Nine at the third line; keeping so still that it represses your natural desires is dangerous, like a burning fire.

Six at the fourth line; keep completely still, there will be no harm.

Six at the fifth line; keep your mouth silent, your words might get you into trouble.

Nine at the top line; stop once you reach the top, and it will be auspicious.

The image; mountain over a mountain, a mountain range; the gentleman does not think beyond his current position.

INTERPRETATION

This hexagram is formed by gen (The mountain) up and down, meaning a mountain range. When two mountains are together, it is significant and firm. The sage, therefore, thought of boundaries and frontiers, which is exactly the meaning of "Gen". When you reach the border, you naturally have to stop, step on the brakes, control yourself, and exert self-control.

In this regard, the sage made a few points:

First; hold your hands and feet, do not reach out, do not get involved.

Second; is to keep your legs checked, do not follow blindly, do not pursue impetuous feelings.

Third; is to keep your waist firm and stand upright, do not lie down or wiggle.

Fourth; is to control the body, do not toss and turn.

Fifth; keep your mouth shut and do not talk nonsense.

Six; is to control the heart (emotional mind). In fact, there is one more important things to control. The sage is not embarrassed to say it clearly. Let me speak for him: control your genitals. This may be implied in the second point. Why? Good folks probably cannot understand it, haha.

In the end, the sage emphasised that there should be no impulse to cross the border. Do not even think about it. "Do not go allow your thoughts beyond the duties of your position". There are two questions here, which are worth thinking about:

> **First;** is the problem of inertia. When we brake, we feel a lot of inertia. Inertia is not just a mechanical phenomenon. There is inertia in various things, such as human psychology, emotions, thinking, ways of doing things, interpersonal relationships, etc. However, sometimes we call it a habit. When we are accustomed to

doing something, we are often unable to stop ourselves and cannot remain still, so something goes wrong. Of course, good habits also make people better. For example, inertia makes our marriage more stable. Inertia is a double-edged sword. So, what should we do? In fact, it is simple; it is just like driving. Where we obey traffic regulations, operating norms, remain calm at the proper speed so the car can be controlled. The basic thing is to turn bad habits into good ones.

Second; is the border issue. Everything has boundaries. Some borders are tangible. As soon as the red light is on, you cannot go on. The intangible boundaries are difficult to draw. Some are drawn in the form of laws and regulations, guidelines and norms, and moral customs. Others may be just some kind of tacit agreement based on judgment. Clarifying and observing the invisible boundary is of great significance to Confucianism. In a society or an organisation, people should focus on things that are within their boundaries. They can take their place, take responsibility, work hard, and be vigilant about being the most harmonious and efficient as a whole. There is an important theory in ancient Chinese management thinking, "do not exceed the boundaries". This is considered very important. There is a boundary between the division of labour, between leaders and subordinates. In the history classic *Comprehensive Mirror in Aid of Governance*, Zhuge Liang was criticised for going against this idea. When it seems that everything must be done personally, one easily exceeds one's functions and meddle in the affairs of others.

In addition, the boundary problem can be extended as a reluctance problem. Some things are supposed to be on the other side of the border. They must be left alone. As for some things, such as some emotions, you take the initiative to draw the boundary between yourself and that thing, then take a step back, carefully, this is the wisdom of life.

Jian: Everything should be gradual

CLASSICAL TEXT

Jian; suggests the marriage of a young lady, and the good fortune attending it. There will be an advantage in being firm and correct.

Six at the First line; shows the wild geese gradually approaching the shore. A young officer in similar circumstances will be in a position of danger and be spoken against, but there will be no error.

Six at the Second line; the geese gradually approaching the large rocks, where they eat and drink joyfully and at ease. There will be good fortune.

Nine at the third line; shows them gradually advancing to the dry plains. It suggests the idea of a husband who goes on an expedition from which he does not return, and of a wife who is pregnant, but will not nourish her child. There will be evil. The case symbolised that might be advantageous in resisting plundering.

Six at the fourth line; the geese gradually advanced to the trees. They may sit on the flat branches. There will be no error.

Nine at the Fifth line; the geese gradually advance to the high mound. It suggests the idea of a wife who, for three years, does not become pregnant; but in the end, the natural issue cannot be prevented. There will be good fortune.

Nine at the top line; the geese gradually advanced to the heights beyond. Their feathers can be used as ornaments. There will be good fortune.

The image; the trigram representing a mountain, and above it that for a tree forms Jian. The superior man, in accordance with this, attains and maintains his extraordinary virtue, and be with good manners.

LITERAL TRANSLATION

Jian; courting, engagement, and wedding, all done by the book, are auspicious.

Six at the First line; the little goose struggles to the shore, the boy was in danger, there was no blame.

Six at the Second line; the goose gradually makes it to the shore, it is eating and happy, auspicious.

Nine at the third line; the goose went astray into the highland, the husband did not return, the woman was pregnant but did not bear the child. A dangerous situation, beware of robbers.

Six at the fourth line; the goose perched on tall trees, they could find stable branches to rest without harm.

Nine at the Fifth line; the goose finally reaches its destination. The woman did not get pregnant for three years, and eventually, she managed to overcome it.

Nine at the top line; the goose flies into the highest point, its feathers can be used for ceremonies and are auspicious.

The image; trees growing slowly on the mountain; gentlemen must keep firm virtues and improve his habits.

INTERPRETATION

This hexagram is formed by Xun (The Penetrating) in the upper part, indicating the wind; the lower is Gen (Keeping Still), indicating the mountain. The mountains are full of trees. In the autumn and winter seasons, the leaves of the trees gradually fall, the branches wither and turn dark, and the mountains are exposed. When spring comes, the trees are full of new foliage. It gets green and dense with colours and pleasant weather. Therefore, the sage named this hexagram as "Jian", which means gradual progress. The sage believes that most affairs should not be rushed; we must be "gradual" in our approach; we must proceed gradually and slowly. Just like the migration of the goose, they do not fly over the long road at once, but fly for a while and then rest, eat something, replenishes physical strength, and then flies again. It is also like a pregnant woman. Before giving birth, there are several months of pregnancy.

Struggling young people often sing this song, 'I am a little bird and want to fly high, but I can only fly low'. In this regard, the sage considers:

First; at the beginning of life, if a bird is on the water's shore, at the lowest place, it is not valued, understood, and it is often criticised and ridiculed.

Second; fighting hard, like a bird flying on a big rock, will eventually, in your thirties, determine a small career, a prosperous life, healthy parents, and lovely children. This is the happiest time in life.

Third; the bird struggled to fly higher, but she felt little fulfilled in her life, then this person faces various middle-aged crises, such as career bottlenecks, ups and downs, and so on.

Fourth; the bird finally perched on tall branches. After going through all kinds of tests, a person has learned well, has been well rounded, and has become flexible. He has finally entered the upper class and entered the higher circle.

Fifth; the bird flew up again and felt cold, lonely, helpless, and tedious.

Sixth; the bird flew up to the top of the mountain, fully feathered and reaching the immortals. However, the old saying, 'If attainting immortality is possible, the path to it is full of vicissitudes'. If the gods care about us, they must be troubled too.

The bird's upward flight is similar to the struggle of the dragon in this hexagram. But here, the main emphasis is on gradual progress. This bird is flying to the height, little by little. It is not flying, explosively, not a rocket, but a stage, a step. Like the eighteen sets on Mount Tai, the steps are level by level, and a walk will take a while.

All things are like this; if there were a success at the first try, everybody would overdo it, like a fat person with food. This is Confucius's so-called "hurry to fail". Quickness is often a sign of inadequacy and can mess things up. When Sima Qian criticised King Hanwen, he did it on the basis that reformers made mistakes because they did not understand the truth of the "gradual" approach. Wang Anshi's reform, the Great Leap Forward, the "shock therapy" of the former Soviet Union, and so on, all failed at this point. In short, treating various matters and grasping the "gradual" approach means to develop a mature mentality, a stable style, and a long-term vision.

In the end, the sage mentioned that we should "attain and maintain one's virtue and make people good". Leaders must take the lead in advocating for good behaviour, promote good morals, change customs, and promote the development of social civility. This is the focus of the Confucian "rule by virtue". In fact, the number of civil servants in the feudal dynasties was very small. The county officials led a dozen or at most two dozens officials. The management of the people at the grass-roots level mainly depended on folk customs and provincial regulations. Therefore, it is particularly important to instil people with proper traditions and to change bad habits. The process of the formation or transformation of customs and styles embodies the characteristics of the "gradual" approach; it cannot be achieved overnight, with a single order, or with a few cuffs and kicks. In recent years, the state has paid more attention to public moral advertisements for social ethics and civility, indicating that high-level attention has been paid to this issue.

Gui Mei: Choose life

CLASSICAL TEXT

Gui Mei; it is dangerous to go ahead with risky endeavours.

Nine at the First line; the marriage of the younger sister can make her the second wife; this can be auspicious.

Nine at the Second line; seeing with one eye, stay in seclusion, this will maintain your integrity.

Six at the third line; marrying a young girl has to wait, she could end up as a concubine.

Nine at the Fourth line; delaying marriage, waiting for the right time.

Six at the fifth line; the king's bride is not as well dressed as the bridesmaids.

Six at the top line; a woman holding an empty basket. A man slaughtered a sheep; there was no feast and no benefit.

The image; thunder over the lake; a gentleman must show restraint and know the drawbacks of his actions.

LITERAL TRANSLATION

Gui Mei; Choose life.

Nine at the First line; the young sister becomes the second wife.

Nine at the Second line; seeing with one eye, stay in seclusion.

Six at the third line; hoping to be a wife, ending up being a concubine.

Nine at the Fourth line; delaying marriage, all in good time.

Six at the fifth line; the bride is more modestly dressed than the bridesmaids.

Six at the top line; the basket is empty.

The image; thunder over the lake. Do not let emotions make you hasty and reckless.

INTERPRETATION

This hexagram is formed by Zhen (The Arousing) in the upper part, indicating the thunder, and the lower is Dui (The Joyous), meaning lake. Thunder sounds, and the raindrops, the situation was in line with the mood of a girl being married. At that time, women were not married as they are now. They did not do it based on love. Maybe they had been living with a "husband" for several years. In ancient times, the bride did not meet the groom before marriage. The husband could be a dog or a chicken, maybe the bride could be happy! They were all "crying". Therefore, for the sage, the scene strikes a chord in one's heart, and he named this hexagram as "Gui Mei" meaning, to marry a girl. Moreover, rarely there are not very positive words from the sage who summarises the hexagrams by saying: it is not profitable to go on with it.

Why is this marriage so unbearable? The sage enumerates the experience of marrying a wife: in the beginning, she wants to be in the spotlight, looking at the faces of her husband and in-laws, looking forward to becoming one of them, and having to compete with other females for power. More importantly, she has to take care of the household meals and do all the housework. Can someone live like this forever? Not necessarily, because maybe one day will they retire. The sage must have never seen Qian Zhongshu's *Besieged City*, where the motto is "People outside want to go in, people inside want out". Still, their views should be consistent, and they are not optimistic about marriage.

This process of being a daughter-in-law can also be understood as a process of getting accustomed to the workplace:

First; starting from a low-level posts, you have no resources available and might try your best to show enthusiasm.

Second; we must be good at looking at things, focusing on our work, being honest, and making few comments.

Third; we must choose the right springboard for climbing the ranks, grasp it, and set foot on it.

Fourth; greatness comes eventually, and we must be good at waiting. Regardless of whether they are institutions or enterprises. Most Chinese higher positions are assigned by qualifications and seniority, but only to varying degrees.

Those who can survive, and work harder, often end up better than those who jump up and down.

Fifth; after being in such a position, be humble, low-key, and diligent.

Sixth; there are ceilings in all workplaces. When you touch this ceiling, you should make other plans. If you do not leave, someone will drive you away.

Our workplace, in the context of the sage, can only be officialdom. It is a scholar's duty to serve the country and serve the king. There is no other way.

When starting from a small office, you are looking at an official's higher rank, looking forward to being promoted to an ideal official position. In order to give play to your talents, you also face competition from peers. During the process, you are constantly labouring and struggling, and maybe you will make some big mistakes, you then can be cut off.

Regardless of marriage or occupation (workplace, officialdom), it is the most important choice for everyone. This choice is often carried throughout life and cannot be bypassed. In this regard, the sage believes that, 'The superior man, in accordance with this, having regard to the far-distant end, knows the mischief that may be done at the beginning'.

So the gentleman knows that this road is difficult to go, and he has to go, and he must be clear about the many difficulties and problems that he may face, deal with them all, and stick to the end. Someone once commented on Confucius' 'who knows the impracticable nature of the times and yet will be doing in them'. The cause he chose was clearly impossible, but he still insisted on doing it because that was his mission and his life! Being a good wife or a good official may be difficult. Still, it is a responsibility, a mission, and a way to realise the value of life. Now that you have chosen it, what else can you say? Stay true to it and stick to it! That is the colour of life, how many are not blooming amid bitterness? Confucian loyalty, patriotism, and idealism are all reflected in the hexagram "Gui Mei".

Some options may not take as long as a lifetime, but as long as they are relatively long-term, they will all face the problem of "having regard to the far-distant end." For example, if I want to write a series of Chinese-style inspirational books, I want to write seven or eight books. For ten years, I must find a publisher to complete the series, but just one, not two of them, nor three of them. When I decide to choose a certain home, I will make this determination of "having regard to the far-distant end. There may be many problems in the long-term cooperation in the future, but I must persist in working with it to the end. Only in this way can we win.

Feng: The wisdom of decision making

CLASSICAL TEXT

Feng; This hexagram intimates progress and development. When a king has reached the point which the name denotes, there is no occasion to be anxious through fear of a change. Let him be as the sun at noon.

Nine at the First line; shows its subject meeting with his mate. Though they are both of the same characters, there will be no error. The advance will call forth approval.

Six at the Second line; its subject surrounded by screens so large and thick that at midday he can see from them the constellation of the Bushel. If he goes and tries to enlighten his ruler, who is thus not disingenuous, he will make himself seen with suspicion and dislike. Let him cherish his feeling of sincere devotion that he may thereby move his ruler's mind, and there will be good fortune.

Nine at the third line; shows its subject with an additional screen of a large and thick banner, through which at midday he can see the small Mei star. In the darkness, he breaks his right arm; but there will be no error.

Nine at the Fourth line; the subject is in a tent so large and thick that at midday he can see from it the constellation of the Bushel. But he meets with the subject of the first line, undivided like himself. There will be good fortune.

Six at the fifth line; its subject surrounding himself with men of brilliant ability. There will be an occasion for congratulation and praise. There will be good fortune.

Six at the top line; the subject with his house-made large, but only serving as a screen to his household. When he looks at his door, it is still, and there is nobody about it. For three years, no one is to be seen. There will be evil.

The image; the trigrams representing thunder and lightning combine to form Feng. The superior man, in accordance with this, decides cases of litigation and apportions punishments with exactness.

LITERAL TRANSLATION

Feng; The virtue of the king is moving; there is no need to be anxious; it is great to shine like the sun in the sky.

Nine at the First line; meet your partner, there is no blame for ten days.

Six at the Second line; the curtains are so thick that even at noon, there is a need to light the lamps. Honesty and richness do not need to be hidden.

Nine at the third line; many flags darken the sky, a broken right arm can still be healed.

Nine at the Fourth line; heavy curtains keep the room dark as to seem to see the stars. Understanding the confusion will make you see the light.

Six at the fifth line; shinning inner light wins blessings.

Six at the top line; living beyond your means, peeping at his palace gate, it seems empty for three years. It is dangerous.

The image; thunder over fire makes 'Feng'; the gentleman uses this to assess and act upon a situation.

INTERPRETATION

This hexagram is formed by Zhen (The Arousing) in the upper part, indicating thunder; the lower is Li (The Clinging), meaning fire. The sage used one sentence to describe this hexagram: thunder and lighting reach everywhere. The sage used two words when describing this image earlier: thunder and lightning. The difference here is that there is "reaching everything" here, and the sage's mind is in this difference. "Everywhere" means that everything is put together. Lightning is coming, electricity is coming, and you can also think that the wind is coming and the rain is coming. What is this called? It is complete, rich, sufficient, comprehensive, thorough, and numerous, so this hexagram is named "Feng" (Abundance). The sage believes that only by knowing the truth of the hexagram "Feng", can a solid judgment be made.

Quite simply, "clear punishment" here refers to legislation, law enforcement, including the use of punishment. "Deprivation of punishment" refers to the sentencing of a case. Indeed, it is still suitable for modern times. The "Laws of Punishment of the Ming" were to be harsher in order to be effective, so in Chinese it sounds like "bitten", like biting something; and what is the most important thing about "judging and sentencing"? Every teenager who watched TV knows that the most important things are "testimony and material evidence", meaning "rich" in evidence.

The whole "Feng" hexagram is about the process of closing a case:

First; we must strive to find important witnesses and material evidence, no matter how much time is required.

Second; be good at questioning the common beliefs. Unselfishness and subjective judgment are necessary to find evidence and judge the case. All operations should be transparent.

Third; the collection of evidence must be based on cooperation to form a better judgment. However, there is both construction and destruction; we should avoid getting into a tiger's lair.

Fourth; when witnesses and physical evidence are available, the case can be finalised.

Fifth; fair judgment and legitimacy for justice in the world have won a great reputation. For example, in *Justice Bao*, the king was called "the son of heaven," but on no other occasion was heaven used to referred.

Sixth; when people have qualifications, when they are in high positions, they will become more and more subjective. They do not like to be in the spotlight. Acting only by imagining the facts and ignoring the evidence will cause many problems.

Confucius once criticised his student's, saying, 'Ah! It is You who could work with half a word to settle litigation!' It would be a grievance to break a sentence based on one-sided remarks. This hexagram also emphasises explicitly; do not dare in a similar way to decide cases of criminal litigation. And the case cannot be concluded if there are false premises. This is the ancient Chinese spirit of the rule of law!

Of course, sages have always been both short-term and far-reaching, and the meaning of the hexagram Feng is by no means limited to judgment. Judgment and decision making in any matter should use the wisdom of the "Feng" hexagram. One should be careful, have a fertile imagination, be on the scene, listen to people's opinions, collect as much relevant information and data as possible, observe, and carefully consider.

The main ethos of The *Book of Change*s is simplicity, but all-important simplicity must be done after "Feng".

 The intention of words

CLASSICAL TEXT

Lu; This hexagram indicates that in the condition which it denotes, there may be some little attainment and progress. If the stranger or traveller be firm and correct, as he ought to be, there will be good fortune.

Six at the First line; shows the stranger is mean of thought and deed. It is thus that he brings on himself further calamity.

Six at the Second line; the stranger, occupying his lodging-house, carrying with him his means of livelihood, and provided with good and trusty servants.

Nine at the third line; the stranger, burning his lodging-house, and having lost his servants. However, firm and correct he tries to be, he will be in peril.

Nine at the Fourth line; this shows the traveller in a resting-place, also having the means of livelihood and the axe, but still saying, 'I am not at ease in my mind'.

Six at the fifth line; the subject shooting a pheasant. He will lose his arrow, but in the end, he will obtain praise and a high charge.

Nine at the top line; suggests the idea of a bird burning its nest. The stranger, thus represented, first laughs, then cries out. He has lost his ox-like docility too readily and easily. There will be evil.

The image; the trigram representing a mountain and above it that for fire forms Lu. The superior man, in accordance with this, exerts wisdom and caution in the use of punishments and not allowing litigations to continue.

LITERAL TRANSLATION

Lu: Passing though, auspicious for the wanderer. A traveller has few friends and so he travels light. Not a good time for long-term planning.

Six at the First line: An inattentive and badly prepared traveller will not enjoy the journey. An agitated mind and attitude leads to mistakes.

Six at the Second line: The wanderer finds a place to stay. It is a good place to rest, but is not good to think of overstaying.

Nine at the third line: Your shelter has burned down and you lost your servant. Your resting place is no longer safe and you have lost the goodwill of others. Time to leave.

Nine at the Fourth line: The wanderer finds an axe, he can settle down and make a living, but it is not what you really want to be doing.

Six at the fifth line: You shot a pheasant with one arrow, it puts you in a good position. You are recognised for your talents, accept opportunities without being boastful.

Nine at the top line: The wanderer's nest burns up, a big loss. Laughing at other people's disgrace will only make yours worst.

The image: Fire over a mountain. The image of movement and restlessness. Moving is inevitable, the traveller can enjoy the journey as long as it is without attachments.

INTERPRETATION

In this hexagram: the upper is Li, indicating fire; the lower is Gen, meaning the mountain. Many mountains are painted with a melancholic hue under the setting sun. One or two people on the mountain road, the bells hanging from the animals clang, adding a little loneliness. Just like in that famous piece of Qu poetry: *A dead tree and old one, a crow, a small bridge, flowing water, wind from the west, and a thin horse, the sun is setting, sinking on a broken gut at the end of the world.* What the sage thinks about are journeys and business trips.

In the "Lu" hexagram, the sage told a tortuous business story. In the oldest era, the hardships of businessmen were like those of the Shanxi businessmen in the *Qiao's Grand Courtyard* series. All that accumulated wealth may not be safe. In the end, it often ends in tragedy.

Regarding business, the sage believes that:

First; the new businessmen must not be speculative, should not engage in crooked ways, and should not counterfeit and scam with inferior products. Once such a basic foundation is destroyed, the career cannot be long-lasting.

Second; is that there is always a chance to get out there. In *Journey to the West*, it is said that there is an advantage in action. Opportunity does come when one is sitting at home waiting, nor does it appear according to a plan or assumption. It is random, unexpected, and comes across.

By getting out there, inspecting, participating in exhibitions, or various business activities, you might not necessarily be able to come across opportunities. Still, there is definitely no chance if one only stays at home. Opportunity is of two kinds: one is for being rich, and the other is for being talented. Get business opportunities and develop your talent.

Third; business people face risks at any time. Risks are normal. To secure wealth requires it.

Fourth; if you make too much money, it will be very hard, and your happiness might pay the price. I sometimes think that money makes a lot of people good-for-nothing's, it can be destructive for those people.

Fifth; there are uncertain gains and losses, and some unforeseen work may achieve great benefits. It is like playing Go. It is often wonderful to play against some good Go players.

Fourth; human beings die in pursuit of wealth, and birds die in pursuit of food. Be vigilant.

The sage was not a businessman, but he had the Confucian attitude of "When I am walking along with two other people, one might serve me as a teacher, the other as a student". He can discover the valuable qualities of business people and learn from their work.

He said, 'The gentleman, in accordance with this, exerts his wisdom and caution in the use of punishment and not allowing litigation to continue'. It means that they learn the careful calculation of business people, and the settlement of daily affairs to make a judgment. Engaging in the management of public relations with a spirit of entrepreneurship and business management is still an important topic.

The careful calculation of business people and the officials' use of punishment without sending to prison, at the end of the day, it can be attributed to one quality: diligence. In this regard, Zeng Guofan and his ingenious *Five directives and achievements* are handy: physical diligence, observing diligence, skill achievement, speech diligence, and mental diligence. It can be said that this is the secret of Zeng Guofan's success. In short, a diligent character takes the lead, and will be earnest, not lazy, or procrastinate, whether it is in business or office, or any other occupation, it will never be the worse.

Xun: Taking advantage of the trend

CLASSICAL TEXT

Xun; indicates that under the conditions which it denotes, there will be some little attainment and progress. There will be an advantage in movement onward in whatever direction. It will be advantageous also to see the great man.

Six at the First line; shows its subject now advancing, now receding. It would be advantageous for him to have the applied wisdom of a brave soldier.

Nine at the Second line; the representative of Sun beneath a couch, and employing diviners and exorcists in a way bordering on confusion. There will be good fortune and no error.

Nine at the third line; subject penetrating only by violent and repeated efforts. There will be an occasion for regret.

Six at the fourth line; an occasion for repentance in its subject passed away. He takes the game for its threefold use in his hunting.

Nine at the Fifth line; shows that with applied wisdom there will be good fortune to its subject. All occasion for remorse will disappear, and all his movements will be advantageous. There may have been no good beginning, but there will be a good end. Three days before making any changes, let him give notice of them; and three days after, let him reconsider them. Thus, there will be good fortune.

Nine at the top line; this shows the representative of penetration beneath a couch, and having lost the axe with which he executed his decisions. However, firm and correct he may try to be, there will be evil.

The image; two trigrams representing wind, following each other, forms Xun. The superior man, in accordance with this, reiterates his orders and secures the practice of his affairs.

LITERAL TRANSLATION

Xun; Bow down to the respected person; it is auspicious to make your intentions known.

Six at the First line; when in doubt, be firm as a martial artist.
Nine at the Second line; kneel by the throne, receive the shaman's blessing. No blame.
Nine at the third line; reluctant to bend the knee into submission.
Six at the fourth line; remorse fades away, the hunter obtains three types of game.
Nine at the Fifth line; remain in remorse, then die being righteous. It was not smooth at first, but eventually, it went well. Bad beginning, good ending.
Nine at the top line; kneeling before the throne, losing your weapons, remain alert against evil.
The image; wind over a tree, or tree over wind; a gentleman must apply order into things.

INTERPRETATION

In this hexagram, both up and down are 'Xun' (The penetrating), meaning the wind. On this hexagram, the wind follows the wind. Naturally, it is downwind, which in turn confirms the meaning of "The Gentle", that is, the meaning of following, obedience, submissive, and patience.

The sage emphasised a few points:

First; the more masculine and stubborn people are, they must understand the meaning of obedience, they must be good at grasping, advance and retreat, and being flexible. If you cannot defeat the other party, join the other party and cooperate with the other party.

Second; people below should learn to worship and obedience to religious believers in order to face society and things. In one of Sima's work on classical history books, there are records of such low-status people. There is nothing that they can do to change their status. They can only be the best servants they can be, and then win the favour and trust of the king. This is exactly the kind of gentleman practice of "being sensitive to his actions, so they speak well"! Two thousand years later, the most elite group of Chinese society, the students of Tsinghua University Student Union, created a slogan "obey and be efficient!" This is said to be the secret of their predecessors becoming the most successful people in contemporary China.

Third; being blindly obedient is unbearable. Lu Xun once criticised, that in the history of China, there is "the era when you want to be a servant" and "the era when you are a servant is temporary". Who wants to be a servant? No one wants it! But why did you become a servant? For survival and development. And so, a grandson can grow to be a grandpa. These vulgar words are the pillar of faith that supports this nation's tolerance for humiliation and develops the world's most forgiving character.

Fourth; is that if you endure it to the end, you will gain something. Legend has it that the Jade Emperor's name before taking the throne was Zhang Bairen (Great Endurance Chang).

Fifth; it is a hero who can tolerate even the most obnoxious people. Endure the moment, calm down, take a step back, imagine a brighter future at all times and all places. As long as one can bear it, the fish will turn to a dragon. The Qumran says, "Allah is with the stoic".

Sixth; obedience brings no harm, but it is too unjust to have nothing after a lifetime. Lu Xun's words hit a key point of Chinese traditional culture. Regardless of following Confucianism, Buddhism, or Taoism, they all emphasised obedience, endurance, and victory through resilience.

In terms of interpersonal relationships, the Confucian hierarchies are based on obedience:

Loyalty, and strict enforcement of prohibitions, submission, and obedience. Filial piety, obey your parents.

Marital harmony, be contented with the man a woman has married regardless of his lot. In terms of the relationship between man, destiny, and nature, it is also said that man must conform to nature.

The sage's statement puts it like this: "The superior man, in accordance with this, reiterates his orders, and secures the practice of his affairs". This is a generalisation of these concepts. However, the sage's attitude is positive. Regardless of dealing with the relationship between man, heaven, and ego, he must be good at taking advantage of the situation. This is like riding downwind and sailing down a river.

Dui: Water like friendship

CLASSICAL TEXT

Dui; indicates that under its conditions, there will be progress and attainment. But it will be advantageous to be firm and correct.

Nine at the First line; shows the pleasure of inward harmony. There will be good fortune.

Nine at the Second line; the pleasure arising from inner sincerity. There will be good fortune. An occasion for remorse will disappear.

Six at the third line; its subject bringing around himself whatever can give pleasure. There will be evil.

Nine at the Fourth line; its subject deliberating about what to seek his pleasure in, and not at rest. He borders on what would be injurious, but there will be cause for joy.

Nine at the Fifth line; the subject trusting in one who would injure him. The situation is perilous.

Six at the top line; the pleasure of its subject in leading and attracting others.

The image; two trigrams representing the waters of a marsh, one over the other, form Dui. The superior man, in accordance with this, encourages the conversation of friends and the stimulus of their common practice.

LITERAL TRANSLATION

Dui; difficulties are easier to overcome when you are at peace with yourself.

Nine at the First line; peace and good fortune.
Six at the Second line; a sincere speech, it is auspicious, and there will no regret in the end.
Six at the third line; there is a tempting offer, it is dangerous.
Nine at the Fourth line; calculating the odds, not yet tranquil, free of disease, there is joy.
Nine at the Fifth line; there is danger in eliminating integrity.
Six at the top line; encouraged to come forth.
The image; lake over Lake; the gentleman makes friends, exchanges, and learns from them.

INTERPRETATION

Dui refers to lakes and marshes. In this hexagram, the upper and lower lakes are connected. It is like two glasses of water mixed, blending, and enriching each other. The sage, therefore, thought of the "the gentleman, in accordance with this, encourages the conversation of friends and the stimulus of their common practice". This is the communication and exchange between friends, mutual benefit, and collective progress.

Regarding friends, the sage thinks that exchange and business are good things, but the exchange is not necessarily good.

First; it should be a harmonious exchange. Two people need to have chemistry, look into each other's eyes, and recognise each other, attract each other. Just like adding sugar to coffee, it can dissolve and makes the coffee taste better, and the sugar will be easier to absorb. It is not normal to add sesame oil to coffee, the oil floats on it and it tastes bad; it is even more abnormal to add mercury. You might not taste it when added to coffee, but it would not be good at all. As for like-minded friends, the sage has a wonderful description: "Act in unison, people with the same ideas have an affinity for each other. Water flows towards the place that is low and damp; fire rises up towards what is dry; clouds follow the dragon, and winds follow the tiger. And so the sage makes his appearance, and all men look to him. Things that draw their origin from heaven move towards what is above; things that draw their origin from the earth cleave to what is below: so does everything follow its kind'. Fish look for fish, shrimps look for other shrimps, and toads look for frogs. When young people meet, they attract each other.

Second; inspire confidence in each other. Friends must treat each other with sincerity and without deceit. Once deceived, friends not only separate, but they will quickly become enemies, which may have tragic results in the end.

Third; come together to exchange. Make friends, let nature take its course, do not force emotional matters. When I left home for school, I was anxious about making new friends, and I was troubled by it. In the end, I found out that friends are found by accident and not through seeking. In the end, who you are friends with and who you are with comes down to fate, that and your will to come together. In addition, we have to understand a kind of mentality and be sure that: Nothing delivered right to your front door can be that good.

Fourth; business exchange. Friends will inevitably have differences and misunderstandings. What should we do? You must discuss, negotiate, and communicate.

Fifth; the world is changing, life is impermanent, and friendship cannot be immutable. Some friends end up in the high ranks, too busy to take care of eating, they may neglect you, but maybe not intentionally. As long as understanding and goodwill remains, friendship never leaves.

Sixth; guidance. There are two cases: one is that of the peach tree that is not attractive, but people admire it when it blooms with fruit and flowers. If you study hard, advance in your career, improve yourself and become a good person. Naturally, someone will take the initiative to make friends with you. The second is that the people who come to interact with you are not necessarily the nicest people. Some villains are good at pleasing others. But remember, happiness among friends is not the most important thing; the most important thing is that it is conducive to survival and development. The villain may be cute, but will hurt you without a second thought.

Between friends, it is like the interaction of two lakes. What more to say? But when two men are one in heart, not iron bolts keep them apart; The words in union used,

Fragrant like orchids perfume diffused. What more to say? When it comes to friendship, there is another famous saying in Zhuangzi; "The gentleman's friendship is as light as water". Of course, if we jump out of the context of the image, we can also talk about love. The word "pleasant" (Yue) in Chinese, which is sympathy between two emotions, is formed with the character for the "lake" (Dui) and "heart" (Xin). As soon as there is sincerity between a man and woman, they can give free rein to their sexual interest. For example, the "guidance" becomes a way to seduce, and the other party also benefits from the exchange. Again: the benevolent see benevolence, the wise see wisdom. This is another charm of the *Book of Changes*.

Huan: Freedom

CLASSICAL TEXT

Heng; indicates that under its conditions, there will be progress and success. The king goes to his ancestral temple; it will be advantageous to cross the great stream. It will be advantageous to be firm and correct.

Six at the First line; shows its subject engaged in rescuing from the impending evil and having the assistance of a strong horse. There will be good fortune.

Nine at the Second line; its subject, amid the dispersion, hurrying to his contrivance for security. All occasion for remorse will disappear.

Six at the third line; its subject discarding any regard to his person. There will be no occasion for repentance.

Six at the fourth line; its subject scattering the different parties in the state, which leads to good fortune. From the dispersion, he collects again good men standing out, a crowd like a mound, which is what ordinary men would not have thought.

Nine at the Fifth line; the subject amidst the dispersion issuing announcements as the perspiration flows from his body. He scatters abroad also the accumulations in the royal granaries. There will be no error.

Nine at the top line; disposing of what may be called its bloody wounds, and going and separating himself from its anxious fears. There will be no error.

The image; the trigram representing water is below, and that for wind moving above the water form Huan. The ancient king, in accordance with this, presented offerings to God and established the ancestral temple.

LITERAL TRANSLATION

Huan; the king calls for restoration of the ancestral temple, which is conducive to public (construction) works on the river, this is conducive to maintaining justice.

Six at the First line; rescued with the aid of a strong horse.

Nine at the Second line; dragged by the flood, confused about the way and with regret.

Six at the third line; swept away by the flood.

Six at the fourth line; swept from the herd, looking for safety on top of a hill.

Nine at the Fifth line; summoned to the palace by the king and dripping in sweat.

Nine at the top line; got away from sorrow, no harm.

The image; tree over water; the king wants to build a temple to the Lord of Heaven.

INTERPRETATION

This hexagram is formed by Xun (The Gentle) in the upper part, indicating the wind; the lower is Kan (The Abysmal, meaning water. In spring, the freezing snow and ice slowly melt, and the wind plays over the water, an image of freedom. Therefore, the sage named this hexagram with the word "Huan", which in Chinese has the meaning of melting away, scattered, flowing, free, loose, and open. Although I have listed these words, they all have the meaning of "Scattering". Still, it is evident that there is a difference between righteous and derogatory. It depends on the situation and the degree of emphasis. The sage's short words are both derogatory and appraising. He says:

First; when things are scattered, we must take decisive and powerful measures to take care of them. In Feng Xiaogang's movie, *A World Without Thieves*, one of the characters says, 'If morality is gone, a team is worthless'. What to do? To uphold the family structure, we must step up in governance. The so-called "embankment of a thousand miles that collapsed because of an ant's nest" kind-of-situation should also be prevented as soon as possible.

Second; when you are out of control, grab something, and stand firmly on your heels. Even if you cannot remain still, do not follow the waves. When the trees fall apart, and everyone is on their own, you need to be calm. People today are fickle, with money on their minds and busy with their selfish interests. You must insist on faith.

Third; when the whole world is turbid, and you are alone, it is dangerous. The perseverance in your heart should not be shaken, but it is not necessary to show it. Confucius said, "Forego conclusions, arbitrary judgment, obstinacy, and egoism". Taoism says, "Swim with the tide, stand aloof from worldly success." Be able to part with things, break, and shatter.

Fourth; an organisation should also have the wisdom to take advantage of a bad situation and form an inherent cohesion in a relatively loose environment. For any organisation, flexibility can maintain vitality and have wolf-like wisdom, courage, and creativity.

Fifth; a policy should be broken down into a number of operational details, which should cover all details. Barriers keeping people from the government must be dismantled, many boundaries must be broken, and policies must be fully enforced.

Sixth; we must ensure a smooth flow, including physical, financial, personal, political, and in other aspects and forms, to be healthy.

From the above, we can see that "scattering" has gradually changed from a crisis to a proactive strategy, and turned from negative to positive.

In the end, the sage's summary is based on a country level, saying that the rulers "enjoy the temple of the Lord of Heaven". They worship with the king and use the values of religion and national spirit to gather the "scattered" people. At the same time, under this invisible cohesion, let the people fully enjoy the freedom of being "scattered", which is conducive to development.

During the "May 4th" period, Hu Shi criticised Li Dazhao. Yet, he should have talked less about doctrines and talk about more about practical issues. But Li Dazhao's insistence on doctrine is important and a means of cohesion. Today's world is also facing many problems caused by "disintegration," and many people think that it can be improved by advocating universal human values. In terms of corporate management, this means rectifying corporate culture and promoting the cohesion and coordination of employees.

However, I think the positive meaning of "scattering" reflected in the "Huan" hexagram is particularly important.

Cai Yan's *Analects* states: The literati should scatter knowledge. When writing calligraphy, you must first relax and not be nervous.

Beautiful things are distributed. In terms of being a person, a person who is too rigid and serious is most annoying when he shows no sign of emotion and generally does not have true skill. We should have an open mind and vision, and maintain a free heart, lively, free, and humorous. Nothing is absolute. You cannot split hairs.

The world itself is scattered, life is free, and order is relative, but there is indeed a spiritual power that maintains this world. The so-called "the form might be lost, but not the spirit", is something everyone must seriously consider.

Jie: Temperance

CLASSICAL TEXT

Jie; indicates that under its conditions, there will be progress and attainment. But if the regulations which it prescribes be severe and difficult, they cannot be permanent.

Nine at the First line; shows its subject not quitting the courtyard outside his door. There will be no error.

Nine at the Second line; its subject not quitting the courtyard inside his gate. There will be evil.

Six at the third line; its subject with no appearance of observing the proper regulations, in which case we shall see him lamenting. But there will be no one to blame but himself.

Six at the fourth line; shows its subject quietly and naturally attentive to all regulations. There will be progress and success.

Nine at the Fifth line; its subject sweetly and acceptably enacting his regulations. There will be good fortune. The onward progress with them will afford grounds for admiration.

Six at the top line; subject enacting regulations severe and difficult. Even with firmness and correctness, there will be evil. But though there will be cause for remorse, it will by and by disappear.

The image; the trigram representing a lake, and above it that for water, forms Jie. The superior man, in accordance with this, constructs his methods of numbering and measurement and discusses points of virtue and conduct.

LITERAL TRANSLATION

Jie; Too much restraint is not beneficial.

Nine at the First line; there is no harm in staying indoors.

Nine at the Second line; it is dangerous not to leave the house.

Six at the third line; lack of self restrain, there will be remorse, but no blame.

Six at the fourth line; keeping safe by exerting self restrain.

Nine at the Fifth line; if the heart is willing to become disciplined, there will be good fortune.

Six at the top line; excessive restraint, there will be remorse and exhaustion.

The image; water over the lake; the gentleman must set the rules of etiquette and be clear about morals and conduct.

INTERPRETATION

This hexagram contains: in the upper part is Kan (the abysmal), indicating the water; in the lower part is Dui (Joyous), meaning the lake. During the flood season, Dongting Lake serves as a flood discharge lake, which then stores a large amount of river water; during the dry season, Dongting Lake supplies the Yangtze River to a certain extent. It can be said that these lakes have a regulating effect on the Yangtze and other rivers so that they can always maintain a relatively stable level of water. Therefore, the saint named this hexagram as "Jie", which means regulation and restraint. The sage believes that human behaviour and development need regulation to be more efficient and less problematic, and summarise this power of regulation as "setting the rules of etiquette and being clear about morality and conduct".

The rules of etiquette, including a clear system of reward and punishment, laws and regulations, norms, rules, etc., these are the external regulatory forces. They influence what people can do, what they cannot do, and how to do it in a compulsory, guiding, and normative manner.

But discussing these topics, including morals, customs, public opinion, etc. This is mainly an internal regulatory force. Discussing exerts its strengths in areas where external rewards and punishments cannot be reached. For example, King Wei Xiaowen once encouraged historians to record their merits and deeds truthfully. Then when the king's rewards and penalties could not be enforced upon them, having them think about historical judgment helped them remember.

How to deal with these regulatory powers? The sage thinks that:

First; there is no standard to refer to. When I do not know how to go about it, I simply let it go for a while.

Second; being too cautious does not work; by always staying at home, you can miss golden opportunities. When you need to reach out, you have to put yourself out there, and when you need to try, you must motivate yourself.

Third; is that things have no intrinsic rules; they must be made and setup. In particular, you need to have self-control. If you cannot manage yourself and you have a problem, you can only blame yourself.

Fourth; is to adapt to the system and free play within the scope of the system. This is how you develop proficiency.

Fifth; let the system serve itself and enjoy the profits. This is success.

Sixth; if you take on the system with bitterness, it will backfire; if you are too restrained, you will not be able to persist for a long time, you need to, even if it is not favourable for a long time.

Life is the game and balance between a person and these regulatory forces. Regardless of external or internal forces, the power of these adjustments is complicated. Flexibility is important in order to adhere to them. It is like drinking water and knowing what is cold and warm for you, and how to embody life's wisdom. For example, Zhuangzi said, 'To make good deeds without looking to make a name for oneself, and to make evil deeds without thinking about the punishment. You do not have to be a moral model, it is too tiring, and you may get sick from it; just do not be a criminal'. Between the two extremes of regulating power, there is ample space to live freely.

From a manager's perspective, how to make good use of the power of these two types of regulation is a top issue.

Zhong Fu: Integrity wins the world

CLASSICAL TEXT

Zhong Fu; moves even pigs and fish, and leads to good fortune. There will be an advantage in crossing the great stream. There will be an advantage in being firm and correct.

Nine at the First line; shows its subject resting in himself. There will be good fortune. If he sought to any other, he would not find rest.

Nine at the Second line; the subject like the crane crying out in her hidden retirement, and her young ones responding to her. It is as if they said, 'I have a cup of good spirits', and the response was, 'I will partake of it with you'.

Six at the third line; its subject having met with his mate. Now he beats his drum, and now he leaves off. Now he weeps, and now he sings.

Six at the fourth line; the subject like the moon, nearly full, and like a horse in a chariot whose fellow disappears. There will be no error.

Nine at the Fifth line; perfectly sincere, and linking others to him in close union. There will be no error.

Nine at the top line; its subject in chanting, trying to reach heaven. Even with applied wisdom, there will be evil.

The image; the trigram representing the waters of a marsh and that for wind above it forms Zhong Fu. The superior man, in accordance with this, deliberates about cases of litigation and delays the infliction of death.

LITERAL TRANSLATION

Zhong Fu; sincerity can change even pigs and fish, act with caution, do not attempt to cross the river.

Nine at the First line; quietly develop your inner mind stability.

Nine at the Second line; a crane calls in the shadows, the small crane replies; I have some good wine and would like to drink with you.

Six at the third line; facing the enemy, or announcing the attack; weeping, then singing.

Six at the fourth line; the moon is not yet full, and a horse got lost, there is no blame.

Nine at the Fifth line; keep your integrity, and it will look after you.

Nine at the top line; the bird's call raises to the sky, beware of evil.

The image; a tree over a lake; the gentlemen should review the case and use the death penalty with caution.

INTERPRETATION

This hexagram is formed by Xun (The Gentle) in the upper part, indicating the wind; the lower is Dui; The Joyous, indicating lakes and marshes. The wind blows from above the lake, through the flowers and the trees, through the birds, beasts, and insects. The wind is the same; no matter how it blows, it does it in the same direction, with the same intensity and the same temperature. The sage, therefore, thought of "Zhong Fu" as being upright, fair, and honest. Here, honesty is the basic principle. Without honesty, how can anything be fair? How can anyone be right? So, in short, the hexagram for Zhong Fu is mainly about honesty.

The sage thinks:

First; of all, being honest is the most worry-free way of life. Just tell the truth, do what you say, say it how you do it, how simple it is. It is much harder to lie. You think one thing in your heart, but to say something else with your mouth. Usually, when a lie is told, it is necessary to make countless lies to round it off, which is a great test for memory. Once the lie is exposed, it may make everything collapse. How high and unrealistic is that risk?

Second; everyone is willing to make friends, cooperate, and share with people of integrity. People need a sense of security, and they want people with whom they work to have roots, not "a newly hatched egg that is called a rooster," there is no root in that. So honesty means more friends, more partners, more development opportunities. Be honest when making friends; life is fun.

Third; in the face of difficulties and problems, honesty is to have a clear attitude and position, not to ride on the fad of the moment, not to be ambiguous, and not to try to please both sides. It also means taking risks.

Fourth; if you make a mistake or have a problem, you must take the initiative to accept and acknowledge it. You must never make a fool of yourself. With such an honest attitude, you often win people's hearts and respect.

Fifth; if you build a credibility system, including both interpersonal and corporate organisation circles, such development will be stable.

Sixth; credit, integrity, fairness, and so on. Such a reputation is certainly good, but it does not have to be promoted for obtaining fame. People are afraid of being put on the spot. There are many similar stories in history. From the common people's officials to acts of kindness of the king. Most people know that one's great achievements jeopardise one's boss' position. Still, they do not know that being the boss is already dangerous. To leave a good impression on the person who decides your destiny, you must have a sense of "wanting to leave". In the end, the sage returned to the proposition that the gentleman (that is, an official) "deliberates about cases of litigation and delays the condemning to death". Meaning, that one must have the spirit of being upright, fair, and honest.

At this point, we can sort out the sage's thoughts in this regard:

First; gentlemen punish according to the law and etiquette, there must be laws to follow and strict law enforcement.

Second; gentlemen do justice regardless of politics and dare not break laws. The legal system must not be false.

Third; gentleman sentences to death when it is due. The judgment of a case must be based on sufficient evidence and cannot be delayed.

Fourth; gentlemen use punishment with prudence, and do not just sentence to jail.

Fifth; the gentleman discuses the law, he must be honest and fair and live up to people's expectations.

Among the sixty-four hexagrams of The *Book of Change*, the sages use mainly five hexagrams to talk about legal matters. Why are they so important? Because this is the State's system, and it has a bearing on the lives of ordinary people. Those good intentions of the sages, can today's bureaucrats appreciate them?

It can also be seen from this that the sage's summary of the hexagrams is closely related to the work of the statesman, and they are all pragmatic and specific. At the same time, they are not limited to practice but are far-sighted and far-reaching, inclusive, and transcendent. The "Honesty" elaborated in the hexagram of "Zhongfu" was later developed into one of the most important values of Confucianism. *The Great Learning* speaks of "sincerity"; *The Doctrine of the Mean* also speaks of "sincerity," and believes that sincerity can be "bred in us and educated". Sincerity is the spiritual bond that connects people and nature.

That is where one's absolute sincerity lies, and sincerity can make metal and stone crack. Zhong Fu, "Integrity wins the world".

Xiao Guo: there are degrees for everything

CLASSICAL TEXT

Xiao Guo; indicates that in the circumstances which it implies, there will be progress and attainment. But it will be advantageous to be firm and correct. What the name denotes may be done in small affairs, but not in great affairs. It is like the notes that come down from a bird on the wing – to descend is better than to ascend. There will in this way be good fortune.

Six at the First line; suggests the idea of a bird flying and ascending until the issue is evil.

Six at the Second line; shows its subject passing by his grandfather, and meeting with his grandmother; not attempting anything against his ruler, but meeting him as his minister. There will be no error.

Nine at the third line; its subject taking no extraordinary precautions against danger, and some, in consequence, finding an opportunity to assail and injure him. There will be evil.

Nine at the Fourth line; its subject falling into no error, but meeting the difficulty of his situation, without over-stepping its boundaries. If he goes forward, there will be peril, and he must be cautious. There is no need for ongoing firmness.

Six at the fifth line; suggests the idea of dense clouds, but no rain, coming from our borders in the west. It also shows the prince shooting his arrow and taking the bird in a cave.

Six at the top line; its subject not meeting the difficulty of his situation, and exceeding his proper course. It suggests the idea of a bird flying far aloft. There will be evil. The case is what is one of calamity and self-produced injury.

The image; the trigram representing a hill and that for thunder above it forms Xiao Guo. The superior man, in accordance with this, revises his conduct to foster humility, in mourning exceeds in sorrow, and in his expenditure exceeds the economy.

LITERAL TRANSLATION

Xiao Guo; prosperity depends on being upright. Deal with small things and not big things for now.

Six at the First line; flying birds meet with bad luck.

Six at the Second line; missed the grandfather, but met the grandmother; failed to catch up with the monarch, but met his minister; no blame.

Nine at the third line; attacked from the rear, advancing forward is dangerous.

Nine at the Fourth line; be on your guard against enemies, be vigilant. Do not push your luck.

Six at the fifth line; clouds are forming but without rain. The Prince tried his best to shoot something hidden in the cave.

Six at the top line; the bird was caught in the net. It is dangerous. This is a disaster.

The image; thunder on the mountain, Xiao Guo; the gentleman behaves in a respectful manner, there is a funeral and is sad, the economy is a frugal.

INTERPRETATION

In this hexagram, the upper part is Lei, indicating thunder; the lower is Gen, meaning the mountain. It is associated with a previous hexagram, "Yi." Thunder below the mountain, this is "Yi." This is an easier way to understand this hexagram. The sage considers the human head as a mountain, and the thunder below the mountain is the sound in the mouth produced by the head, then the "thunder on the mountain" is what? That is what's called "the thunder on the mountain." Why does one's head buzz? It is usually because of overthinking. If you overthink, your behaviour can be easily overwhelmed.

So, what is the difference between this Xiao Guo (small over) and the previous "Da Guo" (big over)? To put it simply, Xiao Guo is more about one's behaviour, and the relationship with oneself; while Da Guo is an external force, it is a relationship with the outside.

Regarding the thoughts and actions of "Xiao Guo", the sage believes that:

First; the initial situation should not be too prosperous. It is like singing, if a tone in the back is too high, it will not be heard. The rush to do everything right from the start is a problem. When you come to a new group, you think about how good and outstanding you are. It is easy to want to be sharp and to show off, which will be strange to others and make them jealous. When a new officer takes office, he immediately starts three fires, which are generally not easy to put out. In this, what if the relations between people were not straightened out. Could this fire spread out? Can it be controlled if it fast?

Second; find a role model to emulate. It is not a bad idea to have a higher idea and a higher ambition. Even if you cannot reach this ideal goal, it is not bad.

Third; the most ideal is the golden mean, not too much, not too little, just right; the most feared is uncertainty, one day higher than anyone else, tomorrow lower than everyone else, that will always be unfortunate and unable to stand up.

Fourth; if you do not have a good grasp, you would rather not do it.

Fifth; keeping a low profile should be the norm in life. Usually do not reveal anything, until you have a firm grasp of the situation.

Sixth; it is better to stay low than to go too far. If something is lacking, and the problem is not big. It can be regarded as having room for improvement; It is like cooking if there is less salt, the dish is light, and you can add salt later on, but if it is salty, you have to throw it away. There is now a consensus in medicine that many diseases have worsened due to overtreatment. People do not die that much, but they are tortured by surgery or harsh treatments — over-consumption, over-competition, over-entertainment, over-education, etc. There is too much over-existence in this society.

A lot of over-small-things is no problem. The sage gives an example, "The superior man, in accordance with this, in his conduct exceeds in humility, in mourning exceeds in sorrow, and in his expenditure exceeds his economy". People should be careful when doing things and should be sad at a funeral.

However, we must be calm and rigorous in major events, and we must not be paranoid or too moderate. We must concede in order to succeed.

Ji Ji: The difficulties of maintaining the achievements of our predecessors

CLASSICAL TEXT

Ji Ji; indicates progress and success in small matters. There will be an advantage in being firm and correct. There has been good fortune in the beginning; there may be disorder in the end.

Nine at the First line; shows its subject as a driver who drags back his wheel, or as a fox with a wet tail. There will be no error.

Six at the Second line; its subject as a wife who has lost her carriage-screen. There is no occasion to go in pursuit of it. In seven days she will find it.

Nine at the third line; the case of one ancestor who attacked the Demon region, but was three years subduing it. Small men should not be employed in such enterprises.

Six at the fourth line; its subject with rags provided against any leak in his boat and on his guard all day long.

Nine at the Fifth line; as the neighbour in the east who slaughters an ox for his sacrifice, but this is not equal to the small spring sacrifice of the neighbour in the west, whose sincerity receives the blessing.

Six at the top line; shows its subject with even his head immersed. The position is perilous.

The image; the trigram representing fire and that for water above it forms Ji Ji. The superior man, in accordance with this, thinks of evil that may come, and beforehand guards against it.

LITERAL TRANSLATION

Ji Ji; In this hexagram, the lines are in balance and the appropriate place for a perfect moment, but they are already changing into something, and it might be something dangerous.

Nine at the First line the wheel is stuck, the little fox gets its tail wet, no blame.

Six at the Second line; a woman lost her veil and did not have to chase it. She recovered it within a week.

Nine at the third line; Yin Gaozong (1250–1192 BC) conquered the badlands; it took him three years. Not a task for small men.

Six at the fourth line; your magnificent clothes become stained, making you nervous.

Nine at the Fifth line; the neighbouring countries to the east sacrificed cattle for the offering. They were not as blessed as the neighbouring countries to the west that made a smaller sacrifice.

Six at the top line; the little fox crossing the river with its head wet, dangerous.

The image; water over fire; the gentlemen should foresee disasters and prevent them from happening.

INTERPRETATION

In this hexagram: the upper part is Kan (The Abysmal), indicating the water; the lower part is Li (The Clinging), meaning fire. In a previous hexagram, "Ding", we see "fire over wood". They both look like cooking in a DaDing (an ancient cooking vessel). Now, this hexagram, "water on fire," shows that people are not paying attention to the burning fire below, but are paying attention to the soup in the vessel. They might even have a spoon ready to try it. In short, this meal is almost cooked. It is like the person crossing the river, finally getting to the other side. Therefore, the sage named this hexagram "Ji Ji", as in already overcome. At this time, is it possible to sleep peacefully? Of course not yet. The truth is that cooked ducks can still fly away.

After all the hardships and trials, one has finally done something. This is not the end, but merely a new beginning. Mao Zedong's poem:

Idle boast the strong pass is a wall of iron,

with firm strides we cross its summit.

We are crossing its summit,

The rolling hills sea-blue,

The dying sun blood-red.

As the road ahead is long and full of crises. The sage raised the following points:

First; when an undertaking is about to be completed, it is still faced with a large number of problems. From entrepreneurship to business obligations, there is still hard work.

Second; there is no need to worry about small gains and losses that have nothing to do with a bigger purpose.

Third; the key for success or failure depends on the people set to do the task, especially in those big moves that need to bet big capital, we must be cautious about finding the right people. The person you want to employ may not have the ability, and you must be honest, he must be able to truthfully report back to you the mistakes and problems he has encountered, so as to avoid further losses. If this person is a utilitarian and his vanity too strong, so he makes mistakes and gives incomplete feedback; this may drag the whole cause into the abyss. It is even more dangerous if this person has a divided heart and a personal agenda. The bigger the cause, the more it can ultimately fail, even more, if it is because of problems with insiders.

Fourth; to be frugal and cautious.

Fifth; we must be pragmatic, pay attention to small gains, and do not covet unrealistic things. Those, if not traps, are often just illusions, they can cost labour and money, and waste energy.

Sixth; for issues that may harm core interests, we must prevent small problems from happening, discover them in time, and resolve them in a timely manner.

In short, it is not easy to start a business, and it is more difficult to achieve success. We must think about the problems and prevent them, and we must maintain a sense of concern to prevent problems before they occur. Understand that life springs from sorrow and calamity. Learn from Bill Gates when he said, Microsoft is always eighteen months away from bankruptcy. Maybe we only need eight minutes of bad luck.

Prevention has been institutionalised in various social undertakings. When a project is approved, an environmental assessment is required; during construction, fire-fighting facilities are required, and in some places, earthquake prevention must be considered. There are even air-raid shelters everywhere; most are usually used as underground shopping malls. There are even foreigners building a Noah's ark.

The Yellow Emperor's Canon of Internal Medicine states that, 'It's too late to treat disease and cure it when it already developed, why cure it later rather than before?' It puts forward that a clever medical approach lies in preventing the disease. In Confucianism it is said, 'If a man takes no thought about what is distant, he will find sorrow near at hand'. Or 'Life springs from sorrow and calamity, so die peacefully'. Also, 'In all things, success depends on previous preparation, and without such previous preparation, there is sure to be a failure'. And many more.

Wei Ji: The path

CLASSICAL TEXT

Wei Ji; indicates progress and success in the circumstances, which it implies. We see a young fox that has nearly crossed the stream when its tail gets immersed. There will be no advantage in any way.

Six at the First line; shows its subject like a fox whose tail gets immersed. There will be an occasion for regret.

Nine at the Second line; its subject dragging back his carriage-wheel. With firmness and correctness, there will be good fortune.

Six at the third line; shows its subject, with the state of things not yet remedied, advancing on, which will lead to evil. But there will be an advantage in trying to cross the great stream.

Nine at the Fourth line; offers its subject by applied wisdom obtaining good fortune so that all occasion for remorse disappears. Let him stir himself up as if he were invading the Demon region, where for three years, rewards will come to him and his troops from the great kingdom.

Six at the fifth line; by wisdom obtaining good fortune, and having no occasion for remorse. We see in him the brightness of a superior man and the possession of sincerity. There will be good fortune.

Nine at the top line; its subject full of confidence and therefore feasting quietly. There will be no error. If he cherishes this confidence, until he is like the fox who gets his head immersed, it will fail from what is right.

The image; the trigram representing water and that for fire above it form Wei Ji. The superior man, in accordance with this, carefully discriminates among (the qualities of) things, and the different positions they naturally occupy.

LITERAL TRANSLATION

Wei Ji; just like a little fox crossing the river, when almost on the other shore, the ice breaks and its tail get wet, there is nothing to be done about it.

Six at the First line; it is a pity that the little fox got his tail wet.

Nine at the Second line; breaking its wheels, it is auspicious to stop in time.

Six at the third line; failing to get through on the first try, rushing in is dangerous, but it might lead to crossing the river.

Nine at the Fourth line; conquering the badlands needs three years of hard effort but can be rewarded by becoming a vassal of the great power.

Six at the fifth line; remain firm and be generous, without complaint and regrets, the gentleman's glory lies on being sincere and honest.

Nine at the top line; to become content with drinking without blame, just like a little fox crossing the river, you will get wet and end up in the wrong place.

The image; fire over water; gentlemen should be careful to distinguish things so that they are all in their right place.

INTERPRETATION

In this hexagram: the upper part is Li (The Clinging), indicating fire; the lower part is Kan (The Abysmal), meaning water. The fire is above the water, indicating that the fire was already on, but the pot containing the water had not yet been put on over a fire. This just started, just before the horoscope was left. Therefore, the sage named this hexagram as "Not Crossed Yet," which means that the matter has not been done yet; it is still struggling and is still marching toward success.

So how do you view this struggle? How to achieve success? The sage said a few things about this:

First, we should try to avoid the problems caused by our thoughts. Many people lose at chess, not because their opponents are better, but because they do not remain firm. Therefore, dedication, caution, and diligence are necessary.

Second; is to regard external difficulties as a chance to discipline oneself. We must believe in "difficulty without blame" and take a positive view of external pressures. The heavier the burden God has given you, the higher your expectations should be. Mencius's phrase, "When Heaven is about to confer a great office on any man, it first exercises his mind with suffering", and that is all right.

Third; is that good, and the bad depend on each other. There are some things you left unfinished for a long time, and then it just happens that you have a chance to accomplish more important things. For example, if you like a girl but do not have any success chasing after her, you might find a goddess walking towards you the next day. Or, maybe an ugly duckling will come to you, and then you will realise that she is the treasure of your life, you will be glad of not succeeding with the previous girl. There is only one life. If you cannot get on one bus, then you catch a different one. When planting flowers intentionally without success, you might inadvertently plant willows that will yield good shade. A reason why those flowers did not bloom is that they are not meant for you, but you did not know it at the time.

Fourth; is that you must be happy in life. Some people do not take into account the time for sleeping, the time for leisure, aging, and the time of doing various chores. There is not much time for real work. In particular, to do what you want, to work on yourself, there is even less time for that. Hold on to this short time and do something you really want.

Fifth; someone open and aboveboard is a good person. How can things develop as wished? But blame in one's heart.

Sixth; we must step out of ourselves and examine our struggle and life with a vision of improvement. Is it a life of obsession?

The sage ended the sixty-four hexagrams; with "not crossed yet," much like Mr. Sun Yat-sen's last words, 'The revolution has not yet succeeded. Comrades, we still need to work hard! We are always on a new road. The sage hopes that these sixty-four hexagrams will help us "distinguish the object" [of study], carefully analyse our internal and external factors, advantages, and difficulties, make a good positioning and choose the right direction. Then, getting back to the road! It is just a matter of time!'

Part Three

Having fun with the *Book of Changes*

"In the Yi (Change), there are four things characteristic of the way of the sages. We should set the highest value on its explanations to guide us; on the way it changes for setting our motives; on its image for specific; and on its predictions for our practice of divination".

I may be frivolous when it comes to this passage, *The Book of Changes*" is the main classic and core of Chinese philosophy. For two or three thousand years, the Chinese have lived in a culture based on *The Book of Changes*.

The value of The *Book of Changes* lies mainly in four aspects: Setting the highest value on its explanations to guide us; that is, the influence of *The Book of Changes* on people's speech and thoughts; "and on its predictions for our practice of divination," which is the core purpose of The *Book of Changes*.

Divination:

"The divination is still in within" refers to the influence of *The Book of Changes* on uses in an abstract way, in space, time and life.

So, how does *The Book of Changes* make a concrete impact in the practice? Below I cite two of the most typical cases, namely *The Sixty-six Tactics and Sixty-four Hexagrams* and *How Zhou People used The Book of Changes.*"

Thereafter, I teach you a simple method of divination that you can learn in five minutes. This is a book focusing on the philosophy and spirit of The *Book of Changes*, but it should also be an interesting book, one just for fun.

Thirty-six stratagems and sixty-four hexagrams

Eight times eight, sixty-four hexagrams. Six times six, thirty-six stratagems. War is central in Chinese thought, it means the rise and fall of a country and the lives and deaths of millions of people. The highest wisdom must be used.

Books on war and military wisdom are great – study them a little and they can be used in work and life. As long as history shows, wars have been fought, and there are many war books. However, the most well known war books for Chinese people, in addition to Sun Tzu's *Art of War*, is the *Thirty-Six stratagems*.

The *Thirty-six Strategies* is indeed very good. It was widely printed after the 1980s, but it has been known to the world for more than thirty years before then. Why? Because it is practical and straightforward. Like *The Book of Changes*, it summarises in a simple paradigm. For different situations and problems, there is a specific paradigm, it is convenient.

The version of the *Thirty-six stratagems* commonly used today is considered to have been compiled by masters of the Ming and Qing dynasties based on the famous Tan Gong's *thirty-six strategies*. Tan Gong was a renowned general from the Northern and Southern dynastic period. It is a tragedy of the Yue Fei style. A jealous king killed him. Then when the king died, he called him the bastard king to get rid of a capable lieutenant, which became a famous saying. In 2009, the media reported a set of the *Thirty-ix stratagems* engraved on the jade piece of the Sui Dynasty. As a result, experts proved that the author of *Thirty-six stratagems* was Tan Daoji. However, whether the contents of the jade piece is a simplified version is consistent with the current popular version; is not something that can be easily proven, no relevant information can be found online. I did not do this research specifically, and I do not want to go deeper. My concern is that each of the *Thirty-six stratagems* quotes and thoughts of *The Book of Change*s, and many of them are quoted from the original text.

So how do the thirty-six stratagems and the sixty-four hexagrams integrate? The following briefly explains it. However, first, let us cover two things: For some unknown reason, the general title and chapter titles in the book *Thirty-six stratagems* (winning tactics, enemy tactics, offensive tactics, melee tactics, combined tactics, and retreat tactics) have been deleted. In my opinion, they are not consistent with the corresponding full text or specific strategies.

The second is that most of the names of each of the Thirty-six stratagems are a generalisation of the content of the stratagems, and some are complements or extensions. However, taking these into account is enough to call it the "shortest book in history"!

*The Book of Change*s is infinitely inclusive. Politicians read it for politics, artists read it for art, military strategists read it for military art, and ordinary people read it for daily life. For us ordinary people, martial arts (the military art) are also a method for living.

Stratagem 01: Cross the sea without the king's knowledge.

The sea and the sky being as big as they are, how could it be possible to hide them? In *The Book of Change*s, the Yin and Yang reciprocate each other. There must be Yang in every Yin and Yin in every Yang; moreover, the more Yang there is, the more yin spots there will be. The more fool proof a place is, the more likely it is for something to go wrong; the more dangerous a situation is, the safer it is. Eventually Yin will be Yang, and Yang will be Yin. This seems to be too philosophical. Let us take an example of an image; male genitals are Yang, so they are called "the yang tool" in Chinese; they are also Yin, so they are called "the stem of yin."

Stratagem 02: Besiege Wei to rescue Zhao: A united enemy is worse than a divided enemy. An enemies Yang is worse than an enemies Yin.

If the enemies forces are concentrated, it will be challenging to go head to head. It is relatively easy to find a way to spread the enemies strength and then focus on breaking each part separately. *The Book of Changes* believes that there must be Yin where there is a Yang, a weakness that has advantages. Avoid the enemies yang side, take a detour, hit the enemies yin side, attack his weakest link, and win.

Stratagem 03: Kill with a borrowed knife: When the question of who is the enemy is clear, and who is a friend is unclear, kill using your friend's hand.

The "Sun" (Lose) hexagram says; "The topmost NINE, undivided, shows its subject giving increase to others without taking from himself". But people also want to obtain benefit, though they often have to withstand consequential losses. However, nobody likes to bear any loss. Between the enemy and me, there are usually several erratic third-party forces. We must find a way to initiate conflict between a third party and the enemy, and at the same time, narrow their relationship with us, to use them to attack the enemy. It is like letting a third party be used as cannon fodder, and deriving advantage from it. Of course, do not treat real friends as "third parties" because you will end up losing them.

Stratagem 04: Wait at leisure while the enemy labours: Trap the enemy without a fight. Lose in order to win.

The hexagram of "Sun" states that; "There is a time when the strong should be diminished". There are overcast days and short days in a month, and good fortune and happiness for everyone. Everything is constantly changing, like in profit and loss; there are different states at different times. Deciding on the outcome of a war depends on seeing who can afford to act first and on waiting until the enemy is in the worst state possible. If your side is united, and the reserve of supply is stable, then a siege can continue without fighting. Just wait for the enemies in the city to run out of food, and become desperate. If you are the defender, you can strengthen the walls and clean the city, wait for the enemies outside to run out of supplies.

Stratagem 05: Loot a burning house: If the enemy suffers harm, take advantage of the situation, and he will be finished.

The "Guai" (Break-through) hexagram states, "We see in the figure the strong lines displacing the weak". Controlling the weaker side by strong is a typical legalist strategy. It is simple, crude, but effective. When the enemy is in a vulnerable state due to natural disasters, human-made disasters, and other factors, seize the opportunity and give a blow to gain an advantage.

Stratagem 06: Make a sound in the east, then strike in the west: The enemy will be in trouble.

The trigrams of Kun on top and Dui below forms the hexagram of "Cui" (Gathering). The hexagram of "Cui" is about many people or other things. Coming together is particularly confusing and prone to unexpected problems. We should find a way to pass a large amount of information to the enemy, both true and false, as to create trouble for the enemy. Let the enemy try to extinguish a fire that might not be there. Then, when it is weak, launch a real attack. The odds will be better.

Stratagem 07: Create something from nothing: A proven lie is also a revealed truth.

*The Book of Change*s believes that the yin turns into yang and the yang turns into yin. In response, Lao Tzu asked the question, 'Do you know the extremes?' When does the fundamental transformation take place between Yin and Yang? This is the most difficult thing to grasp. Remember the story of *Peter and the wolf*, where he lost credibility after calling out falsely two times and so no one believed him when he called for real a third time. We must take the initiative to find a way to achieve the effect of the third call of wolf: I say I'm going to attack you, so you think I was bluffing. In the eyes of the enemy, a third false attack suddenly turns into a real blow.

Stratagem 08: Openly repair the main roads, but sneak through a narrow passage: Show movement, to remain hidden.

The hexagrams of "Yi" (Increase) is formed by Xuan in the upper part, which means wind, submissive action. In the lower part is Zhen, which means thunder, which means violent action. The "Yi" hexagrams say, "Yi is made up of the trigrams expressive movement and docility, through which there is daily advancement to an unlimited extent. The suppleness of the upper part is shown to others, and the toughness of the lower part is hard work in the background. Such a person will surely achieve great success. Push a strategic manoeuvre in a high-profile manner, thereby locking the enemies attention and main forces, while secretly pushing for another strategy, to then, attack the enemy unexpectedly.

Stratagem 09: Watch the fires burning across the river: Yang is in disorder, and Yin is waiting to be reversed. Wait for violence to manifest before acting.

The hexagram of "Yu" states; "the will power will make itself be felt and carried out". Traveling along the water is easy and comfortable, riding along the breeze is brisk and joyful; speaking nicely brings happiness. A well-behaved person should follow along. But do not support that person if he is lazy.

Offer a treat, so everyone is happy. Otherwise, if you insist on acting against this, it will be difficult. This is very important for leaders. When you come up with an idea and implement a set of policies, you must conform to the will of the people to succeed. Sometimes the masses do not understand, so you must do a good job of propaganda, guidance, and communication in the early stage so that people are ideologically ready. In the military, when the enemy is still strong, the generals are arrogant. They commit all sorts of outrages. At this time, if you attack, it is like a reminder that they must be ready and united. Therefore, it is better to wait for them to fall into chaos, and when they become desperate, then you can rush up and help them die faster.

Stratagem 10: Hide a knife behind a smile: Keep faith and peace. Do not make any changes until the trap is set.

The hexagram "Kan" represents water. The shape "strong in the centre, weak on the outside" is part of the character of water. In "The Zuo Tradition," it is written that, when a fire is big, and everyone pays attention and remains aware, few people are killed by the fire. But while water seems calm, people love to get close to it, and many people eventually drown. The insidious villains who are really lethal are often people who seem to be friendly and relaxed. Be careful when someone suddenly treats you well. Militarily speaking of course, it is not possible to show friendliness to an enemy. Still, you can show weakness instead, so that the enemy believes that you are not a matter to be concerned about. While on the other hand, this also gives you enough time to prepare for the offensive.

Stratagem 11: Sacrifice the plum tree to preserve the peach tree: One is bound to be damaged, it is usually the yin that is damaged by the yang.

The hexagrams of "Sun" states; "If there be sincerity in this method of diminution, there will be good fortune; freedom from error; firmness and correctness that can be maintained; and advantage in every movement that shall be made." In many cases, it is necessary to do with less. Sometimes actively losing and some passively, but as long as it is controllable and the reduction is systematic, it will be advantageous. For example, national disarmament, company layoffs, and dismissal of business units may further improve overall efficiency.

Or, as when people have tumours, and cutting away the relevant body tissues will help prolong their lives. All warfare hopes to sacrifice one part for the greater benefit of another. The same is true in life, where one part of the profit is sacrificed continuously in exchange for another (smaller part). Sadly, the result here is always a lost.

Stratagem 12: Take the opportunity to pilfer a goat: you must take any opportunity, get any small profit.

*The Book of Change*s believes that the transformation of Yin and Yang starts from the slightest thing. Lao Tzu said, 'Consider what is small as great, and a few as many; and recompense injury with kindness'. There is nothing trivial to war, and a small flaw can bring a devastating disaster. It is not an exaggeration to say that a horseshoe, if it is not nailed may bring calamity. If war is an art, it must be sophisticated. Be keen to catch any small flaws in the enemy, and seize any opportunity to strike the enemy, because if you do not, it will be the key point in determining your ultimate victory.

Stratagem 13: Stomp the grass to scare the snake: Question the truth, and then move with certainty.

The hexagram of "Fu" states; "Things will return and repeat its proper course. In seven days they will return". Everything in the world is undergoing cyclical changes. For anything, what you see at this moment is often only one side, one state. You need to see a more complete operating cycle and see all its sides to grasp its actual essence.

Regarding the state of the enemy, do not just look at the surface, but think of a way to see its back and inside; do not just look at it while it is static, activate it, make it move, and look at its dynamics. Then, a judgment can be accurate, and you will not fall into the trap of the enemy. The reason why the mafia is sinister is that the people you can see are only one of its many faces.

Stratagem 14: Reincarnate in somebody else's body: Use what has not been used, give it a new use.

The hexagram of "Meng" states; "I do not go and seek the youthful and inexperienced, they come and seeks me". When the other party knocks on your door to ask for advice, you can teach him, and the learning will be better. If you rush and beg someone to let you teach him, you will sell yourself cheap, and that person will not learn well. In war, we need to integrate as many resources as possible, but others cannot lend us things of real value. Unless they have something to lose themselves, we cannot wait for them to do us a favour. Let these resources come to you willingly; this can best reflect the wisdom of leaders. Zhuang Zi said, 'The use of a seemingly useless thing is to be useful for something bigger'. No matter what its use is, change waste material into things of value.

Stratagem 15: Lure the tiger off its mountain lair: Do not go fetch him, hire someone to lure it out, and go back to your safety zone.

The trigram below the hexagram Jian (Obstruction) is Gen, which represents the mountain, and above Kan, the ridge, which represents the water. There is a large river above the mountain, which means that this road is too difficult to walk, what to do? Return to your original place, and slowly find an alternative way, this is a wise choice. Sometimes the enemy is in such a situation that it is best for them to stand still. We must increase the pressure on the enemy to make them feel that they have to abandon the city or use tricks to lure the enemy out of the town.

Stratagem 16: In order to capture, you must let loose: If forced to flee, the will to fight will be pushed by survival instinct, reduce it by giving hope.

The hexagram of "Xu" is about waiting, "with the sincerity declared in Xu, there will be brilliant success," and with a firm yet calm attitude, the light will eventually come to shine brighter. When the enemy is lost, but their forces are still strong, we should follow closely and push on to victory. We cannot let the enemy run away nor push too hard. Pressing too hard will make the enemy think that he cannot run anyway, and turn around for a final deadly battle. The enemy must seek the chance to escape and be unwilling to fight. In this way, they will feel relieved when running away. If they want to fight back, they will not be able to organise a counter strike. When this happens, you will give them a fatal blow, and they will be defeated. It is easy. It is like a cat scratching a mouse that plays dead. There is a typical life example in this. No one can stand a lengthy pursuit. Sooner or later that person will be caught.

Stratagem 17: Tossing out a brick to get a jade gem: offer something useful to get something important.

The hexagram Jian (obstruction) is mainly about education, and it can be further extended to instil and influence others' ideology. In kindergarten, Xiaoming sang a nursery rhyme, and his aunt gave him a little red flower, and other children would think that if he would also sing a nursery rhyme like Xiaoming, he would also get aunt's little red flower. Management is mostly to play with such a trick. Reading history, I found an interesting question: the generals who surrendered during the war all ended up in the same situation; some were relocated immediately, while others were beheaded. Why? Because the former generally happens in the early stages of the war, at this time, there are still many cities to attack. If a prisoner is killed, the enemy generals in the future will not surrender, and they will desperately resist. In the latter part of the war, when the overall situation has been determined. Those who surrender will be shown to their people as an example and be told: you cannot surrender to the enemy when you protect your country, surrender is punished with death.

Stratagem 18: Defeat the enemy by capturing their chief: Maim their strength by eliminating the head, the rest of the body will follow.

The "Kun" hexagram states; "Dragons fight in the wild, the onward course indicated by Kun is pursued to extremity". If the commander in chief goes and fights in the trenches, he will come to an end. Chinese chess is very similar to a simulation of war. At the beginning of the game, the two sides are equal in strength. After a long and arduous fight, there are injuries and deaths, and there are only a few troops left. The veteran of the disadvantaged side is no longer stable, and he dances around the remaining enemy pieces for a long time, until he is finally killed. However, real chess masters do not have to work so hard. After the opening, they do not take many steps. When they grab a vital point, catching the opponent's leader, the horses and cannons become decorations. During the war, extraordinary measures are taken. First, the enemies headquarters is destroyed, just like the KO in a combat match. The match is difficult to solve, and the game ends suddenly. In addition, destroying the enemies elite troops will also destroy the morale of the enemy.

Stratagem 19: Remove the firewood from under the pot: do not attack the enemies forces, attack his supply lines instead.

"Dui (Joyous) is up, and Qian (The Creative) is down", this is the image of the hexagram of "Xu," and the hexagram of "Xu" is about being polite and rules-oriented. If you cannot beat someone, talk to him, mention international law, talk about human rights, talk about democracy, talk about ethics, and talk about the friendship of your common ancestors. At the end, let him feel righteous and to spare you; or let the public criticise him for not behaving morally right. In this way, his momentum dissipates. At first, Mao Zedong could not beat Lao Jiang, but he was better at propaganda, so countless revolutionary youths rushed to Yan An, and the masses cheered for the Communist Party. Lao Jiang felt his American-style equipment was too advanced for the enemy and was arrogant and unjust with his enemy. It is like pulling out the firewood under the pot. In the end, it cools down only a little bit, but once the strength is gone, the momentum is lost.

Stratagem 20: Disturb the water and catch a fish: multiply confusion and push your agenda while people are unaware.

The hexagram "Sui" is about following; in the "Four Books of the Yellow Emperor," there is a section about governing the country. A country, an organisation, and an army must have leaders, ideological values, and brave souls that are followed by everyone. Otherwise, they will fall into a mess. Many years ago, we used to say that we should be alert to the "peaceful evolution" of the West. What is this "peaceful evolution"? In fact, it was about the internalisation of their values, so that we gradually had doubts, dislike, and resistance towards the establishment and the things that we followed. Finally, society felt lost, and then they were ready to surrender. Specifically, in war, it is necessary to establish a strategic idea of "psychological offensive as the best tactic so the attack will get right to the core," we must actively fight psychological warfare.

Stratagem 21: Slough off the cicada's golden shell: Mask yourself by leaving a distinctive trait behind.

The hexagram of "Gu" states; "the idea of Gu is a troublesome condition of affairs verging to ruin" The word Gu in Chinese is also used for a legendary worm, and a worm is patient. It enters the body with eaten food and goes unnoticed until it develops in the stomach, then it starts to grow. In that way, others can be afraid of you, and your situation remains stable. On the other hand, if someone sees your internal crisis and weakness, you may be taken advantage of while in distress. History books record that after the death of many kings, the royal family did not mourn. When the transfer of power was complete, the new court was set up, and the overall situation became stable. During war, after a siege, when the army is retreating, it is the most frightening place to be found by the enemy. If people chase after you, you may lose a lot, so you must create the illusion of maintaining the status quo. Go on quietly.

Stratagem 22: Shut the door to catch the thief: To capture your enemy, you must first make sure there is no other way out.

The hexagram "Bao" (exploitation) is about stripping and losing one's foundation. For small enemies who venture into our country, we should cut off their connection with the rear, turn him into a rootless grass, and wipe them out. Therefore, solitary advancement is often a taboo when marching.

Stratagem 23: Befriend a distant state and strike a neighbouring one: Make allies of distant countries and wage war on closer ones.

The trigrams of fire in the upper part, and marshes in the lower, form the hexagram of "Kui" (Opposition). It has to do with the relationship between the opposites and differences between things. Geopolitics is the science of interpreting peace; follow its development, and the disputes around the world today. Disputes often occur between geographically close countries, and there are fewer conflicts of interest among countries that have no borders or shores. Therefore, on the one hand, Japan insisted on confrontation with our country over issues; such as rights over the Diaoyu Islands; while, on the other hand, actively developing diplomatic relations with the United States, India, and African countries. Similarly, in daily work and life, competition and interests between people often are seen in relatively closed circles, and seeking strong support outside of this circle will help your development.

Stratagem 24: Obtain safe passage to conquer the State of Guo: borrow from allies to conquer enemies, and then use those same resources against your ally.

The "Kun" hexagram states, "If he makes speeches, his words cannot be made good". You are in a weak position. Others do not believe you can fulfil your promises. Others' promises to you are uncertain because they cannot guarantee the expected benefits. As a small country, it is difficult to maintain neutrality between opposing powers, and such a country is bound to be dependent. Who to cling to? In such a situation, you should not look to see which party is more committed to yourself, and which one is more powerful. You can join any strong one. For that one, you can provide an airport and a base. At the same time, you can take advantage of it to strengthen your prestige. Small countries such as the Philippines, which are sandwiched between China and the United States, are now adopting this position. This is also the situation of many young people. Your life begins with an attachment to "adults." If you find a good attachment, you can make it. If you do not, you cannot rise.

Stratagem 25: Replace the beams with rotten timbers: Disrupt the enemy supply lines, harass their patrols, and change the rules of common warfare in order to weaken their foundations.

The hexagrams "Ji Ji" and "We Ji" both refer to "pushing its wheels," which means that the brakes should not be pushed too hard. When the enemy attacks, if the position is concise and fierce, and the elite troops focus on a single target, the pressure will be strong. Find a way to fight the enemy guerrilla-style, from the flank or even from behind. Disrupt the enemies deployment, harass the enemies elite forces, and finally drag the enemy to slow down the pressure on your offensive, until you can achieve a strategic counterattack. Although the Kuomintang and Communist Party's battle against the Japanese army was passive, the objective was indeed to achieve the strategic exchanging space for time. Then, the offensive momentum was curbed.

Stratagem 26: Point at the mulberry tree while cursing the locust tree: Use innuendo and allegories instead of direct accusations to reveal hidden treats by having them talk against you.

The "Shi" (The Army) hexagram states; "There is the symbol of strength in the centre of the trigram below, and it is responded to by its proper correlate above". There is a risk in fighting, but the military fights for strength, not for power. Big fish eat small fish, and a strong country wins over a weak country. Everyone understands this principle. Therefore, when your strength is superior to the enemy, it is often possible to achieve your strategic intention without sending troops, but by simple political diplomacy. Sun Tzu's *Art of War* says, "Anyone who wins a hundred battles must also become a good person, even if at the beginning was not good; a soldier who is a good man without a fight can remain a good person".

Stratagem 27: Feign madness but keep your balance: act as not knowing what you do and see how the enemy lowers its guard.

"Tun" (Difficult at the beginning) hexagram states that the period of career development is extraordinarily difficult. You should plan patiently, hold back, and do not move lightly. Just like a small grass bud, if conditions such as moisture, soil, nutrition, and temperature are not right, the sprouting will emerge from the ground only to be sunburned, frozen, and dried. Therefore, it is better to be quiet than to be foolish or mad. When the time is right, if you do not take off, you will regret it. Some people have also compiled their own set of "Thirty-six stratagems," one of which is "disguise as a pig and eat a tiger", which is related to this.

Stratagem 28: Remove the ladder when the enemy has ascended to the roof: isolate your enemy as much as you can, then cut their lines of communication.

The hexagrams "Shi He" states; "he meets with what is disagreeable and hurtful: his position is not the proper one for him". The original meaning Shi Ke in Chinese is biting. Though it implies biting meat, it might be poisonous meat. For a fish, what looked like food might end up being a fishhook. For corrupt officials that think there is a sweet deal, but they might find it to be bait. This applies to food and sex too. Desire is the driving force and the big trap of life. Soldiers are perverse. All conspiracies and tricks are to seize the weaknesses of human nature and make some people a victim of their desires. In war, we must be good at provoking the desires of the enemy, lead the snake out of the hole, lure the enemy deeper and lead him into the right spot and lay an ambush.

Stratagem 29: Decorate the tree with false blossoms: Make a dead tree look alive, make something of no importance look like it is virulent.

The hexagram "Jian" states; "the geese gradually advanced to the heights beyond. Their feathers can be used as ornaments". A bird perched on the top of a marvellous mountain is divine, and its feathers precious. People worship a stone, carved into a Buddha statue and placed on top of an incense case; for the same stone, when it is built into a step, is stepped on by people's feet. What is the difference? Power! Two college students with the same qualifications, one made it into the Provincial Party Committee, and the other entered the county Party Committee, both are ordinary members, but their situation is quite different. One started a business, and in ten years, became a small boss; the other worked as an executive in a large company and then started a business.

Similarly, their potential is different. Mencius said, 'A man may have wisdom and discernment, but that is not like embracing a favourable opportunity'. Han Feizi believed that "law, skill, and potential" are the three elements that determine success or failure. Potential is everywhere. Just see if you can use it, such as a mountain, wind, water, power, education, momentum, demeanour, situation, upbringing, family support, etc. If there is no potential to dispose of, you can build your own. To make things plain, fake it until you make it; fake education, fake background, fake godfather, fake breasts. Many people who have been longer in their job are all fake except for their mother; it is difficult to say anything else about this.

Stratagem 30: Make the host and the guest exchange roles: use any gap to infiltrate, and then gain power from within.

The hexagram of "Jian" states; "the advance indicated by Jian is like the marrying of a young lady which is attended by good fortune". Everything should be done, step by step, like a woman getting married. First needs a matchmaker, then a marriage proposition, then the wedding, and then get along with the in-laws. After several years, a spoiled girl became a wife, like the character in *Dream of Red Chamber*. In the actual power struggle, there is no such warmth. When an outsider gets through a process of gradual penetration, and finally seizes the opportunity and takes control of the overall situation, this process is somewhat similar. Why do all the kings founding a new dynasty like to kill heroes? It is because they are afraid of being compromised by them. At the same time, there are many stories of opening the doors to a dangerous foe.

Stratagem 31: The beauty trap: send beautiful women to the enemy camp; let them fight among them to win her over.

The hexagram of "Jian" is very interesting. It uses birds that are gradually flying as an image, and the development of a marriage relationship as a reference to tell the truth. The hexagram mentions a crisis of marriage, "a husband who goes on an expedition from which he does not return, and of a wife who is pregnant, but will not nourish her child. There will be evil. The case symbolised might be advantageous in resisting plunderers", the husband goes out on an expedition, but the woman at home is pregnant. Of course, it is a woman's problem, which cannot be a good thing. But it is conducive to resist greater harm from bad people. This exposes an ugly problem in Chinese culture: the objectification of women. When the Allied Forces hit us, some city-guard officials forced many prostitutes to take off their pants and stand against the wall, because people believed that this would make the artillery of the enemy fail. The advanced form of this is that of marrying close relatives. It has been done since the Han Dynasty, marrying a princess to a leader of the Huns in exchange for peace. It can be said this was to adjust to local conditions (or sex politics). The so-called heroes, of course, regard money as dung, and they are not convinced by a knife pressing on their neck so that they are as strong as yang can be. Only women who are supple as yin can restrain them. What is love in this world? It is the one thing that can defeat anything!

Stratagem 32: The empty fort strategy: When weakened, pretend you are overconfident, then your enemy will think you are preparing an ambush. If you do have a hidden force to ambush, then it is even better.

The hexagram of "Jie" is about settlement and reconciliation. As the saying goes, "The strong and the weak correlate", yielding will not cause problems. When the enemy arrives at a yang position, and you are also at a yang position, conflicts will inevitably occur. If you are weak, you will lose. On the contrary, if he is first to the yang, and you are supple as the yin, his strength will quickly dissipate. You can become an active part instead. For example, if someone criticises you, you will easily get hurt if you refute it; if you accept it, he will be at a loss, and others will not believe his criticism. Since femininity has such great power, it implies that there must be a greater hidden power behind femininity. There is no perfect person in the world, and no absolute perfect defence; there will be shortcomings and flaws. If a person is strong enough, there is no need to cover up as much as possible. Maybe others do not think of it as a flaw, and perhaps there is no flaw at all, so think of it as your hidden strength.

Stratagem 33: Let the enemies own spy sow discord in the enemy camp: feed the enemy false information and plant the seeds of discord.

The hexagram of "Bi" (Compare) talks about the principle of closeness. It states, "The movement towards union and attachment proceeds from the inward mind: the party concerned does not fail in what is proper to himself". It is easy for people inside a circle to be close to each other, and they generally do not hurt each other. In everyone's mind, the people they associate with are either insiders or outsiders, which is the same as the concept of Yin and Yang, not an absolute. A group of insiders may become outsiders. We want to be close to the enemy leader to obtain information. The most effective way is to turn an insider against him, instead of sending an outsider to approach him.

Stratagem 34: Inflict injury on oneself to win the enemy's trust: Pretend to be injured to look harmless, or to create the rumour of a different enemy.

In the "Meng" hexagram, it states; "the good fortune belonging to the simple lad without experience comes from his docility and humility". It is a wonderful thing to educate innocent and simple children, and the love of children and teachers will easily and naturally stimulate each other. It is not like teaching adult students, with preconceptions and complex emotions. The feeling between teacher and student is not as good. Under normal circumstances, when a person who has been persecuted by the enemy comes to you, like a lost bird, or a stray dog accepted in a new home, it will be grateful, and our compassion and love will overflow. It is cruel to use this emotional situation to spy during a war though.

Stratagem 35: A chain of stratagems: Have more than one stratagem ready as a follow-up, or play many at the same time as a grand plan.

The "Shi" hexagram states; "he is in the midst of the host, and there will be good fortune". In the military, a general is one of the highest positions; his strategy needs to be right. Though there is luck in victory, when it comes to destiny; non-human power can completely control it. When the enemy has many soldiers and its strength is greater than yours. In this case, you cannot give up hope. You must try your best strategies or a set of systematic tactics to lengthen the time of the war and insist on waiting until the time is right. The changes in the entire external environment might benefit you, and with enough luck, you can overcome the enemy.

Stratagem 36: If all else fails, retreat: When everything fails, then it is time to retreat, choose between surrender, compromise, or escape.

The hexagram "Shi" states; "the host is in retreat, but there is no error". Retreat does not mean failure. Today's retreat is tomorrow's attack, just like the Big Bad Wolf shouted at the end of each episode, "I will come back!" Then he would come back in the next episode, and still managed to challenge the sheep in their never-ending confrontation. A concession is not equal to failure. To give up is not equal to failure. Even escaping is not equal to failure. As long as you shout in your heart, "I will come back!"

How Zhou People used *The Book of Changes*

The *Book of Changes*, as the name suggests, was first compiled by talented people during the Zhou Dynasty. Actually, people from the times of the Zhou Dynasty were closer to the original text.

It is recorded in our earliest history books, The Discourses of the States, and The Zuo Tradition. Here, I have selected these records and briefly explain them. I hope to help you understand the most orthodox way of reading *The Book of Changes* and the method of interpreting hexagrams, as well as the understanding of the philosophy of *The Book of Changes* at that time.

I. *Discourses of the States*

Let us start with the three or four cases in the *Discourses of the States*. Most of the cases described in The Zuo Tradition also belonged to the times of the Spring and Autumn period. These were times when only nobility of the Zhou Dynasty had access to *The Book of Changes*. *The Book of Changes* was an "instruments for the profit of a state that would not be shown to the people.

After the death of King Zhou Wu, Zhou Gongdan assisted the young King Zhou Cheng. King Zhou Cheng and his brother Shu Yu were close playmates. On one occasion, Xiao Cheng Wang cut a piece of paulownia leaves into a shape of an ancestral jade tablet for his brother and said that he should be the new marquis. When Zhou Gong heard this, he told King Zhou Cheng, 'Heaven has no humour to make jests'. So Feng Shuyu was a named marquis, it was roughly 1042 BC, and the Jin Dynasty began from then on.

Jin State has always been a relatively powerful vassal state. Until the end of the Spring and Autumn Period, that is, when the Jin Dynasty was separated. The Jin, Zhao, Wei, and Han families rose, and eventually divided Jin into three states.

Case 01: Duke Xian of Jin attacks Li Rong: He was victorious but unlucky. He used scapulimancy instead of *The Book of Changes*. In 672 BC, Duke Xian of Jin wanted to destroy a minority tribe. The person in charge of scapulimancy was called Shi Su (an officer), and he told Xian Gong that the result of scapulimancy was "victory without luck". The battle was won, but the win was not auspicious, not good, so it was best not to fight. Xian Gong did not listen, and the result was indeed a victory. He returned with a lot of spoils and the beautiful Li Ji. At his return, he then asked Shi Su, 'What's wrong about all this?' Shi Su did not dare to speak in person. He just said that the result of scapulimancy was just what was described. It might not be wrong, but there is no harm on being alert. Afterward, Shi Su privately pointed out to a friend that this "bad luck" would manifest on the ill-fated sorrow of the concubine, Li Ji. At that time, Xia Jie, the last king of the Xia Dynasty, attacked, and brought back a beautiful girl named Mei Xi. Then came the end of the Xia Dynasty. King Zhou of Shang also brought a beautiful concubine from Da Ji, and then the Shang Dynasty collapsed. King You of Zhou also got a beautiful lady as spoils of war, and then the Zhou Dynasty also collapsed.

Sure enough, Li Ji made Xia Jie fall crazily in love and tried her best to make his son a prince. As a result, the oldest prince was isolated and committed suicide. The other two heirs fought over the succession, and the dynasty fell apart.

Case 02: When Prince Wen of Jin returned to his kingdom, he was to occupy the throne: he was first faced with the hexagram Tu (Difficulty at the Beginning), then with Yu (Enthusiasm) in the second interpretation by *The Book of Changes*. Turmoil in Jin State lasted for many years, during which Duke Wen of Jin had been exiled abroad. In 636 BC, the Duke Wen of Jin received help from the kingdom of Qin and was expected to regain the throne of the Jin kingdom. He personally used "milfoil steams" for divination to try and predict whether his expedition would be smooth. The Hexagram obtained originally was "Tun," and the Hexagram derived was "Yu." As shown below:

 Tun (Difficult at the Beginning)

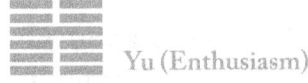 Yu (Enthusiasm)

Now, let us talk about the use of milfoil steams in divination, this is the so-called Long Development Method. Milfoil is also known as yarrow; it is a plant of the family of Asteraceae and also known as wild chrysanthemum.

For divination, the steams are dried, and then trimmed to a length and thickness of about the same size, then they can be used to sort hexagrams during divination. There are some for sale on Taobao, but they are not cheap, anyone interested can check it out. Later generations mostly used chopsticks instead.

Why use fifty yarrows for divination? This is an eternal mystery left to *The Book of Changes* scholars. However, Confucius said, 'At fifty, I knew the decrees of Heaven'. It can be seen that there may be a mysterious connection between the number fifty and destiny.

First, take out one yarrow steam, this one represents Tai Chi, and you place it on the table. The ancients probably placed directly on the ground. Let us not delve into details such as venues, rituals, and methods as I will give a basic explanation how to get a hexagram.

The next step is completed with the remaining 49 pieces.

First, divide these 49 randomly into two groups, left and right, and then take one from the group on the right.

Set aside the steam, then divide each bundle again into groups of 4, so in the end, there is 1, 2, or 3 left in the end. No matter how many are left, take them with the rest already left out and set them aside. If there is nothing left, take out the four from the last group and set aside.

Then, the remaining steams are grouped together and randomly divided into two groups again, the same way as before. Each group is divided into groups of 4, and the remainder is taken out.

Finally, put the remaining steams together again, and take out the remaining, like we did the first two times, do this three times. At this point, how many groups of "4 steams" are there on the table? There are only four possibilities: 6 groups, 7 groups, 8 groups, or 9 groups.

This gives four numbers: 6, 7, 8, and 9. How to assign these four numbers, the Yin and Yang strokes? The ancients believed that 6 and 8 were even numbers, so they were Yin, while 7 and 9 were odd numbers, so they were Yang. Yin nature is down, Yang is up. Therefore, 6 is the lowest, and it is going to be the lowest, which also means that it will change. Consequently, it is called "Shao Yin" (Yin most). For the one representing Yang, 9 is the top, and it is called "Yang most"; 7 is called "Lesser Yang."

Therefore, if the number of steams is 6 or 8 in the end, it means that there is a Yin stroke; if it is 7 or 9, it means that it is Yang stroke. This becomes the first one in the bottom of the image or Hexagram that will come out.

6	Yin Most	‒‒ ‒‒	Changes
8	Lower Yang	‒‒‒‒‒	Doesn't Change
7	Lower Yin	‒‒‒‒‒	Doesn't Change
9	Yang Most	‒‒ ‒‒	Changes

By repeating the above process, you can finally get all the six strokes, a complete hexagram. The image thus comes out.

Knowing this method, we can now go back to the case of the Duke Wen of Jin. Let us first see how his "Tun" hexagram came out on the table below.

Sixth Number Obtained	8	‒‒ ‒‒	
Fifth Number Obtained	9	‒‒‒‒‒	
Fourth Number Obtained	6	‒‒ ‒‒	Tun (Difficult at the Beginning)
Third Number Obtained	8	‒‒ ‒‒	
Second Number Obtained	8	‒‒ ‒‒	
First Number Obtained	9	‒‒‒‒‒	

The Hexagram obtained originally is different.

So, how did the "Tun" and "Yu" hexagrams come about? As mentioned earlier, 6 and 9 represent Yin most and Yang most, both of which are the extremes, so the two, and the stroke obtained from these two numbers contains the trend of the change. The original yin stroke will change to Yang, and the Yang will become Yin.

"Zhi" means to go in Chinese, and it is part of the description for this case. There is a sentence in the textbooks of junior high school that reads, "Do you want to go to far away places in the south?" Do you remember any of them by any chance? Looking at the table above, this time, Duke Wen of Jin's divination result; the first time he was right, but then for the following interpretations, it is "mutating." As soon as they change, the whole Hexagram will turn into "Yu".

Tun (Difficult at the Beginning)		Kan (The Abysmal) Represents water and the people.	8 Doesn't Change		Kun (The Receptive) Represents earth.	Yu (Enthusiasm)
			9 Change			
			6 Change			
		Zhen (The Arousing) Represents a cart.	8 Doesn't Change		Zhen (The Arousing) Represents a cart.	
			8 Doesn't Change			
			9 Change			

Now that we know the method, how do we obtain the original divination? And how does it change?

Let us see how to check the hexagrams. Regarding the results of Duke Wen of Jin, the first time using divination was regarded as "unlucky", but then it would become "good luck" for his son. He said: In the hexagrams of "Tun" and "Yu", the words were clearly written, "Luck will come later", which was conducive to the establishment of the prince. What would have happened, had they not regain the throne of the Jin Dynasty, what about "Luck will come later"?

The lower trigram in "Tun" is Zhen, an earthquake, and there is an image of a cart (the ancient roads were bumpy and shaky for carts); the upper trigram indicates water, (a representation of people on a boat). In the Hexagram of "Yu", there is Zhen, an earthquake, and Kun is the next. Kun represents the land. Moreover, Tun has a sense of accumulation and a sense of joy. There is a cart, the people, the land, virtues, and joy. Isn't this the image of a successful monarch?

There are earthquakes (Zhen) in both hexagrams, and shaking of the earth can also be about war, and water is involved.

Warfare in an affluent fashion, isn't this also a sign of conquering a country? Therefore, with the help of the Qin Kingdom, Duke Wen of Jin decisively returned to claim his kingdom. At that time, the Minister of the State of Jin, Dong Yin, greeted him at the border, and he was stunned. He asked Dong Yin, 'What will it be from now on?'

(Can I succeed?) Dong Yin first pointed out the positive signs from astrology, and then said, 'I asked specifically about it and got the "Tai" hexagram'. The Hexagram is the image of a monarch that is mediating between heaven and earth.

The Hexagram shows "there will be good fortune, with progress and success". The former monarch is small, and you have to be big. So you will succeed!

Sure enough, Chong Er successfully took over the Jin Dynasty, became Prince Wen of Jin, and showed grand ambition, making the Jin Kingdom the overlord of the Spring and Autumn period.

Case 03: Duke Cheng of Jin returns to claim the throne: "Qian" (The Creative) becomes "Fou" (Standstill).

In 607 BC, Duke Ling of Jin was assassinated, and the ministers summoned his son of Duke Cheng of Jin, who was abroad. He was to become the heir to the throne. In the meantime, someone asked the oracle about the fate of Duke Cheng of Jin, who was also known as Hei Tun. He obtained the hexagram "Qian" and the hexagram "Fou". As described in the next table:

Qian (The Creative)			
	— —	7 Doesn't Change	— —
	— —	7 Doesn't Change	— —
	— —	7 Doesn't Change	— —	Fou (Standstill)
	— —	9 Changes	— —
	— —	9 Changes	— —
	— —	9 Changes	— —

At that time, the result was interpreted as: "It will get what is deserves, it will not be done for, but the ruler will leave three times". What does, "It will get what it deserves" mean? This means roughly the following: This Hexagram is "Qian", which means heaven and has the image of a monarch. Therefore, Hei Tun could successfully sit on the throne of the king of Jin.

However, the first, second, and third lines of Hexagram are "9s", Yang most strokes that will change.

Editor's note; *There are 4 possible numbers you can get when consulting the I Ching: 6, 8, 7 and 9. These are respectively: Big Ying, Small Ying, Small Yang, Big Yang. I translated them as Ying most, Lesser Ying, Lesser Yang, Yang most to make it like a continuum from least to most.*

So it becomes the Hexagram of "Fou", which means impassable. Inappropriate in the short-term, and then "unfinished". However, historically, Duke Cheng of Jin himself had a good ending and passed on his throne to his son.

Therefore, later generations interpreted it that Duke Cheng of Jin's descendants would eventually lose control of Jin State, "but not end it". This was inevitable. The king would eventually be ousted. About 150 years later, the Jin Dynasty began to be divided up by the Zhao, Wei, and Han clans.

What does, "The ruler will leave three times" mean? Later generations combined historical facts and figured that Duke Cheng of Jin, and his successor monarch did leave three times, or some major set back before taking office, or was forced to flee abroad while in office. This was the second time for Duke Cheng of Jin; Duke Li of Jin was killed in the year 573 BC, and his son was taken abroad to become the king. He was Duke Dao of Jin. So this was the second time the Jin had to be outside their kingdom. The last time was when the kingdom started to split; their heir was expelled from the country in the year 458 BC.

So, how is this "The ruler will leave three times", reflected in the Hexagram? Quite simple. The three strokes in the lower part of the "Gu" hexagram change from Yang to Yin, from Qian to Kun and from monarch to Minister.

The part of "The Zuo Tradition"

There are over twenty references to *The Book of Changes* in *The Zuo Tradition*, mainly divided into two kinds: one is to quote the hexagrams in *The Book of Changes* and their explanation, and the other is for divination and interpretation of the Hexagram. In the following section, takes examples from the *Discourses of the States*:

Case 04: Is there a dragon in the real world?

In "The Zuo Tradition", during the twenty-ninth year of Duke Zhao of Lu (513 BC), a dragon was seen on the outskirts of Jin State. At that time, Wei Xianzi, the governor of the Jin Dynasty, sought his most trusted historian Cai Mo (621–687) to inquire about dragons. Cai Mo told him that during the reign of King Dashun (2294–2184 BC), there were officials who were responsible for raising dragons, and their descendants were "Longlong" and "Yonglong". Under their management, the dragon could even carry the king. But during the Xia Dynasty, the dragon died, and the official in charge served the King Kong Jia the dead dragon's meat. Kong Jia thought it was delicious and wanted more. The official then panicked at the idea of having to kill a dragon and ran away.

Since then, there were no officials who could handle dragons, and so, everything was in conflict. No one can control the dragon, so the dragon is always lurking hidden somewhere, almost invisible. All over *The Book of Changes*, we can see examples: "The dragon lies hidden in the deep", "The dragon shows himself and is in the field", "The dragon is flying in the sky", "The dragon exceeds the proper limits", "the host of dragons appearing were to divest themselves of their heads". And in the "Kun" hexagram, "dragons fighting in the wild". If the dragon was not something that ancient people saw day and night, how could they talk about such an image?

Case 05: Man Man has no Morality and is Greedy

In "The Zuo Tradition", during the sixth day of the Xuan Gong emperor (603 BC), two nobles from the vassal state of Zheng chatted together. One of them, Man Man, was ambitious and said that he was fighting for a high position. The other was called Biao Liao and knew that Man Man loved compliments, and so he complimented him, 'You're great, work hard, and do not forget your brother after you rise'. Later, he went around telling people in private: Man Man is ungrateful and greedy, just as in the sixth line of the Feng hexagram in *The Book of Changes* states, "its subject with his house-made large, but only serving as a screen to his household. When he looks at his door, it is still, and there is nobody about it. For three years, no one is to be seen. There will be evil". With insatiable greed, living in a luxurious house, but not knowing that something is missing, danger is on the way. Sure enough, Man Man was killed a year later.

Case 06: The hexagram of "Master" (Shi) in the Battle of Jin versus Chu

In "The Zuo Tradition", during the twelve-year of King Xuan Gong for (597 BC), King Chu Zhuang led an army to attack the vassal state of Zheng. The famous allusion, "You cannot see how big a bird is until it squawks"; is about the King Zhuang of Chu. During the first three years of his reign, he did not do anything in politics and slept all day. After three years, he changed his personality. He quickly sentenced a group of adulterers, appointed Sun Shuo and other famous ministers. He worked hard to control the country's strength, thus possessing the power to challenge the then overlord of Jin.

The state of Zheng was a small ally within Jin's sphere of influence. And after being beaten by the Chu, Jin had to send elite troops to rescue him. However, when the Jin army was approaching, it became known that Zheng had surrendered to the Chu. The commander of the Jin army wanted to withdraw his troops at first, and then later take back Zheng State after the Chu army withdrew.

Most other generals agreed with this decision, arguing that King Zhuang of Chu's battle against Zheng was difficult to deal with. There was no chance of winning the war, and he should "see the advance of the enemy and then retreat when he learns about the difficulties". However, the deputy commander of the Jin army first firmly opposed the move, thinking that if he went back like this, it would be too embarrassing. How could face be saved in this situation? You can withdraw, but I will fight by myself. And so it was that the detachment of the army under the deputy crossed the Yellow River without authorisation to fight against the Chu army.

At this time, a general named Jiu Shou pointed out that the army was in danger. He quoted from the first line of the "Shi" hexagram, "The host going forth according to the rules. If these be not good, there will be evil". The army must be strictly disciplined and must be obedient; otherwise, it will be dangerous. At the same time, from the perspective of the hexagram, he pointed out that the hexagram "master" (Shi) is formed by Qian (The Creative), and Kan (The Abysmal). And Kan indicates water, and the water follows the flow.

If this first line changes, Kan becomes Dui (Joyous), Dui represents lakes and marshes. And so the mountains and rivers divert water into lakes and marshes. In short, when there is a problem in military discipline, there is danger.

However, the deputy was worried that if he were defeated first, he would not be able to blame himself as the commander, so he had to bravely lead the army across the river. In the following battles, military discipline issues always plagued the Jin army. In the end, the battle ended with the victory of the Chu army. A few years later, Chu replaced Jin as the spring and autumn period new overlord.

Case 07: The doctor discusses the fate of the King of Chu based on the "Fu" hexagram.

In "The Zuo Tradition", during the twenty-eighth year of King Xianggong (545 BC), a court physician from the state of Zheng visited the kingdom of Chu. Previously under the rule of King Chuzhuang and then under King Zhuang of Chu. The country was stable, and so power passed to King Kang of Chu. He was even more treacherous and often bullied the state of Zheng. The physician returned from his visit and reported to the rulers that King Chu Kang was about to die. Since he took the throne, he had not worked on state politics, but he coveted other countries' resources and had heavily used his troops. How could he last? As the "Fu" hexagram says, "all astray on the subject of returning". "Set to regain one's desire for glory, but to abandon its cause, and return to nothing, is it not to say that you are lost, can it be inauspicious?" Wanting to revert to his vision, but not knowing what path to follow. This is "confusion". How can it not be inauspicious? An order was given to prepare to send a funeral party to King Chu Kang. In the next ten years, Chu would be in civil strife and could finally be taken back.

Sure enough, King Chu Kang died that year, and his successor's son was slaughtered four years later. After that, the state of Chu did not have the strength to invade Zheng.

Case 08: The physician from Qin and Duke Ping of Jin's disease

In "The Zuo Tradition" during the first year of King Zhao Gong (541 BC), Duke Ping of Jin, the monarch of the kingdom of Jin became ill. In the state of Zheng, a well-known politician, Zichan, gave condolences, and had a discussion with the Minister of Jin, Uncle Xiang, on the condition of Duke Ping of Jin. Uncle Xiang said that ghosts and the gods might cause the monarch's illness. Zichan pointed out that the disease was caused by too much work and no rest, excessive diet, and grief, and had nothing to do with ghosts and gods. Zichan said, 'A gentleman has four periods in a day: a time in the morning for listening to the court discuss the government, a time during the day for visits, a time in the evening for recovering, and by night things will be settled down'. Work when you have to work, and rest when you should rest, if it is so vitality will flow free, and there will be no illness; Duke Ping of Jin's disease was caused by uncontrolled sexual conduct.

Soon, the Jin court called the state of Qin's most famous doctor, He, and the diagnosis of He was, "The Illness seems like a worm on what has been spoiled (Gu)". He said that women's genitals could be close to each other, but when there is an infection, problems occur. In addition, when the infection damages the yin energy of the women, it can spoil the rest". The disease caused by having sex with such women damages both the body's yang and yin, disrupting the body's Yin and Yang balance. It is like a venomous insect is in the stomach, and it cannot be treated. This is precisely what the "Gu" hexagram means: a mountain, and below that wind, the woman is bewildering the man.

Here we have to add one more point. Gossip is a basket, where you can put all kinds of things in it. As long as we mark a limit, everything within this range can be in *The Eight Trigrams*, and there will be a corresponding interpretation to a hexagram.

The Yi scholars, with numerous schools, devoted much energy to this kind of "putting things in the basket" kind of work.

In addition to the basic, the most common are the sky, earth, mountain, swamp, wind, thunder, water, and fire, which correspond to Gan, Kun, Gen, Dui, Zhen, Kan, and Li. The situation corresponds to each hexagram:

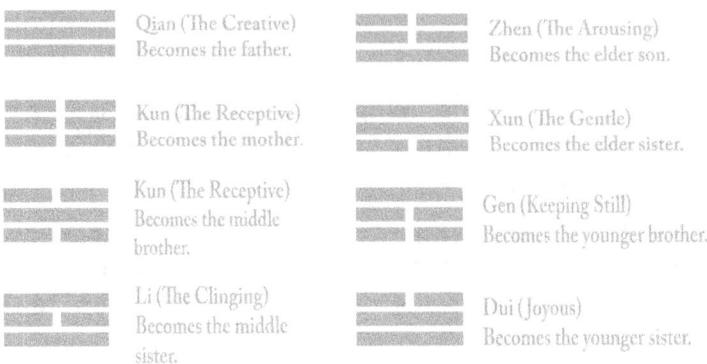

Why doing that? It is pretty visual. There are six kinds of Chinese characters: pictographs, Ideographs, Phono-semantic compounds, Compound Ideographs, Transfer Characters, and Rebus. The pictograms and Compound Ideographs can be used for the analysis of hexagrams in *The Book of Changes*. Zhen is the first trigram with a yang stroke, so it represents the eldest son. Xun is the first trigram with a yin stroke, so it represents the eldest daughter. This is how Compound Ideographs work.

Then, let's look at the hexagram of "蠱" (Gu). The top trigram is Gen, indicating a young man; the bottom is 巽 (Xun), meaning the eldest daughter; in turn, it becomes a mature woman lying with a naive young man, so it is called "Women confuses men". Along this line of thought, it looks like the sixty-four hexagrams become a sort of pornographic picture, haha.

Case 09: Shi Mo discusses the impermanence of monarchs and princes referring to the "Da Zhuang" hexagram.

In the "The Zuo Tradition" during the thirty-two years of King Zhaogong (510 BC), Duke Zhao of Lu died in Jin seven years after exile. He had previously been defeated in the battle by three major members of the Ji family led by Ji Pingzi: Uncle Ji and Meng Sun, and he was driven out of the state of Lu. Since then, Lu Pingzi had been in control.

In response to this situation, Jin politician Zhao Jianzi asked his aide Shi Mo, 'The Ji family is treacherous, why do the people of the state of Lu still support them? And other vassal states also recognise him?' Shi Mo answered, 'The Ji family has assisted the monarch of Lu for several generations. All these monarchs have been indulgent and careless. They all left the administration of the country for Ji to handle, and new generations of Ji government officials were diligent. Ordinary people have long forgotten the existence of the monarch, and so Duke Zhao died without them caring about it'. "Gods rarely respect rulers, and monarchs rarely give up their position – since ancient times it has been so". The gods of mountains and rivers do not always favour one side, and the flow of power is not static for the king and court. In the *Book of Songs*, there is this passage; "The crags on the hill-tops fall. High banks become valleys. Deep valleys become hills". The descendants of kings are now ordinary people. In *The Book of Changes*, the "Zhen" trigram moves on top of the "Qian" trigram, this means "big and strong". In the law of the jungle, the strong feast off the weak, this is the will of heaven. Therefore, "the monarch most be careful and recognised, and cannot let others make their ruling".

We will now take a look at the case of divination in "The Zuo Tradition". We will, again start from the top. Do not be dizzy, haha.

Case 10: Tian's legacy was predicted 300 years before its time

In "The Zuo Tradition", during the 22nd year of King Zhuanggong (672 BC), civil disturbances occurred in the state of Chen. Duke Li of Chen's son Chen Wan fled to the kingdom of Qi for refuge and received the courtesy Duke Huan of Qi, one of the overlords of the spring and autumn period. Because of the ancient pronunciation, "Chen" and "Tian" sound are similar. At the same time, for security reasons, Chen Wan changed his name to Tian and became Tian Wan (so Chen and Tian originated at the same period). After several generations of operation, Tian became the patriarch of the Qi Kingdom and gradually took control of the state. In 481 BC, the sixth descendant of Chen Wan, Sun Tianchengzi slaughtered Qi Jiangong and put on the throne the monarch Qi Jinggong as a puppet king. In 386 BC, Chen Wanxian's grandson Tian He dethroned Qi Kanggong and established himself as the monarch. He was sent by the then king of the Zhou Dynasty and continued to use "Qi" as the country name and title to add to the family title "Tian's clan of Qi." By this time, Chen Wan's native country, the state of Chen, had been destroyed for more than 100 years.

When Chen Wan was a child, one day, one of the royal families of the Zhou royal family came to Chen Ligong with a set of *The Book of Change*s, and Chen Ligong asked for a reading for Chen Wanzhan. The hexagram was "Guan" (Contemplation), and the change headed towards the hexagram "Fou" (Standstill). The fourth line is a changing line, and the corresponding text is; "one contemplating the glory of the kingdom. It will be advantageous for him, being such as he is, to seek to be a guest of the king". As in the following table:

Guan (Contemplation)		Xun (The Gentle) represents wind.	7 Doesn't Change		Gen (Keeping Still) represents a lofty mountain.	Qian (The Creative) represents heaven.	Fou (Standstill)
			7 Doesn't Change				
			6 Changes				
		Kun (The Receptive) represents earth.	8 Doesn't Change			Kun (The Receptive) represents earth.	
			8 Doesn't Change				
			8 Doesn't Change				

A Zhou state's historian recorded the event and hexagrams, thinking that the descendants of Chen Wan will become king in a foreign country.

In the "Guan" hexagram, after the lines change, the trigram Xun becomes Qian; that is, the wind becomes heaven, and heaven represents the king. Below both hexagrams is Kun, indicating the land; then it changes to "Gen" trigram representing mountains. It is the image of a monarch because it has the elements of mountains and heaven and earth.

Popularity is not part of the image, so it is interpreted as occurring in a foreign country. "Guan" means waiting and watching, so it should be something for future generations. So, which country is this? The Zhou historian believed that it should be Qi. Because the ancestor of the Qi Kingdom was Jiang Ziya, and he was the "Grand Duke Jiang", which corresponds to the Gen in the hexagram.

However, the historian of Zhou pointed out "one thing cannot be two," what does it mean? There is a passage in *The Yellow Emperor's Four Classics*, telling that "the one with horns doesn't have fangs", and animals with horns on their heads do not have sharp fangs.

When good things happen, they do not leave you alone. Therefore, when Chen Wan's descendants became foreign kings, the state of Chen must have fallen.

This historian really liked to offer good news, haha.

Case 11: Job Hunting hexagram for the state of Wei's Ancestor Bi Wan

In "The Zuo Tradition" during the first year of Min Gong (661 BC), Duke Xian of Jin led the army to destroy several small nations. After that, he rewarded his man, Bi Wan, for his military achievements by appointing him lord of the Wei state. After that, the descendants of Bi Wan took Wei as their surname and gradually grew stronger. Finally, in 453 BC, together with the states of Zhao and Han, "three families divided Jin" and the Wei rule was established. Therefore, Bi and Wei have the same ancestors.

Bi Wan was a nobleman of the Bi Kingdom. After Bi Kingom's demise, he came to the Jin state to seek employment as an official. As described in the next table:

Tun (Difficult at the Beginning)						Bi (Compare)
		Kan (The Abysmal) Represents water.	8 Doesn't Change		Kan (The Abysmal) Represents water.	
			7 Doesn't Change			
			8 Doesn't Change			
		Zhen (The Arousing) Represents the older sibiling, a cart, a foot or the image of a cart.	8 Doesn't Change		Kun (The Receptive) Represents the mother, the earth or the image of a horse.	
			8 Doesn't Change			
			9 Changes			

The diviner thinks: it is auspicious.

Tun (Difficult at the beginning) means to consolidate; it means to be close and integrated. This shows that an officer can be stable and can earn the trust of the monarch.

What is more, the Zhen under "Tun" represents an earthquake, and it changes into Kun. As mentioned earlier, Zhen is the eldest boy and Kun is his mother, which means that he was protected by his brother and mother. According to the "basketing" theory mentioned earlier, Zhen also corresponds to a foot and a wagon; Kun also corresponds to a horse (as in the Kun hexagram line, "what is great and originating, penetrating, advantageous, correct and having the firmness of a mare") and the land. Stepping on the ground, the horse and the wagon go with great ease and freedom, like the nobles.

Case 12: Duke Huan of Lu gets a reading for the future heir; he gets the "Qian" hexagram and "Da You".

In "The Zuo Tradition", during the second year of Min Gong (660 BC) rule, Lu was in chaos, and the monarch Lu Minggong was killed. Minister Ji, You helped to turn the tide and assisted Duke Xi of Lu to ascend the throne, ensuring the state of Lu survived the crisis.

Ji You was the youngest son of Duke Huan of Lu. When he was born, through scapulimancy, it was determined that he would be a boy, and he could assist the state in the future. When looking at *The Book of Changes* in the hexagram "Da You", and one of the trigrams is "Gan," as shown in the following table:

Da You (Abundance)		7 Doesn't Change		Qian (The Creative)
		6 Changes		
		7 Doesn't Change		
		7 Doesn't Change		
		7 Doesn't Change		
		7 Doesn't Change		

The diviner concluded: "As the Father, he will be respected as king". This child will be as noble as his father, and people will respect him as much as the monarch.

This conclusion may be combined with the rhetoric of the fifth line in "Da You", "the sincerity of its subject reciprocated by that of all the others (represented in the hexagram). Let him display a proper majesty, and there will be good fortune".

The transfer in good faith is prestigious and auspicious. Moreover, the lines in the hexagrams of "Da You" and "Qian" indicate heaven, and they have the image of a prince. Later, Ji You's descendant was called Ji Sun's. Although he was not the monarch of the kingdom of Lu, he controlled the government for many years.

Case 13: The two hexagrams of Duke Hui of Jin and Duke Mu of Qin

In the first sections in the "Discourses of the States", Duke Xian of Jin appears confused by a concubine. Soon he abolished the prince, and his two sons were exiled. The "Discourses of the States" only recorded Chong Er's divination (another name for Duke Wen of Jin) but did not mention the case of Duke Hui of Jin. However, there are two related records in The Zuo Tradition. Before Chong Er, Duke Mu of Qin first helped Yi Wu return to Jin's country and became Duke Hui of Jin. How can Duke Mu of Qin be so helpful? He was undoubtedly conditional. Duke Hui of Jin was quick to promise, no matter how much land and how much money he needed, he will give it all. Moreover, there is another reason why Duke Mu of Qin's wife, Mu Ji is the daughter of Duke Xian of Jin, the eldest sister of Yiwu and Chong'er, and Duke Mu of Qin and their brother-in-law and little sister-in-law. To make a long story short, after Jin Huigong successfully ascended the throne, he broke up the agreement with the Qin monarch.

Under such circumstances, a famine occurred in the Jin State, and the Qin State still called for a large amount of food to help the people of Jin. Shortly afterward, the Qin State faced famine. The Jin State not only did not help but also attacked Qin while it was weak. So, in the fifteen years of Duke Xi of Lu, according to "The Zuo Tradition", Duke Mu of Qin was furious and led a large army to attack Jin. Before he left, he asked for divination and got the "Gu" hexagram (蠱)

The official in charge quoted the hexagram, "Thousands of times, three times, after three trips, the fox was caught" (this is not the actual text of hexagram in *The Book of Changes*), implying that Duke Hui of Jin is the "fox," and he will be captured.

Also, the trigram below in "Gu" is Xun, indicating wind; the upper is Gen, meaning mountain. Now it is autumn, the autumn wind blows strong, and the mountains and trees are enduring it, which is the image of the army sweeping the Jin Dynasty.

Sure enough, the Qin monarch prevailed and captured Duke Hui of Jin. Fortunately, Mu Ji's concubine begged with tears and begged some more. So Duke Mu of Qin did not kill Duke Hui of Jin after a comprehensive political arrangement. Jin Huigong, who had become a prisoner, remembered that before her sister married, she once got the hexagram of Gui Mei, and the following one was Kui (Opposition). Such as the following table:

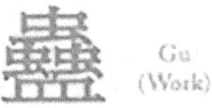
Gu (Work)

Gui Mei		Zhen(The Abysmal) Represents a cart.	6 Changes		Li (The Clinging) Represents fire.	Kui (Opposition)
			8 Doesn't Change	— —		
			7 Doesn't Change			
		Dui (Joyous) Represents a swamp.	8 Doesn't Change	— —	Dui (Joyous) Represents a swamp.	
			7 Doesn't Change			
			7 Doesn't Change			

The person in charge of divination at the time thought: this is not good.

He quoted the rhetoric of the sixth hexagram of Gua Mei (Basically the same as today's version); "The man slaughtered a sheep without seeing blood, and a woman laboured without success". Moreover, Kui means to be tired of each other. This is definitely not good for marriage. In addition, "Gui Mei" has Zhen as the upper trigram, which means thunder, and "Kui" has Li, which means fire, but also thunder and fire. A sign that one must not quarrel every day. Zhen, the earthquake, also means a cart, one that was burned by fire. In short, not good.

Duke Hui of Jin complained to his subordinates, 'If the dynasty physician had listened at that time, and he did not marry his sister to the Qin state, there might be no such troubles'. But his minister, Han Jian, immediately quoted the words in the *Book of Songs*, "the calamities of the lower people, do not come down from Heaven. A multitude of good words, and hatred behind the back. The earnest and determined pursuit of this is from men". This means that a disaster in the world does not come from Heaven, and life is actually smooth; disasters happen because of you.

However, the physician's interpretation of the hexagram was inaccurate. Actually, this was an inaccurate example, haha. If it were not for Mu Ji's help, there might not have been such a thing as Jin Wengong's hegemony in the future. How can we say this was "not good luck"?

Case 14: Duke Wen of Jin's gets his hexagram

In The Zuo Tradition, during the twenty-five-year of Duke Xi of Lu (635 BC), Duke Wen of Jin just had taken the throne for a year. He wanted to revitalise the Jin Dynasty and dominate the vassal states. There was an opportunity right in front of him. Previously, civil strife broke out under the rule of the royal family of Zhou, and King Zhou Xiang's brother conspired with the tribesmen from the western border of Zhou state to usurp the throne, and King Xiang of Zhou was forced into exile. The Minister of Duke Wen of Jin suggested, 'Rush troops to save the throne' and to protect the king and calm down the rebellion. This was an excellent opportunity to win the respect of the princes.

So Duke Wen of Jin First used the scapulimancy to get a good omen. He thus used *The Book of Changes* for divination, and got the hexagram of Da You; the interpretation was that for Kui (Opposition), as shown in the following table:

Da You (Abundance)		Li (The Clinging) Represents fire and a day.	7 Doesn't Change		Li (The Clinging) Represents fire and the day.	Kui (Opposition)
			8 Doesn't Change			
			7 Doesn't Change			
		Qian (The Creative) Represents heaven.	9 Changes		Dui (Joyous) Represents a lake.	
			7 Doesn't Change			
			7 Doesn't Change			

The interpretation was then: good fortune.

He pointed out that the change in the hexagram of "Dayou" was, "The public enjoys the heavenly son". He told him, 'You are the duke, and King Xiang of Zhou is the heavenly son'. This is exactly what the king wanted to hear. The lower trigram of "Dayou" is Qian, which means heaven. After the change of the three lines, Qian becomes Dui, which means lakes and marshes. Above in both hexagrams, there is Li, indicating the sun. Heaven descends and greets the sun with the humility of lakes and marshes, just as after the success of the battle, King Xiang of Zhou was thankful.

Sure enough, Duke Wen of Jin's battle was successful, gaining fame and fortune, and a solid step towards hegemony.

Case 15: The hexagram "Fu" and the Battle of Fuling

In "The Zuo Tradition", in the turn of the sixteenth year of Duke Cheng of Jin (575 BC). The kingdoms of Jin and Chu contended for control of the Zheng state. Duke Li of Jin and King Gong of Chu led the two armies to battle in Fuling, what is now Yanling county in Henan province. The Jin army had shamed King Chu Zhuang more than twenty years earlier by defeating the Chu army. During the climax of this battle, there was a duel between two champions. One of them was General Wei of the Jin Dynasty, who shot an arrow right in the eye of King Gong of the Chu, which created turmoil for the Chu army. Then, the King of the Chu called the archer Yang Youji, and he, in turn, shot General Wei in the throat with just one arrow, instantly killing him.

Before the battle officially started, Duke Li of Jin got the "Fu" hexagram during divination, and the hexagram read, "The south will shoot true in the eye" (there is no such sentence in *The Book of Changes*), which means that the southern state, (Chu State was in the South) was meant to shoot into the eyes of a King.

Case 16: Mother Jiang's and the Sui hexagram

In "The Zuo Tradition", during the nine years of Xiang Gong (564 BC), Duke Cheng of Lu's mother, Mother Jiang, died in a small palace outside the capital. Previously, she had a lover when she was a queen. This lover wanted to use her to achieve his political goals. Eventually, things were messed up, and the mother and the child broke ties. Mother Jiang had to stay away from politics, apart from his son and moved into a small and deserted palace. When she first moved in, Mother Jiang consulted the oracle and drew the hexagram "Gen" (Keeping still), and the following hexagram was "Sui" (Following). As described in the next table:

		9 Changes		
Gen (Keeping Still)		6 Changes		Sui (Following)
		6 Changes		
		9 Changes		
		8 Doesn't Change		
		6 Changes		

There are five changes in this hexagram. When the occupants interpreted the hexagram, they did not emphasise the meaning of the original hexagram "Gen".

One can make a detailed analysis of the meaning of hexagram "Sui". It is believed that "Sui" suggests, going out. This small palace was not suitable for living, and she should be moved out immediately, so as to say in the hexagram "Sui," "there will be great progress and success. But it will be advantageous to be firm and correct. There will then be no error".

At this time, Mu Jiang was disheartened. She had already consulted *The Book of Changes*. She said, 'The characters in this hexagram can be interpreted individually; if so, then they represent four virtues of a man: benevolence, courtesy, righteousness, and justice. I have none of these four virtues. How can I be "without error"? "Gu" is to remain still as a mountain, so I will just stay here and die'.

Case 17: Cui Wuzi married Tang Jiang and got the "Kun" hexagram followed by "Da Guo"

In "The Zuo Tradition" during the twenty-fifth year of the rule of Xiang Gong (548 BC), Cui Wuzi, the governor of Qi State, killed Duke Zhuang II of Qi, which was motivated by an affair between Duke Zhuang II of Qi and Cui Wuzi's wife Tang Jiang. After the tryst, the duke got hold of Cui Wuzi's hat and gave it away to someone. The "green hat" (being a cuckold) expression may have something to do with it. In short, Cui Wuzi became angry. One day, Duke Zhuang II of Qi secretly entered Cui Wuzi's house and was killed by an ambush of royal guards. Later, Cui Wuzi's younger brother became the monarch, namely Duke Jing of Qi. Duke Jing of Qi was always jealous of him and forced him to commit suicide two years later.

Had Cui Wuzi obey the divination and not marry Tang Jiang, then this tragedy may not have existed. Tang Jiang was originally Qi Tanggong's wife. When Qi Tanggong died, Cui Wuzi offered his condolence, and was suddenly fascinated by her vulgar beauty, and had to marry her. When his servants performed divination, they got the hexagram "Kun" (Difficult), and he got the following hexagram of "Da Guo." As described in the next table:

Kun (Oppresion)		8 Doesn't Change		Da Guo (Mayor Demerit)
		7 Doesn't Change		
		7 Doesn't Change		
		6 Changes		
		7 Doesn't Change		
		8 Doesn't Change		

The interpretation was then; good fortune. His good friend Chen Wenzi pointed out that as the third line changed, the interpretation clearly stated; "He enters his palace, and does not see his wife. There will be evil." It was a clear omen; he should not marry this woman.

However, Cui Wuzi disagreed, 'This "evil" should be for her ex-husband, Qi Tang, and it was not for him'. So he got married. Fate is inevitable.

So why did he think it was a good omen? Probably because in the "Da Guo" hexagram, there are words about an old husband who marries a young wife. Or just because his servants wanted to please Cui Wuzi and only say good things.

Case 18: San Bu of the Shu clan was killed by a cow(ard)

In the "The Zuo Tradition", during the fourth year of Duke Zhao of Lu (538 BC), Sun Bao of Lu from the Shu clan died. Many people may not be familiar with this name, but many of his famous sayings have been heard. That happened when he was as an envoy to the state of Jin, his minister, asked him; 'The ancients said,

"Dead yet immortal". Do you know what it means?' He replied, 'I've heard that three steps lead to heaven, achieve virtue, render meritorious service, and achieve immortality from one's writings'. This is how you do not remain among the living. These "three steps of the immortals" have become the ultimate life ideal of Chinese elites.

People get confused about such great ideas. When he was young, Sun Bao, fled to Qi State because of something, and slept with a woman on the way, leaving her pregnant with his child. Later, the woman found him and brought the child to him. Before that, Sun Bao had just had a nightmare, in which he was rescued by a man called a Niu (Ox) in his dream. Upon seeing this child, Sun Bao found that the child was very much like the man in his dream, so he named him a Niu (Ox), and he trusted blindly in the future. However, this Niu was a treacherous Ox. He grew up jealous of his two stepbrothers, so he devised a rumour to wreck their relationship with his father, Sun Bao. Eventually, the two brothers died or fled. At the end, when Sun Bao was gravely ill, he refused to let others visit him, and he starved his father. Later, he supported another relative as his father's suzerain, Sun Zhao of the clan Shu. Sun Zhao, did not appreciate it and mobilised the clan to kill the Niu.

When Sun Bao was born, his father used *The Book of Changes* for clarity about his future and obtained the hexagram "Ming Yi", and the following was "Qian". As described in the next table:

Ming Yi		Kun (The Receptive) Represents earth.	8 Doesn't Change		Kun (The Receptive) Represents earth.	Qian (Modest)
			8 Doesn't Change			
			8 Doesn't Change			
		Li (The Clinging) Represents fire and the day.	7 Doesn't Change		Gen (Keeping Still) Represents the mountain.	
			8 Doesn't Change			
			9 Changes			

The interpreter of the oracle concluded that this child would have a period of exile, and then will return to inherit his position as the suzerain. He will be close to a whisperer, and the villain's name was Niu (Ox), and he will eventually starve him to death.

Then he explained. The first thing to do was to see the change from the first interpretation, "flying, but with drooping wings.

When the superior man is resolve to his going away, he may be for three days without eating. Wherever he goes, the people there may speak derisively of him. From here came the image of exile, and the image of calamity.

The hexagram Ming Yi is a sign of departure; the lower part is Li (Clinging), meaning the sun. This is also the image of a public official and contains the virtue of the Qian hexagram, so it is enough to interpret it as he was inheriting the position of the suzerain.

The trigram below in "Qian" is Gen, which means mountain; the trigram below "Ming Yi" is Li, which also means fire. When a fire burns big, it corresponds to human affairs, which is to say bad things.

The "Li" hexagram states, "Let its subject also nourish a docility like that of the cow, and there will be good fortune". Therefore, this evil man who played with fire and destroyed his father should be related to "cattle".

In the end, as the master of the divination, you will become, you will make this sort of interpretation. By combining this hexagram as a sign of inadequacy, an inevitable conflict was predicted.

Case 19: The Trigram of Wei Linggong's Succession

In the "The Zuo Tradition", during the seventh year (535 BC), Xiang Gong of Wei died. He had only two sons, both born from a concubine, so no successor was established before his death. At this time, according to tradition, the elder was set as the next in line for the throne, and Ji Meng Zheng should take the throne, but he had a disability.

Moreover, the minister in charge and another powerful minister at the time had the same dream. In the dream, the founding father of the kingdom, Ji Kang Shu, instructed them to support the younger brother Ji Yuan as the monarch. As a result, the minister consulted *The Book of Changes* and obtained the hexagram of "Zhun" (Difficult at the beginning); he also asked about Ji Meng Zheng and obtained the hexagram "Zhun," and the following hexagram was Bi (compare). As described in the next table:

		8 Doesn't Change		
▦ Tun (Difficulty at the beginning)		7 Doesn't Change		▦ Bi (Compare)
		8 Doesn't Change		
		8 Doesn't Change		
		8 Doesn't Change		
		9 Changes		

The historian of the dynasty believed that the hexagram "Tun" was straight to the point. "There will be great progress and success". That was clearly talking about the youngest; there is no doubt about it. The minister hesitated: because of an alternative meaning of one of the characters, this should be about the elder brother. The historian answered that in the dream, they were asked to choose Ji Yuan because that character was part of his name. The hexagram interpretation should be taken from the change on the First line, "difficulty in advancing. It will be advantageous for him to abide by correctness and being firm". The elder had trouble walking. He should recuperate at home, not be set for succession to govern the state. Moreover, the divination agreed with the dreams, and Li Jiyuan was an excellent successor.

Therefore, it was decided that the younger one should rule. He was only seven years old. He was crowned Linggong of Wei. Linggong of Wei's fame in later generations is large. Partially because of his homosexual relation, and also because of an ambiguous relationship between his wife Nanzi and the above-mentioned minister. It is all mentioned in the *Analects*.

Case 20: The Nan Zhao Rebellion and Occupation

In the "The Zuo Tradition", during the twelfth year of Duke Zhao of Lu (530 BC), another minor turmoil occurred in Lu. At that time, Ji Pingzi, who had just taken over the state of Lu, had a family member named Nanzhao. He was among the ranks of scholars of the same level as Confucius. In those days, the social stratum was clear, including the monarch, the officers, doctors, and scholars, and then all levels below. Many ideas of Confucianism are about how "the gentleman" should be. Things like self-cultivation, keep a harmonious household, governance, peace, and the like. There is a saying about this "household harmony" that says that running the state is like managing a house. Now going back to the story, this Nan Zhao also had certain resources and power. He was dissatisfied with Ji Pingzi, and so he launched a rebellion that failed.

Before deciding on the rebellion, he consulted the oracle and obtained the hexagram "Kun" (The Receptive), and the following, which was "Bi" (compare). As described in the next table:

Kun (The Receptive)		8 Doesn't Change		Bi (Compare)
		6 Changes		
		8 Doesn't Change		
		8 Doesn't Change		
		8 Doesn't Change		
		9 Changes		

The fifth line changes and the word is "The Yellow lower-garment; there will be good fortune". Nan Zhao was overjoyed and showed it to his friend, Hui Bo. He looked at him and asked, 'I want to raise something big. Based on this hexagram, what do you think?' Hui Bo shook his head, saying, '*The Book of Change*s cannot assess the risks. Dangerous and unrighteous things must not be taken for granted'.

If you are consulting about faithful things, then this line, "the Yellow lower-garment; there will be great good fortune". This of course is a good sign. Yellow is the colour of neutrality, which means faithfulness; the lower-garment implies humility. Now, you are going to rebel against the king. What virtue is there in this? What good is then to talk? This then means defeat!

Case 21: Yang Hu understand the hexagram

In the "The Zuo Tradition", during the ninth year of the rule of Duke Ai of Lu (486 BC), he wanted to grant land to his ministers, but there was no land to give, so he occupied part of the Song state and was defeated by the Song. The situation became critical. The state of Zheng asked the Jin kingdom for help, and Jin's ruling minister, Zhao Yang, used divination before deciding, and the three divination masters judged that the Zheng could not be rescued. Then, he used *The Book of Changes* again, but he asked the famous Yang Hu for a reading. Yang Hu was also the head of a clan. He successfully influenced the Lu rulers for more than twenty years. He also had a grudge with Confucius. He has a famous saying attributed to him; "to become rich is to become heartless". He was later defeated in the struggle for power in the Lu Kingdom and fled to Qi State to resettle under Zhao Jianzi patronage in the Jin State. Yang Huz divination obtained the "Tai" (Peace) hexagram, and the following hexagram was "Xu" (need). As described in the next table:

Tai (Peace)			
	— —	8 Doesn't Change	— —
	— —	6 Changes	———
	— —	8 Doesn't Change	— —
	———	7 Doesn't Change	———
	———	7 Doesn't Change	———
	———	7 Doesn't Change	———

(With Xu (Need) hexagram shown at right)

Yang Hu interpreted paying particular attention to the fifth line; "reminds us of King Yi rule about the marriage of his younger sister. By such a course, there is happiness, and there will be good fortune". King Yi was the king of the Shang Dynasty, and his successor was the well-known king of the Shang Dynasty. King Yi's eldest son was Wei Ziqi, who, because he was not born from a legitimate wife, did not succeed in getting the throne. After the demise of the Shang Dynasty, Wei Ziqi was taken prisoner by the Song under Emperor Zhou Wu rule. This is how the Song inherited the rituals of the Shang Dynasty and became the founding ancestor of the Song Dynasty. The state of Zheng was established relatively late. The mother of an earlier Zheng dynasty monarch was the Princess Song. The relationship between the states of Song and Zheng can be regarded as the relationship between an uncle and his nephew. In other words, the marriage of the king's daughter can be understood as the monarch of Song marrying his sister to the ruler of Zheng. Therefore, the result of divination was that the Song state could not send troops to fight against their own.

There are so many recorded consultations. They seem to be accurate predictions. Why? In my opinion, most stories may conceal the political conspiracy. The so-called "push people towards virtue by the threat of final retribution" is only for foolish people, and it may also be an interpretation of later generations.

From these examples of divination, it can be seen that the reading of hexagrams is eclectic, especially when including hexagrams changes. For more than two thousand years, there has been no consensus on how to interpret the hexagrams. This is the so-called "secret that protects itself", so that there is always a sense of mystery and bluff. However, if you are interested in studying these Zhou Dynasty examples, you should think about them for a while.

The study of *The Book of Changes* in the past dynasties sheds a splendid light, and one should pay attention to "Image, numerology, principles, and divination". Principles are at the centre of this book *Conducting Life Affairs*. In the analysis of the sixty-four hexagrams and its meaning, images are the starting point. Numerology and divination are also important.

Divination

Time to tell fortune, mister!

I mean, dear sir, whatever issue you might have right now, you can now help yourself – in five minutes you may have an answer.

First, let me introduce the simplest method of divination. In this way, you do not need to read the entire book, and you do not need to know the terminology. The intention is that you commune with the spirits of Heaven and earth and find your destiny in your heart.

This divination method delivers quick answers: toss a coin and let it fall freely, like this, you randomly get a positive or negative result. Keep a record of it.

The positive side is yang, so draw a full line on the paper:

The negative side is Yin, and thus draw a Yin line on a paper.

Then, repeat it six times to get the six lines of a hexagram, and arrange them in order (from bottom to top). Which hexagram is it? You can refer to the "Sixty-four hexagrams (above) and their Names" **on the diagram on the next page**.

The answer you seek is in this hexagram. You can read the interpretation of this hexagram by going to the page number of the hexagram in the table of contents. But the key point is to look at the literal translation.

It is not over. A hexagram consists of six Yin and Yang symbols, and one of them is more specific about the question you are asking about. Which one is it? It is easy, look at the time. Now, what time is it? Get that number and divide it by 6. The remainder is the number of the line.

For example, at 16:29, you can get the number: 1629. Divide 1629 by 6 to get 271, and the remainder is 3, which is the third line. You must focus on the meaning of the third line. If there is no remainder, then check the sixth line. This is the simplest method of divination; I invented it by referring to the *Plum Blossom divination* by Shao Yong, a master of The I Ching from the Northern Song Dynasty.

By using coins, we can get the image and the numerology at the same time. The image of the hexagram, the numerology of the lines, they are all there.

The key is your "tossing intent". It is best to have a sense of ritual. The ancients said, 'If a question is dishonest, do not ask it, if it's immoral, do not ask it, if there no real doubt about it, do not ask it'. Since it is a date with the spirits of Heaven and earth, of course, you must be sincere to be able to communicate with the gods. Certainly, you cannot ask about doing wrong; Heaven is busy, do not mess with it.

Zhun (Sprouting)

Meng (Youthful Folly)

Bi (Holding Together)

Xiao Xu (Small Accumulating)

Tong Ren (Fellowship)

Da You (Great Possession)

Gu (Work of the Decay)

Lin (Approaching)

Bo (Splitting Apart)

Fu (Returning)

Da Guo (Geat Exceeding)

Kan (Gorge)

Dun (Retreat)

Da Zhuang (Great Power)

Kui (Opposition)

Jian (Obstruction)

Guai (Breakthrough)

Gou (Encountering)

䷄	Xu (Waiting)	䷭	Sheng (Pushing Upward)
䷉	Lu (Treading)	䷲	Zhen (Arousing)
䷎	Qian (Modesty)	䷷	Lu (Wanderer)
䷓	Guan (Contemplation)	䷼	Zhong Fu (Inner Truth)
䷘	Wu Wang (Innocence)	䷮	Kun (Oppression)
䷝	Li (The Clinging)	䷳	Gen (Keeping Still)
䷢	Jin (Progress)	䷸	Xun (The Gentle)
䷧	Jie (Deliverence)	䷽	Xiao Guo (Small Ponderance)
䷬	Cui (Gathering Together)	䷰	Ge (Revolution)
䷴	Jian (Development)	䷵	Gui Mei (Marrying)

If you have patiently read the previous content of the book, especially the part of divination practice, I have introduced the most authentic divination method in it: the "Long Development Method" with fifty sticks as it is recorded in the Biography of Chuxi. It also introduces the most basic terms, such as the original hexagram, the trigrams, and changes.

Let me introduce you to a relatively simple "Short Development Method" invented during the Han Dynasty: Use three copper plates, which can be replaced with regular coins. Hold them in your hand, shake them, and throw them on the table.

At this time, there are only four kinds of positive and negative outcomes, which correspond to: 6 Yin most, 7 Lower Yang, 8 Lower Yin, and 9 Yang most. As described in the next table:

Refer from coin tosing:	Symbols:	Line
Positive, negative, negative	6 Ying Most	— —
Negative, positive, negative	8 Lower Yin	— —
Positive, negative, negative	7 Lower Yin	— —
Positive, negative, negative	9 Yang Most	— —

Then, after repeating it six times, a hexagram and its two trigrams can be obtained. The method of hexagram change can also be interpreted using this book; if you want to go deeper, you can refer to the stories of the Zhou Dynasty.

There are many other ways of divining. There are many different ways. But let us stop here and we will talk a little more. The meaning of life is easy, and *The Book of Changes* is about survival in its basic sense. The biggest confusion about survival lies in destiny. The older a person is, the more awed he is about destiny because the more unfortunate things happen, the more experience one gets. Every time you recall an incident, you can find that you have walked through more than a dozen nodes of choices in a row and rushed to that precise point of time and space, and then the incident happened. Take for example one of my unlucky incidents which is also related to divination.

A few years ago, one day in early February, I was resting after dinner, and I used toothpicks to enlighten myself with Long Development Method, to see how lucky I was at the moment. The result was the hexagram "Song" (lawsuit), and the hexagram is "Guan" (contemplation). Should I sue someone? Not long ago, my WeChat public account of "Zhongguolizhi" was blocked, and I was trying to sue Tencent for this. Maybe this was it. Unexpectedly, on February 14, I went out to buy things for New Year, and because of a small matter, I ended up arguing with a stranger. In the end, the other guy got wounded and ended up in hospital.

And so, during the New Year festival, I had to ask for help, and got to think about it at the police station, I had to pay for some damages, which cost a lot but I had the funds. I thought about the reading; "unequal to the contention. He returns to the study of Heaven's ordinances, changes his wish to contend, and rests in being firm and correct. There will be good fortune".

I do not specialise in divination. I only played around with it whilst studying *The Book of Changes*. I often use the "time divination method" with friends. There are two insights from my experience: one is that the practice of interpreting the hexagrams can provide a better understanding of *The Book of Changes*. The other is that the hexagrams can be accurate. Many people who have consulted *The Book of Changes* have the same feeling. Why? Why are there divinations and beliefs throughout the world and human history? The world-famous psychoanalyst Jung proposed the principle of "synchronicity", and I understand that one's development in the real world is influenced by another form of the self in another dimension. For example, we see a video on a computer, and this video is completely different from what we see, but the two are absolutely the same.

From general experience, if I feel right because after something happens, like a person who goes to a meeting with the reading of divination in his mind, and then because of it, he feels it is right, so the relation becomes accurate. This is a psychological issue.

Similarly, there is the "law of attraction" in psychology, a concept that is now fashionable. Because when you make a prediction and a judgment, whether you resist it or like it, it will "attract" you to it.

Therefore, Xunzi said, 'The good do not change'. The more proficient people become at using the I Ching, the less likely they are to use it for divination on themselves.

Zeng Guofan (1811–1872) said, 'If you are meticulous and do a good job, people rely on it, and will serve from a distance, then the gods will help you, and this is better than burning incense". As long as you are kind to people, do good deeds, and make sincere efforts, you do not need divination, the gods of Heaven and earth will bless you!

Part Four

Leadership

Methodology I – The way of leadership

According to the records in *The Zuo Tradition*, *The Book of Changes* mainly served during the early days of the Zhou Dynasty. The royal family and the monarchs of the vassal states, like the Ji, are not in this book. It can be seen that *The Book of Changes* was originally for the rulers, that is, to help the rulers manage, and to represent political power in a symbolic way. Like a cheat sheet for leaders. This is indeed the case. The kings of all dynasties drew management ideas from *The Book of Changes*, and many dynasties drew ideas from it, such as the Tang Dynasty and the "Meiji" of Japan. Zeng Guofan's diary contains many notes on reading the book.

The management ideas in *The Book of Changes* are rich and profound. I only choose the following four topics to discuss with you: Great rule of law; A general outline of Chinese leadership wisdom; the framework of Chinese management thought; and, the summary of Chinese management thought.

Great rule of law; The sages, in accordance with this spirit-like way, laid down their instructions, and all under heaven yield submission to them — Guan, Emperor Wen's *Explanations of the Hexagrams*.

Religion and politics are twins, and religion is the elder. In the vast universe, the earth is just a drop in the sea, and a person is just a particle of dust.

Oldness and sickness, dead, sadness and happiness, all sufferings must be passively endured. Lao Tzu said that heaven and earth are not kind, and everything is impermanent. Human beings and everything are under the powerful will of the universe, but they are as insignificant as dogs made of straw. Even if you try to fight a mountain and be extraordinary, you will be destroyed, like a cockroach. Moreover, if we watch some science and education films and understand those beasts that lived on the earth millions of years ago, we can imagine that the earliest humans had no tools, and not much intelligence, and how great the pressure for survival was. How accidental it was for humans to survive and develop as a species.

People struggle on the verge of death, surrounded by fear and confusion. In our time, some people said that there is one thing that dominates everything and decides everything. It is God, and he is the representative of Heaven. As long as everyone listens to him, they can reduce the pain and enjoy the joy of life. And have serenity upon death, and convince people of his magnificence by some magical means. So, with spiritual guidance, everyone feels better. Then, if someone feels superior, he will tell everyone that he is also the second-level representative of God, and this other person the third-level representative of God. You can let them reach more people, so more and more will feel the warmth brought by religion. Then an organisation is gradually formed, and political power is also gained like this.

From primitive witches to later Buddhism, Judaism, Christianity, Islam, Taoism, etc.

The emergence and development of all religions is roughly the same. And all political ideas, movements, and even the establishment of political power, in the generation and development of ideological level, is generally the same. Kings of all ages claimed to be the Son of Heaven. Heaven is the supreme god. He is the son of Heaven and was ordered by Heaven. Is this ridiculous? Is not ridiculous at all.

Liu Bang, founder of the Hand dynasty, was originally a rogue but became a king. Was anyone not convinced? No problem. He wrote a myth, saying that his mother was conceived by a dragon in a field. The earlier Shang, Zhou and Qin dynasties had similar stories. The king of the Shang Dynasty and the king of the Qin Dynasty both said that their ancestor's grandmother had swallowed an egg laid by a large black bird and became pregnant; the Zhou dynasty's ancestor grandma stepped on a giant's footprint and became pregnant. Other cultures were also creative. Jesus said his mother was a virgin while she was pregnant. In short, they all emphasise that they are closer to the gods.

Confucius said, 'The people may be made to follow a path of action, but they may not be made to understand it'. Lao Tzu said, 'The sage, in the exercise of his government, empties their minds, fills their bellies, weakens their wills, and strengthens their bones. He constantly tries to keep them without knowledge and without desire'. All emphasise that rulers should make good use of the policy of fools.

Today, science, education and the media are well developed, but are the people still "foolish"? What is the sense of justice for something that is promoted by "foolishness"? We still have to be positive. 95% of people in this world believe in some religion. Furthermore, it is said that those who do not have a clear religious belief turn to religion when faced with cancer or other extreme conditions of life. The "foolish" seed of religion has been deeply rooted in human genes since the birth of human beings, and it just became less obvious in some people.

When Marx was talking about "religion as the opium of the masses", was he seeing that more than one religion is fascinating? Or, how many things are just religions in disguise?

Religion is a double-edged sword. Countless ambitious people in history rely on it to mobilise thousands of people and harm thousands of people. But if we use its goodness and learn from it, starting from a young age, it will also have positive meaning – regardless of a religion, or a "disguised religion", it is always a powerful way of domination.

A general outline of Chinese leadership wisdom

All the following quotations are from *Emperor Wen's Explanations of the Hexagrams;*

"When the mover is able to use the multitude with correctness, he may attain to the royal sway".

"If he occupies the God-given position, and falls into no distress or failure action will be brilliant".

"It is only the superior man who can comprehend and affect the minds of all under the sky" – Ton Ren,

"The value set on talent and virtue should come with the power to keep the strongest in restraint: this shows the great correctness" – Da Chu

"When the nourishing is correct, there will be good fortune" – Yi,

"What is great should be correct. Given correctness and greatness in their highest degree, and the character and tendencies of heaven and earth can be seen" – Zhuang

"Let the father be the father, and the son the son; let the elder brother be the elder brother, and the younger brother be younger brother, let the husband be the husband, and the wife wife. Then will the family be in its normal state. Bring the family to that state, and all under heaven will be established" – Jia Ren.

"The advance is made according to correctness: might rectify his country". – Jian.

A plaque hung above the Qing Palace, where the Qing Dynasty king dealt with governmental affairs that read: Open and aboveboard. After king Yongzheng (1722–1735), the names of the heirs to the throne were written in a small box in advance and hidden behind the plaque. "Open and aboveboard" and the imperial power are closely linked. Why is this? Because the imperial power represented the highest power, and "Open and aboveboard" was the highest wisdom. This wisdom comes from T*he Book of Change*s, and no book emphasises integrity like *The Book of Change*s.

In this regard, Confucius also summarised; "To govern means to rectify". Integrity is the general outline of Chinese leadership wisdom. Programs are open to the public. Leaders have made this integrity word solid, and all aspects of work will achieve good results. If you cannot get this outline, you may be shocked when something sooner or later happens.

How to get it? To put it simply, there are two aspects: first, internally, you must be morally positive and check your conscience. Like Wang Yangming's emphasis on "being cognitive", anyone doing anything should be cognitive of it being correct.

Regardless of competitors or subordinates, we must always maintain a moral high ground and always be on the right side. Serving people with virtue makes people happy and sincere. If you lead the people with correctness, who will dare not to be correct?

The second is, externally, to straighten out various relationships. People and things need to know where they belong, and this should be normalised. We have all kinds of household items in our house. The TV is placed in the living room, the bed is placed in the bedroom, the toilet is in the toilet, and the cooking utensils are in the kitchen. Everything is in its own place. A dad is like a dad, doing the work of a dad; a child is like a child, doing the work of a child; a wife is like a wife, doing the work of a wife. In this way, everything is positive, it is harmonious; otherwise, it is chaotic.

Separately, the meaning of the word "principle" is too broad. But simply put is: Let it be justice. Leadership must be achieved with justice. If an official was bribed, everyone will be definitely not convinced. If the throne was snatched by your uncle, there must be a sound reason to give everyone peace of mind. A career must be just, so everyone can pursue it and keep morally right. It is not fair for the United States to monitor the privacy of citizens. So Snowden felt uneasy when he expose it, and work against the state.

That was right. Righteousness is the right approach, and with masculinity, can help people to improve. Just do it right. Not to the extreme, not excessive, find the golden mean. Be normal.

In *The Caigentan* it is said; "The real taste is not thick, true taste is light"; only the sages can do magic, and for them is not magic, it is just normal.

Keep the normal state of a normal person, do not cajole the public clap-trap, do not start something new just to be different, do not pretend to be aggressive, do not act aggressively, keep upright, slow and steady wins the race.

Be authentic. Maintain a pure character.

Exert positive energy. Be optimistic and positive, be kind to people, be like a breeze of fresh air. Face problems with a rational mindset. Stay rational and objective, and avoid letting yourself down because of emotional interference. Be fair. Show honesty in your public life. Stand your ground. Go all out, stay focused, and stick to your mission. Be honest. Control desire and persist in faith. Be positive. Hold on. So, evil ways can never prevail!

Framework of Chinese management thinking

The great attribute of heaven and earth is the giving and maintaining of life. What is most precious for the sage is to gain the highest place, in which he can be the human representative of heaven and earth. What will guard this position for him? Men. How shall he collect a large following round him? By the power of his wealth. The right administration of that wealth, correct instructions to the people, and prohibitions against wrong-doing; these constitute his righteousness.

This passage is the framework of China's management thinking, and its general meaning is as follows: Survival and development are the theme of all things in human society, as well as everyone's psychological and behavioural drive.

Every system of management must be based on this. The one who follows it will succeed. The one who defies it will ignore the needs of people's survival and development. Such management will inevitably fail.

To play a big role in the development of human society, a person must obtain the status of a leader. History is about the people, but leaders have always shaped the direction of history.

How do you achieve leadership? It takes talent, appropriate means, and merit to convince people. Then, everyone feels that someone is worthwhile to support. In this way, you will be supported and people will be united around you. We see that this is exactly what Mao Zedong achieved.

How to ensure long-term support? After all, you need to let people make money, survive, or get better, allow development, let people get wealthy and better their livelihood conditions. If you only bring poverty and misery, even if you are noble like the Buddha and Confucius, not many people will follow.

What is "righteousness" in a good leader? What is considered appropriate? The most important thing is to do these three things: One is financial management. Have fun with the money. To ensure that people's material needs are met, to ensure that they have a solid foundation for survival and development, and to enable people to live a solid life. And make it so you have money to reward, money to punish, reward and punish, and incentive.

The second is proper speech. We must standardise cultural thinking. To ensure that people's spiritual needs are met, let people find a spiritual home in a universally recognised culture, work for it, forgive it, and live and die for it. Make sure to have a general organisational culture, a vision, and make people live comfortably and hopefully.

The third is police the people. It is necessary to have a system to guarantee the first two, both material and spiritual, and to regulate people's behaviour so it keeps on the track set by leaders.

Deng Xiaoping was in power in China for more than ten years, laying the foundation for China's rapid development. The focus of his management thinking was to "grasp with both hands, and keep both tight"; reform and opening up with one hand, crackdown on crime with the other, economic construction with one hand, democracy and legal system with the other, reform and opening up with one hand, and fighting corruption with the other. Focus on material civilisation and spiritual civilisation in the other. Roughly the above three kinds of "righteousness".

A framework of Chinese management consolidation

"The superior man finds himself in a carriage" – Bo, Lesser *Treatise on the Symbolism of the Hexagrams*

The car you are driving is for you. Your brothers support this table. Your employees promote your company. The people give your power. "Min" (The people) has been repeatedly emphasised in *the Book of Change*s, and only the *Treatise on the Symbolism of the Hexagrams*" mentions the people. People are society and humanity.

People-oriented is the grasp of Chinese management thought. A leader is a person; a manager is a person. All thoughts and work revolve around people. Find people, stay close to them, win them, motivate them, and control them. If there is no one, only the person in charge, that kind of work will definitely not be considered management. And you can have fun; you can do it all, once everything is done! How to be people-oriented and how to do a good job with people? Let us read a few words from the sages; "while noble, he humbles himself to the mean, and grandly gains the people" – Tun, Lesser *Treatise on the Symbolism of the Hexagrams*.

Say this while toasting; "The right mind makes the big respect the little". Leadership is relatively high rank position, and being objective, human nature is full of vanity and envy, the more successful the more this will be triggered. To win in the face of a proud person, you must be humble, lay low, let the other party feel like your equal, eliminate the sense of competition, and satisfy their vanity. In this way, that person will be cool, and only then will the urge to hunt become useful, and he will work for you.

Liu Bei used this trick for Zhuge Liang. Lao Tzu said, 'He is the King of Hundred Valleys'. The sea is so big because it is lower than all rivers.

"The satisfaction of the people in consequence of this is without limit" – Yi, King Wen's *Explanations of the Hexagrams*.

Emotional flattering is not enough. It must also be practical and to the point. We must understand that "If you are kind, this will enable you to employ the services of others", to make people derive benefits, to get people together, and to share profit! I think in Sima's *Comprehensive Mirror in Aid of Governance*, "when the crisis is at stake, the leader's last move is to distribute the treasure and private possessions to the soldiers, so that the morale is boosted, and so the chance of winning the last fight is greatly improved. When such pleasure goes before the people, and leads them on, they forget their toils; when it animates them in encountering difficulties, they forget the risk of death" – Dui, Emperor Wen's *Explanations of the Hexagrams*.

Leaders need to take the lead. We must maintain a spirit of optimism and the belief that we must win. The ancient king sometimes led expeditions himself, not because the generals who watched him were not useful, but for the effect on moral.

"The small man is not ashamed of what is not benevolent, nor does he fear to do what is not righteous. Without the prospect of gain he does not stimulate himself to what is good, nor does he correct himself without being moved. Self-correction, however, in what is small will make him careful in what would be of greater consequence; and this is the happiness of the small man".

The vast majority of people are "small minded". Only interests, authoritarianism, rewards and punishments cannot control them by morals, but often with very small benefits and reward and punishment, results can be obtained. This is really a blessing for managers. A pharmacy implemented a marketing strategy, it advertised: the first customer will receive a free bag of toilet paper. Next day, there was a long line waiting for the opening. He he.

"They carried through the necessarily occurring changes, so that the people did what was required of them without being wearied".

This paragraph points directly to two major weaknesses of human nature: one is that it is easy to get tired of things that do not seem to change, and the other is that it is easy to dislike strange things. For the first point, managers should be good at changing patterns to keep people sharp. People sometimes complain about everything. In fact, if they do not, they will get even more frustrated.

With regard to the second point, we must be good at transforming "mountains into stones" with readily available things. And get good at refining complex ones into simple ones. The same is true when writing a book. A writer wants to tell the truth about the world and the people, but who will listen? So Li Yu (1610–1680) put these truths in the novel *The Before Midnight Scholar*, and claimed that "to change social traditions, you need power and leadership, then it is an easy task". But the reader may not follow his thinking. That is about it, but it is not enough. Regarding people, Confucius' two sentences are thought provoking; "The benevolent man loves others" and "The benevolent knows he is of the people." My experience is that people management is the core of management, and the spirit above it is love. If you love everyone, everyone loves you; love is the highest kind of management.

Methodology II – The way of doing things

One

As the saying goes, before doing anything, make sure you are doing it for the right reasons. In life, some people are successful in certain things, but have problems with others. Whilst some people do well, but are not strong.

What can we do about it? In my opinion, it is still a matter of level. The highest masters, such as Zeng Guofan, can integrate everything and everyone into carrying on to get things done.

Regarding the way of doing things, the sixty-four hexagrams each have their own theme. Here we select the essentials from the essay and supplement the previous interpretation of the hexagrams.

There are roughly seven ways to do things:

First; you must have a rough grasp of what will be done: where to start, and where to end.

Second; make an assessment of whether this is the right thing to do.

Third; when we start to do something, we need to know how to have progress while maintaining stability.

Fourth; if one thing needs to be done for a long time, you simplify it.

Fifth; must have patience.

Sixth; when faced with problems, know why you are to continue.

Seventh; change at the right time.

To change means to restart the next cycle of the above seven items. Each item is divided into seven sections.

Two

Study the laws and seize opportunities; "The operations forming the change are the method by which the sages searched out exhaustively what was deep, and investigated the minutest origins of things".

Our pursuit of the value of life requires our own business. This business may not make much money, but it must make you feel motivated. When you decide to do it, it is still only a starting point, but you will imagine that in the future it will continue to develop in the direction you want. Your imagination is based on the understanding of the law, and your imagination is not accurate, if it is not based on your deep understanding of the law. "Research" is the process of igniting imagination, and "depth" is the process of directing the kind of imagination to carry on into deep rational thinking. As we mentioned earlier, these two points are the key to learning and grasping the rules.

Why do most young people feel confused and do not know what to do, but in the eyes of many successful people, there is gold everywhere, and there are many opportunities? Not because of how many additional resources the latter may have, but because they have more experience and insight. The so-called experience is to know the general law of something. The so-called vision is the ability to judge the development of things according to this law. When a novice plays a card and someone plays an Ace, you will see only an

Ace; but when a master plays a card and you play an Ace, he knows what your next card is from the insight he has.

So where does this experience, this vision, and this understanding of the law come from? Personal experience of course, the most direct and true, but the most time-consuming. Everybody will get it at some point, but you might be too old and even dead, and you have no chance then.

Therefore, it is most economical for a young person to learn to gain experience and improve the understanding and grasp of laws. How to learn it? Two aspects:

One is to learn from previous masters. Including parents, leaders, brothers, seniors, etc. They all have experienced all kinds of problems, so try and turn their experience into yours. There are others who are not older than you, but are ahead. Like the same problem for you, Americans may have experienced it ten years ago. How to succeed and how to fail? Learn fast, you might be ahead of the people around you, many successful business models in China started like this.

The second is to learn from books. Books, especially some historical books, can present universal examples. The span of time is larger. It can be the lifetime of a person, or the span of an era or even a thousand years. There is deeper and more unique understanding, beyond the eyes of ordinary people.

No one can say that they have fully grasped the laws of heaven and earth. This is a process of continuous cultivation and deepening, and opportunities arise in this process. The sage said about opportunity; "Those springs are the slight beginnings of movement, and the earliest indications of good or ill fortune. The superior man sees them, and acts accordingly without waiting for the delay of a single day.

The Master said; "Does not he who knows the springs of things possess spirit-like wisdom?"

Real opportunities have tiny signs that are not easily noticed by ordinary people. Even a person can discover an opportunity often because of some mysterious contingency, as if God deliberately arranged it for you to see it. What then? "See what you can do, do not hesitate for long", act without delay. In the *Historical Records*, a statement is mentioned many times "Heaven does not take blame, there is only you to blame". God gives you free will, so if you do not do, do not blame Heaven. If you do not show your face, it will make you unlucky.

There are only a few opportunities in a person's life. The power of destiny is the most real among these opportunities. Grab them with gratitude and go to the next stage in life.

In Chinese, Ji is part of both the word opportunity and nearly. It also means "almost" and "a few", which means a little bit. It was used also in "Research". Later, it became an important issue in Chinese philosophy, reflecting the importance Chinese people attach to details and laws.

Acting according to one's capability.

"Virtue small and office high; wisdom small and plans great; strength small and the burden heavy".

There are countless professions, countless careers. There are all kinds of successes and opportunities, and there are many good projects and good development ideas, but they may not be suitable for you. When the time comes or a plan is in front of you, consider whether you are qualified and able to undertake it.

Not being virtuous and holding a high office. A person that has no credit or reputation, but has a high position. Can he be secure? Of course not. In the *Annals of the Warring States*, there is a well-known anecdote known called *Chu Long persuades King Zhao*. After sending troops, the king was reluctant to send reinforcements because his favourite son was held hostage, but the old minister Chu Long finally persuaded him when he explained the value of filial piety. Chu Long said that loving his child should be part of a long-term plan. This hostage experience will make prince Chang An contribute to the country and lay a solid foundation for his future development. Many private enterprises are now facing the situation of shifting leadership from fathers to sons. Letting the new generation stand on their own, achieve good performance, gaining reputation in the company, and be able to convince the public. This is a prerequisite for shifting. The ranking of seniority in the government is also based on this principle. Qualification is relatively restrained, and new members are brought up at a young age. It is not easy for social mobility.

Knowing little but planning a lot. IQ is not enough, experience is not enough, knowledge is not enough, but an idea can be very big.

Do you know failure? There are many such stories. For example, in Sima's *Comprehensive Mirror in Aid of Governance* he mentioned a man named Wang Rong who lived during the Northern and Southern Dynasties. He was arrogant and became a public official before the age of thirty. Because of his being from noble ancestors, he did have a head start. In just a few years, he became a good official, but he still was far from his goal. So he convinced a royal family member to fight for the throne. But in the end, he failed and was killed. He was only twenty-seven years old when he died.

A bit of power is only burdensome. In *The Analects of Confucius* he states; "A gentleman must not only be brave, but have long term endurance". Can a person be successful if he has both virtue and talent? It depends on whether you have a broad and strong mind: A mind must be broad, capable, and brave; but most important, be persistent, knowing that there is a long way to go. To put it plainly, it is necessary to have good psychological and physical qualities; otherwise, it is difficult to take full responsibility. I have seen several small entrepreneurs develop into a comfortable business. But then they want to be bigger and stronger, and get a lot of loans. In the end, they cannot play, and they lose. Some people are crushed and become seriously ill. In fact, Zhuge Liang (181–234) did the same. When Liu Guanzhang and his three brothers were gone, he could not continue anymore, and so went on a northern expedition.

According to Zhuangzi; "those who are too comfortable cannot become wise, and those who are short on resources cannot sink much deeper". Can a small food bag hold a cow? No. To pack a cow, you need a building. If the well is deep, you cannot do with a short windlass. People have different faces. The difference between a person's internal image and ability is the same as its height and weight. Some people are like Yao Ming internally, others are like Eric Tsang internally. If you have an accurate portrayal of your inner image, you can decide what to do and what not to do. There are hundreds of trades. There is always one that suits you. Even if you are weak, you can still achieve a certain level in a job that suits you, and your life will still be good.

Striving for stability

"The superior man in a high place composes himself before he tries to move others; makes his mind restful and easy before he speaks; settles the principles of his intercourse with others before he seeks anything from them. The superior man cultivates these three things, and so is complete".

Those who do great things should the take precaution of visualising how things could go wrong in advance. Usually you think about how to do something first, but you should try to think about how things can fail. Then, try your best to avoid those problems, and be undefeated before you win. In short, be cautious, sound, and thorough. The sage gave three examples:

Compose yourself before you try to move others into action, you should first see if you have a firm foothold. If you want to be promoted, you must first see if your work and character are fully recognised by leaders and colleagues. If not, you are in a hot spot and you are as good as "dead". If your company wants to develop rapidly, innovate and increase yield (with the inevitable high-risk that comes with it), you must first see whether the actual business can achieve stable development and income. Otherwise, a new business will not do well, and the old business may also fail. Mess this one up, and everything will be lost.

Rest your mind and get it at ease before you speak. When you give someone some advice, you should first evaluate the relationship with the other party and the possible reaction from the other party. Or at least, calm down your heart before speaking, and do not open your mouth in anger. It is important to feel the emotional state of the other party, and to understand their concerns. Some people cough two times before speaking, or clear their throats. They use this cough to think about how to say something.

Settle the principles of the exchange with others before you seek anything from them. When you are going to ask someone to help you, it is best to establish the right relationship with the other party first. What would happen otherwise? It is said that there was an official who sent a large payment to a well-known senior official as a bribe, but the senior official had little contact with him before, and his reputation was spotless, so he immediately made a display of his integrity and refused a bribe. Then he asked the disciplinary inspection department to investigate where the bribe came from, and later sentenced the culprit. In any work, you need to have a clear "contract of rights and responsibilities". You have the right to ask for this.

Simplification is the golden key to doing things

"He who attains to this ease of Heaven will be easily understood, and he who attains to this freedom from laborious effort of the Earth will be easily followed. He who is easily understood will have adherents, and he who is easily followed will achieve success. He who has adherents can continue long, and he who achieves success can become great. To be able to continue for a long time reveals the virtue of the wise and able man; to be able to become great is the heritage he will acquire. With the attainment of such ease and such freedom from laborious effort, the mastery is had of all principles under the sky. With the attainment of that mastery, the sage makes good his position in the middle between heaven and earth".

The simpler you convey your thoughts and ideas to others, the easier it will be to understand them; "Heaven will fully mobilise the power of emotion and will to support you if he understands this relationship based on the double foundation of reason and emotion, Then it can last long".

You arrange for someone to do a job. The simpler the job, the easier and more efficient he will do it; then, it will be easier for such a job to achieve larger results quickly; then, you can keep growing.

People who are doing well in an enterprise now dream of becoming a hundred-year-old company and being among the top 500. A hundred-year-old company is really old, and a top-500 company is really big. This takes a long time and needs a lot of space for growing. The first goal is the survival and development of everything in the universe. And this goal starts with simplicity. Those who truly understand this truth and fully practice have the world at their feet. The previous is a Literal translation of the text from the sage.

Simplification is the golden rule to doing things, whether it is a national matter, a major policy or a daily chore. If there is any secret to success in the world, it is this golden rule. To open the treasure of *The Book of Change*s, you also need this golden rule.

The three major schools of Confucianism, Taoism, and Buddhism that have influenced Chinese people the most, all rely on simplicity. They all have numerous classics, but in the process of dissemination, they have emphasised in simplicity. For example, the themes of each school can be summarised in one or two words: Confucianism talks about benevolence, Taoism talks about inaction, and Buddhism talks about emptiness. In this way, ordinary people can easily understand and accept them. Later thinkers have all been influenced by these characteristic. For example, Wang Yangming (1472–1529) only talked about two things: the conscience, the unity of knowledge and action.

Political propositions of politicians or parties emphasise simplification. The great heroes began from lower positions and say so to other so they join them: we can all get rich and prosperous. During peasant uprisings, of all ages, the poor had to be recruited, they all wanted to have a better distribution of the fields. In order for the party to gain the support of the people, the party emphasised that its purpose was "serving the people wholeheartedly'. When Deng Xiaoping was in charge and required vigorous development of the economy at all levels. What did he do? He only said one phrase; 'No matter whether it is a black cat or a white cat, if it catches a mouse it is a good cat'.

To establish a brand image, a company's slogan must be popular. Think of it, the slogans we remember are simple. It can be said that few people remember more than two characters out of a seven-character poem. So modern marketing has a well-known point: every word takes a lot of space in the mind of the reader.

Regarding "simplicity", here are two more sentences: At the operational level, simplification means professionalisation and standardisation. Good companies are simple and clear. Quick profit model with a clear market division. The division of internal business processes and technological processes are also very clear. Similar to the assembly line, each post is responsible for simple tasks. Each piece is simple by itself, but the combination of all parts is a huge thing.

For a person to achieve success, he also needs to be professional.

It is amazing to focus only on one thing throughout life. Moreover, focusing on one thing, focusing, needs to be done for a long time.

Greatness is getting through all sorts of ordeals.

"If acts of goodness be not accumulated, they are not sufficient to give its finish to one's name; if acts of evil be not accumulated, they are not sufficient to destroy one's life".

To accomplish anything, you must rely on the accumulation of skills. Regarding accumulation, there are many qualities involved, the most important of which are: attention to detail, frugality, hard work, and being consistent.

As mentioned in the hexagram of Sheng (Pushing Upward), accumulation means accumulation from small to large. If you do not accumulate by small steps, you will be thousands of miles away from your goal. Without the accumulation of small streams, there will not be a sea. This is what the Kuomintang Chairman, Lien Chan, said in his speech at Peeking University on his first visit to the mainland: "Bits of hard work have been accumulated into our long and peaceful relationship. Many entrepreneurs are thrifty champions. Saving a bit of money means earning a bit of money, and that is pure profit".

Hard work happens when someone, instead of playing on WeChat and Weibo, works hard; while others pick up girls, you work; while others travel, you work; while others sleep, you work; while others work eight hours, you work twelve hours. Being constant means accumulating all your life, being frugal all your life, and working for the rest of your life. Failure is the result of a life time gone, waste not days, months, years, or even some decades.

Therefore, persevering is a life effort. I have written about perseverance many times, and here I say it again, 'follow a dream'. I insist on it. What is a dream? A dream is something that you often think about when you are okay, but you that have never been able to achieve; always frustrated, but never have never thought of giving up on it; you must persist as the result is important. This line is a from a movie, ha; "If that thing is so easy to obtain, why is it called a dream?" For the past twenty years, the thing I have persisted with is with calligraphy. Although I have always had a good eye, and my skill is not that good, my aesthetic level remains higher than my creativity. I cannot always write something that I am satisfied with. Still, I do not give up. Because I have a dream: I want my calligraphy to be at a national exhibition. For many people, this dream seems ridiculous, as some have achieved this in their early twenties. When I compare myself with them, my frustration increases sharply, but it does not affect my love for it, just like some love-relationships give frustrating pain and happiness.

Therefore, we must employ a laser focus. It is more efficient to focus on one thing at a time to maximise that time. Note, the matter you focus on should be as cumulative as possible. It should be something where you can do more or do better because you invest more and more time on it, and enough so it can be supported your whole life.

There is a well-known 10,000-hour rule; to become an expert in a certain field, it usually takes 10,000 hours of practice. It is difficult for us to focus on one thing for more than two hours every day, so it will take more than ten years to achieve success.

In short, greatness comes from getting through all kinds of ordeals, and it is the same for all positive things in life.

The root of all problems is in yourself.

"It is he himself that tempts the robbers to come: on whom besides can we lay the blame?" – Jie Lesser *Treatise on the Symbolism of the Hexagrams*.

If you have money, do not take it all out and show it outside. This is a deliberate attempt to tempt a thief. If you dress yourself like a devious woman, won't that attract those bad men to come and tease you? Many times, you have bad things coming your way, they are self-inflicted, and you cannot blame others. Therefore, those suffering must be in a difficult situation.

Similarly, Confucianism has spoken a lot about this throughout the book. I cannot add to its perfection so I will just offer a few paragraphs here:

The Doctrine of the Mean says; "He does not murmur against Heaven, nor grumble against men. When the archer misses the centre of the target, he seeks for the cause of his failure in himself". When you encounter problems or troubles, you cannot blame heaven, you cannot blame others, and you can only find the cause within yourself. Just like in archery, you cannot blame your arrows; you can only blame yourself for not shooting well. Is that useful?

In *The Analects of Confucius* he states; "What the superior man seeks, is in himself. What the mean man seeks, is in others". Good guys blame themselves, bad guys blame others. Bad people put the responsibility for problems on others; the good man only on himself and corrects mistakes to improve himself.

Mencius states; "If a man love others, and no responsive attachment is shown to him, let him turn inwards and examine his own benevolence. If he is trying to rule others, and his government is unsuccessful, let him turn inwards and examine his wisdom. If he treats others politely, and they do not return his politeness, let him turn inwards and examine his own feeling of respect. When we do not, by what we do realise what we desire, we must turn inwards, and examine ourselves in every way. When a person is correct, the whole kingdom will turn to him with recognition and submission". You love someone, but that person is not close to you, then you must reflect on whether you are benevolent; if you govern a group of people, but fail to keep them safe, then you must reflect on whether you are wise; if you treat others with courtesy, but they mistreat you, then you must reflect on whether you are respectful. For all the problems you encounter, look back to see if you are not doing something well. If you are 100% sure, you will be able to get through everything without any obstacles.

"I do not murmur against Heaven. I do not grumble against men, if you treat others politely, and they do not return this politeness, turn inwards and examine your own feeling of respect." This has been the most important way of doing things for the Chinese elite for more than 2,000 years from Kong Meng to Zeng Guofan. In short, it is all about you.

It is easy to think everyone is the same, at the same time it is easier for them to change, but your own nature is difficult to change. Therefore, even if the problem lies within someone else, it is difficult for us to change that person. It is futile to report grievances, and we can only adjust ourselves.

Changing at the right time

When change takes place in the proper way, "occasion for remorse disappears" – Ge, Emperor Wen's *Explanations of the Hexagrams*. When a series of changes has run its course, another change ensues.

When it comes to a career, you may have a good grasp of the opportunities and a project that might be suitable for you. If you are also stable, and the path is right, you can introspect and persist, but you will still face problems and difficulties. Because at any time in the world, all things are constantly changing. You are still the original you, but the environment is not the same, and the world is not the same. What to do?

Zeng Guofan said that; 'Those who have achieved great things should change at the right time'. This is exactly the spirit of the Ge (Reform). Zeng Guofan had three changes in his life: In his life as a Beijing official, and in his previous life, he was a Confucian. He used the idea of self-cultivation and governing others. Then he founded the Xiang Army and found that the Confucian morality was not good enough, and he became a legalist, and embraced severe punishment. Draconian law came to rule the army and the people. Later, it was discovered that the strength of the Legal School offended both the superiors and other colleagues. Since he could not use it anymore, he began to integrate the Taoist thought, paying special attention to the ideas of compromise and concession, harmonious work, and profitability.

Chinese elites generally have a similar transformation process as Zeng Guofan. In the early days of entrepreneurship, the Confucian spirit of struggle and cooperation was required; in a mid-term business, legalist management skills were required; in the later period, Taoist principles gradually returned the business to a more selfish and indifferent state. This kind of change is sometimes passive and helpless. For example, Kai-Fu Lee, after getting cancer, found that he was not the wisest and regretted not having spent more energy on health and family. In terms of career alone, it is necessary to maintain innovation and keep up with changes in the market.

As ordinary people, we are often tired of our lives and work, and at the same time we have a hint of something to worry about in the future, so we all yearn for change. But few people really change because we have always believed that persistence is both a virtue and an opportunity, and change is always risky. There are many situations requiring prioritisation in life. If you feel that the prioritisation you are doing is slow, change it. Then find what can go faster. If Kai-Fu Lee had stopped working hard early, would his wife and children be as well off as they are? Can they regret it in the end?

Therefore, change is really the most tangled issue in life. What to do? Let us see what the hexagrams say. In this kind of entanglement, many people boil like frogs in warm water for a lifetime. However, in an almost unchanged life, the Chinese people cut out the word "adaptation" from *The Book of Changes* to deal with specific issues.

The theme of *The Book of Changes* is change, and the final "Wei Ji" hexagram points out that we are all still on the way of change. We must be cautious in changing the trajectory of life, but the change and improvement of life structure and life state should always be the theme of life.

In order to see far away, strive for further improvement. I would like to encourage you with this book!

If you enjoyed this book of

The Simple Book of Changes,

you may also enjoy our other books of

Chinese heritage.

Please see our Chinese catalogue on

www.heartspacepublications.com

www.ingramcontent.com/pod-product-compliance
Lightning Source LLC
Chambersburg PA
CBHW060521010526
44107CB00060B/2643